Who's buried where in England

Douglas Greenwood

Who's buried where in England

Constable · London

First published in Great Britain 1982
by Constable and Company Ltd
3 The Lanchesters
162 Fulham Palace Road
London W6 9ER
Second edition 1990
Reprinted 1991, 1994
Third edition 1999
Reprinted 1999
Copyright © 1982 by Douglas Greenwood
ISBN 0 09 479310 7
Printed in Great Britain by
BAS Printers Ltd
Over Wallop, Hampshire

A CIP catalogue record for this book
is available from the British Library

Contents

Acknowledgements

The author and publishers wish to thank the following for their help and for permission to quote from material in which they held the copyright: *The Oxford Companion to English Literature*, fourth edition, in the section on writers; *Pears Cyclopaedia* (Pelham Books, London). And while biographical facts have also come from many other sources we would acknowledge in particular *The Dictionary of National Biography*; various Oxford and University Press histories; the authorized biographies of many lives; and the National Portrait Gallery for the illustrations on pages 52, 59, 72, 73, 80, 82, 96, 100, 103, 109, 129, 133, 155, 158, 167, 181, 203, 208, 217, 227, 233, 247, 252 and 296.

Of the many readers throughout the world who have sent me their comments and suggestions, I must thank especially Mr George Frobisher, FRGS, and Dr R. J. Hetherington, whose specific and detailed suggestions I have been glad to incorporate.

Illustrations

All photographs are by the author except those illustrations from the National Portrait Gallery (see Acknowledgements)

Introduction

Among the peoples of the English-speaking world, especially those of us who live in England, there is an almost spiritual affinity to the past. Even those whose home may have been in another land for generations, the language they have been born to, or have acquired, seems to compel them to visit this country by the millions in search of historical roots and where it all began. Where better to find them than in a burial place?

It can be a strangely moving experience to stand beside a famous grave. One feels a closeness to our heritage that no other form of contact with the past ever brings; we recognise an unsuspected instinct for pilgrimage. 'We ought to quicken our memories of the great, and where they lie, by such a visit occasionally,' says Ethelberta in Hardy's *The Hand of Ethelberta*. We experience a strong feeling of reverence, frequently unbidden, for those men and women of the past whose final resting place is so close to us. We are reminded of the line from Gray's poem *Elegy in a Country Churchyard*: 'The paths of glory lead but to the grave' – true, but the fame lives on! Unless the grave is provided with a notice that gives us some biographical information, however, our knowledge is generally restricted to what is engraved on the tombstone, which gives us little information with which to conjure up the past. But if we can relive those remarkable lives through a knowledge of what they did, our pilgrimage becomes doubly worthwhile. Shakespeare's 'graves . . . Have wake'd their sleepers – op'd and let them forth' (The Tempest, Act V scene 1) is perhaps an important cue for us to pick up. Thus, to reach back over the centuries to an understanding of our heritage and our roots, it is necessary to seek the resting places of the famous; those who have shaped our history.

A personal pilgrimage can have reasons other than a desire to commune with history. Painters, photographers, brass-rubbers, stonemasons and history scholars in search of their particular needs will also want to trace such graves.

This is not a guide to interesting graves as such, or even to those currently classified as national or historic monuments: it is a guide to the resting places of many of the most illustrious men and women of history who were buried in England. It is impossible to include in one volume every person of past renown – even some of the earlier kings have been omitted – but the graves listed here represent, I believe, those of the more famous figures mentioned in standard histories and encyclopaedias; and these persons have been categorized in a comprehensive index. Only the briefest biographical details have been given, to save space and thus provide a more exhaustive coverage. It has been a daunting and rather humbling task to presume an ability to arbitrate between illustrious lives; who to include, who to leave out. Space has indeed been an arbitrary and harsh censor, as well as fame. Where omissions do occur it is sometimes because a grave location has remained stubbornly untraceable. Also there are many illustrious churchmen whose tombs are to be found in the cathedrals and churches of England, but their inclusion would mean a list of almost book length in itself. If any reader does feel that a serious omission has occurred then his or her suggestion will be welcomed and considered for any further edition of the guide.

There will be instances when a person listed under one section could equally well be included in another. For example, Disraeli was both writer and statesman, as was Lord Macaulay. I have included them in section 3 rather than section 6. General consensus would also surely place Shakespeare in section 6, although he was an accomplished actor. Such overlaps are inevitable. Should any reader disagree with my categorization I hope they will bear with me.

Where no actual grave exists to mark the resting place, as, for example, in the case of Queen Boadicea, whose grave is somewhere beneath platform 10 at King's Cross Railway Station, and Richard III, the reasons are given. Where English sovereigns have been buried on foreign soil, and therefore strictly outside the scope of this guide, they have nevertheless been included to avoid breaking the complete list of English monarchs in the guide. They are: William I, the Conqueror; Matilda; Henry II; Richard I, the Lionheart; James II; and George I. With the exception of George I, who was buried in Germany, all were buried in France. I should perhaps mention here that as the main royal line, from which the present queen claims descent, begins with the house of Wessex, I have begun my survey of English monarchs with them. In no other instance have I been able to include any figures, however famous, who were buried outside the borders of England, not even if those persons were buried within the British Isles. If, at some stage, a broadened guide is generally called for, Scotland, Wales and Ireland will then be included.

Many of the persons listed in the guide have close connections with the United States of America, either before or after its independence from Britain; some, even, are American born but lie buried in England. For the interest of American readers, I have stressed the connection with the United States in the biographical information. Among such persons are Sir Ferdinando Gorges, the first Governor of Maine; William Penn, the founder of Pennsylvania; Sir Hiram Stevens Maxim, the American-born inventor of the machine gun; T. S. Eliot, the American-born poet, whose ashes lie buried at East Coker in Somerset, and Francis Bret Harte, the short-story writer born at Albany, N.Y.

Now a word about the pinpointing of the precise location of a grave. As a piece of sound advice, I recommend the purchase of a good road map, one listing the smallest villages and side-roads. Such a map is invaluable. Once there you will discover that most churches are sign-posted. But, where there is no signpost, or the map lets you down, all you need do is ask your way. Most persons in the locality will know where a famous grave is. Generally you will have little difficulty in finding it. Inside a church it is easy, whilst outside most historic graves tend to be either just by the east end of the church, near a path, or the east or south-east of the graveyard. Generally, of course, most churches are orientated east to west, with the tower at the west end. Some of the larger London cemeteries have plans to help you locate the grave you are looking for. Cemetery office staff are always obliging and will usually go out of their way in a large cemetery to direct you to a site.

One of the more frustrating facts about contemporary life is the locking of certain churches against vandals. Mostly this is done in large towns and cities, but even some remote country churches are now locked for large parts of the day, although the graveyards remain open at all times. Cemeteries with a gatehouse usually remain open during the morning and afternoon but it is as well to bear in mind the possiblity of closure, for nothing is more exasperating than to arrive and find you cannot gain entry.

In a few cases burial places are privately owned, as in the case of Kirklees Abbey, which contains the grave of Robin Hood, or Shaftes-bury Abbey, where Edward the Martyr's remains were buried. That, however, is currently open as a museum for a small fee. With regard to photographs I had of necessity to be selective, and those reproduced here, I feel, are the most typical of the sites listed.

As an itinerary for a tour, such a pilgrim's path can show us parts of the country rarely seen on the usual tourist routes; parts of timeless England that otherwise might be seen merely as an accident of aimless peregrination. There is no question that this rich soil of England 'contains a richer dust concealed'. Rupert Brooke's words say it all with poetic economy.

DOUGLAS GREENWOOD, 1990

Preface to the Second Edition

In this new enlarged edition of *Who's buried where in England*, so many additional lives, illustrations, revised and extended biographies are included that it is virtually a new book. Here are also included those who have, alas! died since the publication in 1982 of the guide. I should like to again mention that pompous memorials or witty epitaphs are not the emphasis of this book. Sometimes less important members of the family have more elaborate tombs. Sometimes, also, important members were buried under a floor with no monumental tomb, such as the third Earl of Southampton at Titchfield, the earls of Pembroke in Salisbury Cathedral and Admiral Rodney (the monument is his wife's) at Old Alresford. Some, such as Ian Fleming, Fanny Burney and others, have neither monument nor gravemarker but just a presence in a graveyard or church. Thomas Hollis (Section 6) desired the unidentified corner of a field! King Edward the Martyr is also of special interest in this respect (see Section 1). And the scattering of ashes has its own gentle eccentricity (see Beatrix Potter, Section 6).

Also in this connection one has to remark on the sad fact that 'Old' St Paul's Churchyard is now merely the name of a busy London commercial street, while the National Gallery in Trafalgar Square covers most of what used to be St Martin's in the Field burial ground. (See also Geographical Check-list by County, at the end of the book.) I have nevertheless, for record purposes, cited those locations where immortal fame earlier rested under a discrete site. It is disturbing to reflect that similar obliterations of such graves in both London and the rest of England could occur – or have already been carried out. St Anne's church, Soho, is one example and many years ago the present greensward in Salisbury Cathedral Close was marked by memorial stones. 'Old' and 'New' Minsters of Winchester, of course, no longer exist.

Some readers of the first edition have kindly suggested burial locations that have been deemed appropriate to now include. But it is opportune to point out here that suggestions have also included such as Drake, Keats, H. G. Wells, Oscar Wilde and others who were all buried abroad. Drake, for example, was buried at sea off Porto Bello, Panama as was Admiral Sir John Hawkyns, Drake's second-in-command, off Puerto Rico. Here I should mention that there are several instances where a memorial does not stand over or mark a grave: 'Jenny' Lind's statue in Brompton Cemetery does not mark her grave (it is in Great Malvern); T. S. Eliot, Keats, Gray and some others in Poets' Corner were not buried in Westminster Abbey; D. H. Lawrence (ashes in Taos, New Mexico but a stone in Eastwood Cemetery, Nottinghamshire) is another example. General Gordon's recumbent effigy in St Paul's Cathedral does not mark his grave, but I have included it as an exception and as a mark of respect.

For general information I should also mention that Golders Green Crematorium, where such as Freud, Anna Pavlova, Ivor Novello and others found ultimate rest for their remains, provides a key to unlock the various 'Columbariums' in which urns are placed and before which respects can be made. There is also a Garden of Rest where, for example, Peter Sellers' ashes were placed near his parents' together with a plaque.

It is hoped that this greatly extended compilation will be found of value not only as a spur to pilgrimage, but also as a ready reference in the growing popularity of history that is with us today.

Preface to the Third Edition

In this Third Edition of *Who's Buried Where in England* in which the Princess of Wales and Emad 'Dodi' Fayed have among others been included, plus about fifty other sites all told, we have also taken the opportunity of making some typographical adjustments and minor corrections.

While given in the various categories of the guide-sites, several persons were cremated at Golders Green Crematorium. A list of many others who found rest there since 1902 is also included as a concise supplementary guide. It was provided by the establishment. (See below and also the Preface to the Second Edition.) The fact that persons were cremated here does not mean that there will always be urns here (T. S. Eliot and Sir Herbert Beerbohm Tree, for example). Ashes are frequently taken away (e.g. Bebe Daniels', see below) for alternative private disposal. Also they are often spread in The Garden of Rest here (Peter Sellers', for example). Shaw's also were scattered at his former Ayot St Lawrence home.

PLACES OF EXECUTION

Historical places of execution exist all over England. Tyburn (the Tyburn Tree, named from the small river that flowed here; now underground) saw executions from 1196 to 1759. A small stone slab marking where the triangular gallows stood is on a traffic island at Marble Arch, London. There are no memorials here. Smithfield ('West' Smithfield), another execution place, where martyrs were burned, Wat Tyler (d. 1381) slain and Ann Askew (1521–1546) (Protestant martyr of Grimsby, turned out by her husband, tortured after attempting divorce and burned for heresy), saw numerous memorial plaques placed on the outside wall of St Bartholomew's Hospital.

Sir William Wallace, 'Braveheart' (c 1274–1305) was hanged, drawn, beheaded, quartered and his pieces sent to Newcastle, Berwick, Stirling and Perth with the intention that they discourage others from continuing the struggle for Scottish independence. After winning the Battle of Stirling Bridge (1297) he was elected governor of Scotland. After the Battle of Falkirk (1298) where he was beaten by Edward I Wallace went to France. Eventually caught, at first unrecognised, near

Glasgow it is said, he was taken to London where he was tried in Westminster Hall and condemned to death.

A splendid memorial to him was placed on St Bartholomew's Hospital wall.

Persons Cremated at Golders Green*

Kingsley Amis: Author (1922–1995)

Sir William, Lord Birkett of Ulverston: Lord Justice (1883–1962).

Sir Arthur Bliss, composer and conductor (1891–1975).

Dr Eric Blom: Musicologist (1888–1959).

Bracken, Brendon, 1st Viscount (1901–1958).

Jack (Walter) Buchanan: Actor, writer and matinee idol (1890–1957).

Sir Philip Burne-Jones: artist (1861–1926).

Eric Coates: composer and conductor (1886–1957).*

Sir Charles Cochran: impresario and producer (1872–1951).

Princess Louise of Prussia (m.) Arthur, Duke of Connaught, Q. Victoria's 3rd son (1860–1917).

Edward, Lord Dalton of Forest of Firth: Labour M.P., Chancellor of the Exchequer 1945–1950.

Bebe (Phyllis) Daniels: American comedienne (1901–1971).

Sir James Dewar: kt. 1904: Inventor of the thermos flask (1842–1923).

Charles Doughty: Poet and explorer (1843–1926).

Sir Alexander Fleming: Discoverer of penicillin and Nobel Prize winner (1881–1955)*

Sir George James Frampton: Sculptor (1860–1928).

Sigmund Freud (and Mrs Freud): Psychoanalyst (1856–1939).*

Hugh Gaitskell: Leader of the Labour Party 1955–1963 (1906–1963).

Sir William Garstin: Engineer (Aswan Dam) (1849–1925).

Sir William S. Gilbert: Of Gilbert & Sullivan fame (1836–1911).*

Elinor (née Sutherland) Glyn: Writer of romantic novels (1864–1943)

Arthur Greenwood: Labour politician (1880–1954).

Anthony, Lord Greenwood of Rossendale: Former chairman of the L.C.C. (1911–1982).

Tommy Handley: Radio comedian – 'Itma' (1892–1949).

Arthur Henderson: Home secretary 1924, foreign secretary 1929–1931, Nobel Peace Prize 1934 (1863–1935).

Lesley Henson: Musical comedy actor/comedian (1891–1957).

Dame Myra Hess: Pianist (1890–1966).

Holman Hunt O.M., R.A.: Painter (1827–1910).*

Sir Henry Irving: Actor (1838–1905).*

Rudyard Kipling: Author and traveller (1865–1936).*

Sir Alexander Korda: Film director (1893–1956).

Tom Mann: Founder member of the British Communist Party.

Prince Monolulu: Racing tipster.

Anna Pavlova: Ballerina (1881–1931).*

Sir Isaac Pitman: Inventor of shorthand (perhaps cremated at Woking) kt. 1894 (1813–1893).

Harry Pollitt: Chairman of the British Communist Party (1890–1960).

Reading, 1st Marquess of Reading: Statesman and British Ambassador in Washington (1918–1921) (1860–1935).

Peter Sellers: Actor, one of the 'Goons' (1925–1980).*

George Bernard Shaw: Playwright (1856–1950).*

Bram (Abraham) Stoker: Author of 'Dracula' (1847–1912).

Marie Stopes: Pioneer advocate of birth control (1880–1958).

Vesta Tilley (Lady de Frece, née Matilda Alice Powles): Music hall artiste (1864–1952).

Sir Herbert Tree: Actor/manager (1853–1917).*

Ralph Vaughan Williams: Composer (1872–1958)*

*See also general index.

[1] Sovereigns

Arthur (c.496–d.539?)
Glastonbury Abbey (ruins), Glastonbury, Somerset.

Legend has it that he was the illegitimate son of Uther Pendragon, king of Britain. Arthur was a Romano-British general who controlled much of the south-west of England and his existence is a matter of controversy. Perhaps the securest document is the *Annales Cambriae* of Wales that records his leadership at the Battle of Badon, where he halted the advance of the West Saxons in 515, and his death at the Battle of Camlann in 539. Further details are given by the ninth-century monk Nennius and the twelfth-century Geoffrey of Monmouth. At that time monks are said to have found a tomb near Glastonbury which contained two caskets with male and female remains. The male had a skull wound, whilst the female had traces of yellow hair and was thought to be that of Arthur's wife Guinevere. The bodies were re-interred in Glastonbury Abbey on the order of Edward I, who was present at the ceremony.

Boadicea (d.c.60–61AD)
Under Platform 10, King's Cross Station, London.

Queen of the Iceni and widow of King Prasutagus. When the King died he left half his kingdom to the Emperor Nero and half to his daughters. The Queen was reputed to have been flogged by the Romans and her daughters raped; and when the Romans began to despoil the kingdom she led the Iceni in revolt, massacring large numbers of Romans at St Albans, Colchester and London. The Roman Governor, Caius Suetonius Paulinus, met Boadicea in battle on the present site of King's Cross Station, its former name being Battle Bridge. The Queen's forces were routed and she and her daughters took poison. By legend, Boadicea now lies buried somewhere beneath platform 10. Other places, however, do lay claim to be her burial ground: Parliament Hill, between Highgate Road and the Vale of Health, Hampstead, London; Soldier's Hill, Garboldisham Heath, Suffolk; and near St Andrew's Church, Quidenham, Suffolk.

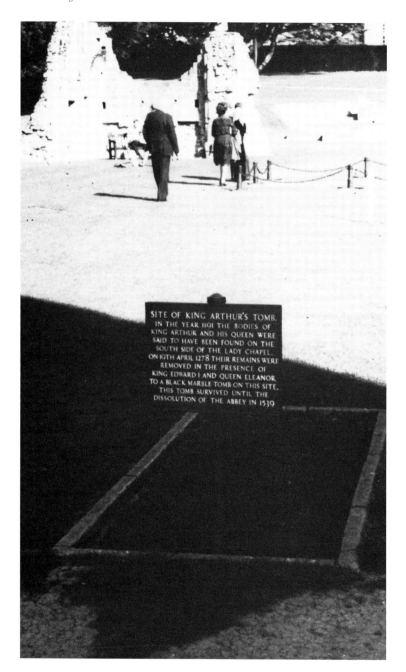

SITE OF KING ARTHUR'S TOMB.
IN THE YEAR 1101 THE BODIES OF
KING ARTHUR AND HIS QUEEN WERE
SAID TO HAVE BEEN FOUND ON THE
SOUTH SIDE OF THE LADY CHAPEL.
ON 19TH APRIL 1278 THEIR REMAINS WERE
REMOVED IN THE PRESENCE OF
KING EDWARD I AND QUEEN ELEANOR
TO A BLACK MARBLE TOMB ON THIS SITE.
THIS TOMB SURVIVED UNTIL THE
DISSOLUTION OF THE ABBEY IN 1539

Edmund, Saint (c.840–870)
Abbey of Bury St Edmunds (ruins), West Suffolk.

Became King of East Anglia in 855 whilst still a boy. In the year 870, the Danes, who had been wintering at York, marched through Mercia into East Anglia and the King engaged them in battle at Hoxne, some twenty miles south-east of Thetford. Edmund was slain, whether in battle or later as a martyr is not certain, but the widely current version of the story, which makes him fall a martyr to Danish arrows after refusing to renounce his faith or to hold his kingdom as a vassal of the Danes, may very probably be true. His shrine became one of the most famous in England and there are churches dedicated to his memory throughout the country. The date of his canonization is not known.

Ethelbald I (d.757)
The crypt of St Wystan's Church, Repton, Derbyshire (by repute).

King of Mercia, an Angle Kingdom, and not to be confused with King Ethelbald of Wessex who died in 860. In 731 Ethelbald was the acknowledged overlord of the southern kingdoms in England, having subdued the neighbouring rulers in battle. Despite his reputation as a liberal benefactor his treatment of his Saxon subjects was believed to have been oppressive. In 752 Ethelbald led his Mercian troops against the West Saxons, meeting them at Burford, near Oxford. After a hand-to-hand combat with the West Saxon Ealdorman, Ethelhun, Ethelbald's 'spirit weakened' and he fled the field leaving his troops still fighting. They were soon routed. From that victory stemmed the gradual ascendancy of Wessex. Later, Ethelbald was reputed to have been slain by his own bodyguards.

Oswy or **Oswio** (c.612–670)
Whitby Abbey (ruins), Whitby, Yorkshire.

King of Northumbria who succeeded in making the majority of the Britons, Picts and Scots tributary to him. He appears to have consolidated his power with the aid of the Church and by a series of judicious matrimonial alliances. In 655, he defeated Penda of Mercia at the Battle of the Winwaed, in thanksgiving for which he founded the Abbey of Whitby. In 664, at the Synod of Whitby, Oswy accepted

Site of Arthur's grave, Glastonbury Abbey (ruins), Glastonbury, Somerset

Tomb of King Sebert and Queen Ethelgoda, South Ambulatory, Westminster Abbey, London

the usages of the Roman as opposed to the Celtic Church, which led to the appointment of Wilfrid as Bishop of York.

Sebert or Saba (d.c.616)
Westminster Abbey, London.
A tomb, said to be that of King Sebert and his Queen, Ethelgoda, now lies in the South Ambulatory of Westminster Abbey.

First Christian King of Essex who was converted and baptized by Mellitus, the first Bishop of London. Legend has it that Sebert was the founder of Westminster Abbey. In 1308 his tomb was reported to have been opened for relics, and his right hand and forearm were found to be perfectly preserved.

THE SAXONS OF WESSEX

Egbert (d.839)
Winchester Cathedral, Hampshire, in gilded mortuary chest, made to contain the bones of the pre-Norman rulers, which rests with other similar chests on top of the Presbytery screen.

Son of Ealhmund, an under-king of Kent. He was exiled in about 789 and spent his exile at the court of Charlemagne, returning to England possibly in the year 802 when he was accepted as King of the West Saxons. He waged constant war against neighbouring kingdoms and against the Welsh of Cornwall and Wales. Eventually he obtained the overlordship of the rest of the English kingdoms though he could never claim to be the actual first King of England. He repelled the incursions of the Scandinavians and at the Battle of Hengestdune in 837 routed the forces of the Danish pirates and the Cornwall Welsh.

Ethelwulf (d.858)

Winchester Cathedral, Winchester, Hampshire. His bones are contained in the mortuary chest on top of the Presbytery screen.

King of Wessex who succeeded his father, Egbert, in 839. During his reign he was under constant attack from Danish pirates, whom he finally defeated at the Battle of Aclea in 851. His attempts to subjugate the Welsh were unsuccessful. In 855, accompanied by his youngest son, Alfred, he made a pilgrimage to Rome, and on his return journey married Judith, daughter of Charles II (the Bald) of France. During his absence from the country, his second son, Ethelbald, had assumed power and when his father returned Ethelbald retained the crown of Wessex, Ethelwulf ruling only in Kent until his death.

Ethelbald (d.860)

Sherborne Abbey Church, Sherborne, Dorset.

King of Wessex who, during his father Ethelwulf's absence abroad on a pilgrimage to Rome, assumed power, refusing to relinquish it when his father returned. When his father died in 858 he married his widow, Judith, daughter of Charles II of France.

Ethelbert (d.866)

Sherborne Abbey Church, Sherborne, Dorset.

Third son of Ethelwulf, King of Wessex and Kent. On the death of his father in 858 he succeeded him as King of Kent and, in 860, on the death of his brother Ethelbald, King of Wessex, he united the two kingdoms under his rule. His reign was beset by Danish incursions, the invaders even sacking Winchester. A combined force of Hampshire and Wiltshire men defeated them but in the winter of 864–865 Danes landed in Thanet and were bought off by the men of Kent. An extant Anglo-Saxon document codifies Ethelbert's laws.

Part of Ethelred I's marble tomb lid in Sanctuary of Wimborne Minster, Dorset

Ethelred I (d.871)
Wimborne Minster, Wimborne, Dorset, where a fifteenth-century brass bears his effigy.

Fourth son of Ethelwulf who succeeded his brother, Ethelbert, as King of Wessex in 866. His reign, like his brother's, was spent in constant war with the Danish invaders. The Battle of Ashdown in 871 in which the English were victorious was followed a fortnight later by a defeat at the Battle of Basing. Two months later at the Battle of Merton the English were again defeated and soon afterwards the King died on 23 April, possibly from a wound received in the battle.

Alfred the Great (b.849 r.871–901)
In Winchester in King Alfred Place off Hyde Street is St Bartholomew's Church, said to contain stone from Hyde Abbey. This was the parish church of Hyde, where Hyde Abbey used to stand. Alfred and his wife founded a nunnery near the site of the Old Minster, and he was first buried there. Later, in the ninth century, King Edgar combined the two minsters and the nunnery was moved to Hyde. Alfred's body was moved to the abbey, and some remains found where it stood are believed to be his. Their site is marked by a flat stone under which they were placed in the churchyard outside the east wall of St Bartholomew's Church. The old gatehouse of the abbey is virtually all that remains of the abbey; the 'Old' and 'New' minsters were close to the present Winchester Cathedral. Little Driffield Church, Humberside, also lays claim as a burial site of Alfred's body, claiming that it was brought to the Priory at Little Driffield where his sister was Prioress.

Youngest son of Ethelwulf, who succeeded his brother Ethelred I as King of Wessex in 871. Alfred realized, at his succession, that his forces were inadequate to repel the Danish advance, and therefore he offered them tribute, known as 'Danegeld', as a means of keeping the peace. During the next few years he gradually built up the strength of his army and navy, and then renewed his war against the invaders. Just after Christmas 877, the Danes invaded Wessex and found little resistance, overrunning Somerset without a fight. The king retreated to Athelney in the marshes and it was during this period that the legend of the burning of the cakes was born. Supporters rallied to Alfred's cause and, seven weeks after Easter 878, he marched out of the marshes at the head of a large force and defeated the Danes at the Battle of Ethandun (Edington). The Danes and their king, Guthrum,

Probable site of King Alfred the Great's remains, St Bartholomew's Church, Winchester, Hampshire agreed to leave Wessex and to accept baptism. Following this peace, known as the Peace of Wedmore, the Danes were restricted to the territory known as the Danelaw, north of the River Thames, leaving the south and west of England under the sole control of Alfred. In 893, Danes defeated by King Arnulf of Germany descended on Kent and Sussex and Alfred once again went to war, which continued almost constantly until 897 when the invaders withdrew.

Alfred was an ardent supporter of scholarship and it is to him that we owe the *Anglo-Saxon Chronicle*, for it was at his bidding that it grew from the older and local annals of the church of Winchester. It is a unique history and during Alfred's reign served as a contemporary narrative of the most stirring years of his life. As a ruler he introduced many important legal reforms and it is from his times that many of the precedents of the English Common Law stem. His writings include English translations from the Latin of Gregory the Great's *Pastoral Care*, Boethius' *Consolation of Philosophy* and St Augustine's *Soliloquies*. In Boethius' work Alfred put a lot of his own thoughts, while his translation of Orosius has Alfred's own account of voyages made by Norse explorers.

Edward the Elder (d.924)
'New' Minster, Winchester, Hampshire, on the site of which Hyde Abbey was built, the gatehouse of which is all that remains in Hyde Street.

Succeeded his father, Alfred the Great, as King of Wessex and overlord of the Angles and Saxons in 901. During his father's lifetime he played an active rôle in the fight against the Danes and may even have been co-ruler with Alfred. At his succession he had to contend with his cousin, Ethelwold's attempts to gain the throne with the help of the Danes. After Ethelwold's death at the Battle of Holme, Edward, with the help of his sister, Aethelflaed, the Lady of the Mercians, gradually subdued the Danes, forcing upon them the Peace known as 'the Laws of Edward and Guthrum'. Fighting off Viking attacks from overseas he fortified former Danish strongholds, extending his rule throughout England until he had established his sovereignty over the entire country including Northumbria and parts of Wales.

Athelstan (b.895 r.924–940)
Abbey Church, Malmesbury, Wiltshire. The tomb is now empty but it once contained the bones of the King.

Son of Edward the Elder, possibly illegitimate, whom he succeeded in 924. A favourite of his grandfather, Alfred, he had been brought up by his aunt, Aethelflaed, the Lady of the Mercians. Whilst his father succeeded in establishing his rule throughout the country, Athelstan was the first Saxon king to be acknowledged as King of England, receiving the homage of the other kings at the Congress of Emmet in 926; and after the Battle of Brunanburh in 937, where Athelstan defeated a coalition of princes, his supremacy and that of his house was unchallenged. William of Malmesbury wrote that Athelstan may have been in possession of the famous Spear of Longinus, or Destiny, with which the centurion pierced Christ's side on the Cross, at the Battle of Brunanburh. He is reputed to have given it later to Otto the Great as a wedding present and it is now in the Hofburg Museum, Vienna. Athelstan was an able ruler who introduced many new and just laws, reducing the previously severe penalties for young offenders. He pursued an imperial policy, allying himself dynastically with foreign rulers, marrying his sisters to French and German princes.

Edmund I, The Magnificent (b.921 r.940–946)
Glastonbury Abbey (ruins), Glastonbury, Somerset.

He succeeded his half-brother, Athelstan, in 940. His accession was marred by an invasion of Vikings and the King was forced to yield much of his territory in East Anglia and Northumbria. He reconquered northern Mercia and in the peace that followed the Viking Kings, Anlaf and Raegenald, were baptized. Towards the end of his reign, in 944 or 945, the peace was broken and Edmund expelled the two Viking Kings from Northumbria. Edmund was stabbed to death at the royal villa of Pucklechurch in Gloucestershire by an exiled robber called Liofa, and his body was taken to Glastonbury Abbey which, in 943, he had entrusted to Dunstan.

Edred (r.946–955)
'Old' Minster, Winchester, Hampshire; its site is no longer traceable with any accuracy.

Youngest son of Edward the Elder, he succeeded his brother Edmund as King of England in 946. At his accession he received the submission of Northumbria but in 947 the Northumbrians chose the

Norwegian, Eric Bloodaxe, as their king. Edred ravaged the kingdom eventually receiving its submission. The King's public policy was largely influenced by St Dunstan and it was his statesmanship that brought peace between the King and the Danes by allowing the Danes to retain their own laws.

Edwy (b.940 r.955–959)
'Old' Minster, Winchester, Hampshire; its site is no longer traceable with any accuracy.

Eldest son of Edmund I, he succeeded his uncle, Edred, in 955, being crowned by Archbishop Odo at Kingston-upon-Thames. He offended his nobles at the coronation feast when he withdrew to pay court to a girl; he was persuaded to return by St Dunstan, which was one of the probable reasons for the King's resentment of the saint. Relations between the two deteriorated to such an extent that St Dunstan was forced into exile in Flanders. That same year the Mercians and the Northumbrians chose Edwy's younger brother, Edgar, as their king but the death of Edwy in 959 prevented civil war.

Edgar (b.c.943 r.959–975)
Glastonbury Abbey (ruins), Glastonbury, Somerset.

Younger son of Edmund I, he had been chosen during his brother, Edwy's, lifetime as king by the Mercians and the Northumbrians. His brother's early death in 959 seems to have prevented war and he succeeded peacefully as King of England. He recalled St Dunstan from his exile in Flanders and together they initiated major ecclesiastical reforms, as well as confirming legal autonomy to the Danes, thus keeping the peace so carefully negotiated by St Dunstan during the reign of King Edred.

Edward the Martyr (b.c.962 r.975–978)
Shaftesbury Abbey (ruins), Dorset. Bones, presumed to be those of the Martyr, were given a conditional resting-place in the Russian Orthodox sect's church at Brookwood cemetery in 1989 pending a legal decision about contested ownership. There is considerable doubt that these bones were his; they were unearthed from a place more than 50 feet away from where his sanctuary tomb was located. The bones, discovered 35 years ago, were in a small lead box, and since they were near the crypt steps in what was the north transept of Shaftesbury Abbey it is highly likely that they are merely the bones of

some person of quality who had been buried there. I believe the martyr's bones still rest undisturbed somewhere in the ruins here. At Wareham, Dorset, there is a roundish stone receptacle in the Church of Lady St Mary that is said to have once held the king's body before it was translated to the Abbey by St Dunstan.

The eldest son of Edgar, he succeeded his father with St Dunstan's support in 975. His accession was contested by Edgar's second wife and widow, Queen Elfthrith, who was anxious to secure the throne for her son Ethelred. She was joined by some of the nobility and Edward's control of the kingdom was weak. His brief reign was marked by anti-monastic reaction. On 18 March 978 Edward was murdered at Corfe Castle, Dorset, probably at the instigation of his step-mother Queen Elfthrith. The king seems to have been personally popular and the poem on his death in the *Anglo-Saxon Chronicle* calls his death the worst deed in English history.

Ethelred II, The Unready (b.c.968 r.978–1016)
'Old' St Paul's Cathedral, London.

Son of King Edgar by his second wife, Elfthrith, he succeeded in 978 after the murder of his half-brother, Edward. A weak and vacillating king, Ethelred was unable to resist the renewed onslaught of the Danes, his situation being made worse by the treachery of his commanders. To keep the peace he was forced to pay tribute, Danegeld. On 2 December 1001, Ethelred, determined to be rid of his enemies, ordered the slaughter of 'all the Danish men who were in England'. The slaughter was great. It did not have the effect of ridding the King of his enemies but provoked fresh attacks from Sweyn, King of Denmark, and from then until 1013 Ethelred gradually lost control of his kingdom. In that year, Sweyn was acknowledged as King of England and Ethelred fled to Normandy, his wife Emma being the daughter of Richard I, the Fearless, Duke of Normandy. In February 1014 Swyen died and the Witan recalled Ethelred on the condition that he ruled better in future. Sweyn's son, Canute, returned to claim the crown the following year and was advancing across the country to London when Ethelred died there on 23 April 1016. 'Unready', the epithet by which Ethelred is known in history, means 'without council'.

Edmund II, Ironside (b.c.980 r.April to November 1016)
Glastonbury Abbey (ruins), Glastonbury, Somerset.

Son of Ethelred II by his first wife, Aelfgifu. The death of his father on 23 April 1016 led to a double election to the English crown: London and some of the Witan choosing Edmund; the rest of the Witan meeting at Southampton electing Canute. Fierce fighting ensued and Edmund's courage earned him the appellation, Ironside. At the disastrous Battle of Assandun (now Ashingdon) in Essex, Edmund was defeated and, in a pact with Canute, they partitioned the realm. Edmund, however, died one month later and Canute was suspected of having poisoned him.

THE DANES

Canute (b.c.994 r.1016–1035)
Winchester Cathedral, Winchester, Hampshire, in mortuary chest on top of the Presbytery screen.

Proclaimed King of all England in 1017 shortly after the death of Edmund II, he also became King of Denmark on the death of his brother Harald in 1018. Earlier, upon the death of his father in 1014, Canute had been forced to withdraw from England through a general uprising of the Anglo-Saxons. He returned a year later and ultimately partitioned the kingdom with Edmund before acceding to the whole. To avoid dynastic disputes he married Queen Emma, Ethelred the Unready's widow, who bore him a son, Hardicanute. His reign, after the initial conflict, was peaceful and brought stability to the realm.

Harold Harefoot (r.1035–1040)
Originally buried on the present site of Westminster Abbey, but his body was disinterred, beheaded, thrown into a fen before being rescued and finally buried 'with honour by the Danes' in St Clement Danes, Strand, London, though the precise location is not known.

The illegitimate son of Canute and Aelfgifu of Northampton, he claimed the throne on the death of his father. A compromise was reached whereby he would remain regent whilst the legal heir, Canute's legitimate son, Hardicanute, was in Denmark. Harold's mother, however, managed to persuade the Witan to accept her son and he was elected king in 1037. Whilst Hardicanute was preparing to invade England to claim his throne, Harold died at Oxford on 10 March 1040.

Hardicanute (b.c.1019 r.1040–1042)
'New' Minster, Winchester, Hampshire.

Legitimate son of Canute and his second wife, Emma. He became King of Denmark on his father's death in 1035 and was in Denmark when his half-brother, Harold Harefoot, claimed the throne. He was in the process of invading England when news of his brother's death reached him. He arrived with an invasion fleet of 62 ships but his succession was peaceful. His brief reign was oppressive but to avoid dynastic conflict he recalled his step-mother, Queen Emma, from exile in Normandy, together with Edward, her son by Ethelred II, the Unready, whom he named as his heir. In 1042 he died of convulsions at a marriage feast for Tostig the Proud.

THE SAXONS OF WESSEX RESTORED

Edward the Confessor (b.c.1004 r.1042–1066)
Chapel of St Edward the Confessor, Westminster Abbey, London. The central shrine was constructed on the orders of Henry III.

Son of Ethelred the Unready and his second wife, Emma, daughter of Richard I Duke of Normandy, he was brought up at the court of Normandy whilst his mother remained in England as the Queen of Canute. Acknowledged by Canute's son, Hardicanute, as his heir, his accession was peaceful. An able but not a strong leader, Edward found himself in opposition to the more forceful nobles, chief of whom was Earl Godwin, whose daughter, Edith, the King married. The cause was the King's favouritism of the Normans. Godwin rose in rebellion but the King, with the help of the Earls Leofric of Mercia and Siward of Northumbria, subdued him and he was forced into exile, along with his family. During his absence, Edward is believed to have named William of Normandy as his successor. Godwin soon returned and asserted his influence over the King, forcing him to accept Stigand of Winchester as Archbishop of Canterbury. Thereafter, Edward lost the effective control of the kingdom and turned his attention to religion, earning himself the appellation, Confessor. On his deathbed he is reputed to have named Godwin's son, Harold, as his heir.

Shrine of St Edward the Confessor, Westminster Abbey, London

Harold II (b.c.1022 r.January to October 1066)
Waltham Abbey, Essex. There is a stone marker in the abbey gardens.

Elected King of England on the death of Edward the Confessor who was married to his sister, Edith, although he had been the *de facto* ruler of the country since 1053. Having defeated an invasion led by King Harold Hardrada of Norway and Tostig, Harold II's brother, at the Battle of Stamford Bridge on 23 September 1066, he learned that William of Normandy, who claimed the English crown, had landed at Pevensey. Harold marched his troops southwards and engaged the Normans at the hill of Senlac, near Battle. There on the 14 October 1066, in what has become known as the Battle of Hastings, Harold was said to have been killed by an arrow that pierced his eye. The high altar of Battle Abbey, now in ruins, stands over the exact spot where Harold was killed.

Stone marking the burial site of King Harold

THE NORMANS

William I, The Conqueror (b.c.1027 r.1066–1087)

Buried in France at St Stephen's Church, Caen, Normandy. The tomb was desecrated in 1793 but a plain slab marks its original site.

Illegitimate son of Robert the Devil, Duke of Normandy, and Arletta, a tanner's daughter. When his father left on a pilgrimage to Jerusalem in 1034 he induced the baronage of Normandy to accept his bastard son as his heir, Robert having no legal son. The following year he died on his journey and William, although still a child, was accepted by the Normans as Duke. In 1051 William visited England and it is believed that during the visit his kinsman, Edward the Confessor, promised him the crown. In 1064, Harold, son of Earl Godwin and Edward's chief counsellor, accidentally found himself at William's court. There is strong belief that he too agreed to acknowledge William's claim to the English crown. This broken promise of support was one of the chief reasons for William's invasion of England after Harold's accession. The defeat and death of Harold at the Battle of Hastings on 14 October 1066 brought William to London where he was crowned at Westminster on Christmas Day 1066. However, five years were to elapse before he had the entire kingdom under his control, and a Norman aristocracy established. When he was firmly in control he ordered the compilation of the Domesday Book as a survey of the country. He died at Rouen in Normandy on 9 September 1087 after being thrown from his horse.

William II, Rufus (b.c.1056–1060 r.1087–1100)
Winchester Cathedral, Winchester, Hampshire, in front of the lectern. There is also a memorial marking the spot where he was killed in the New Forest: following a signpost at the turn-off on the Cadnam Road.

William, known as Rufus, was the third son of William I and Matilda of Flanders, and his father's favourite. On his deathbed England was bequeathed by the Conqueror to William, Normandy going to his eldest son, Robert. Rufus was crowned at Westminster on 26 September 1087, just fifteen days after his father's death. There were uprisings in favour of Robert and the hereditary principle which brought William into conflict with his brother. In 1096 Robert, who wished to go on the Crusade, gave Normandy in pledge for money to William, and there can be little doubt that William determined to remain in lasting possession of the duchy. The *Anglo-Saxon Chronicle* says of the King that he was 'hateful to nearly all his people and odious to God'. He was killed by an arrow whilst hunting in the New Forest.

Henry I, Beauclerc (b.1068 r.1100–1135)
Reading Abbey (ruins), Reading, Berkshire.

The youngest son of William I and Matilda of Flanders. Hearing of his brother William Rufus's death he seized the treasury at Winchester. His elder brother, Robert Duke of Normandy, being at the Crusade, Henry was elected King. He married Edith of Scotland, daughter of Malcolm III and the Saxon princess, Margaret, granddaughter of Edmund II, Ironside, thus uniting the Norman and Saxon lines. At his coronation, he issued the famous charter which redressed grievances and rid the court of vice. His English government was severe and grasping, but he 'kept good peace'. After the death of his legitimate heir, William the Aethling, in the *White Ship* in 1120 he

Tomb of William II, Rufus, in Winchester Cathedral, Hampshire

NEAR TO THIS SPOT
WAS BURIED
KING HENRY BEAUCLERC,
WHO FOUNDED
READING ABBEY.
JUNE 18. 112.

UNVEILED 18,1921

Stone marking the burial site of Henry I, Reading Abbey (ruins), Reading, Berkshire

forced the baronage to recognize his daughter Matilda, widow of the Emperor Henry V, as his heiress by doing homage to her, first in 1126 and then in 1131 after her marriage to Geoffrey Plantagenet, Count of Anjou. Henry died at Gisors on 1 December 1135.

Matilda (b.1102 d.1164)

Buried originally at the Abbey Church at Bec; her tomb is now in the Cathedral Church of Rouen, Normandy, France.

Daughter of Henry I and his first wife, Edith of Scotland. She was married to the Emperor Henry V but at his death after eleven years of marriage she returned to England. In 1126, her brother William the Aethling having died earlier in the *White Ship* disaster, the Great Council of England did homage to her as her father's heiress. In 1129 she married Count Geoffrey of Anjou, and in 1133 gave birth to the future Henry II. On the death of Henry I in 1135, the nobles of England and Normandy accepted Stephen of Blois, a grandson of William I, as King; but, with the help of her half-brother, Robert of Gloucester, she invaded England and succeeded in capturing Stephen in 1141. Proclaimed Lady of Normandy and Queen of England at Winchester she entered London, but her arrogance alienated the nobles and the Papal Legate, Henry of Winchester. Routed at Winchester by forces loyal to Stephen, she was forced to exchange the King for Robert of Gloucester, and thereafter her cause steadily declined. She retired to Normandy in 1148, her husband having secured possession of the duchy, and lived to see her son crowned King, having renounced her claims in his favour. She died on 30 January 1164.

Stephen (b.c.1094–1097 r.1135–1154)

Faversham Abbey, Faversham, Kent. The base of the tomb was discovered in 1965.

Third son of Stephen, Count of Blois and Chartres, and Adela, daughter of William I. His nineteen-year rule was known as the reign of the 'nineteen long winters' owing to the continuous struggle with his cousin Matilda and, after 1149, with her young son, Henry, whom his parents had invested with the Duchy of Normandy in 1150. In 1141 Stephen was captured by Matilda and imprisoned, during which time she was proclaimed Lady of Normandy and Queen of England. After six months forces loyal to Stephen captured Matilda's half-brother, Robert of Gloucester, and she was forced to exchange him for Stephen. Owing to her unpopularity her cause declined and she retired to Normandy in 1148, assigning her rights to her son. In 1153, worn out by the conflict, Stephen agreed, after the death of his son Eustace, to acknowledge Matilda's son Henry as his heir. Thereafter until Stephen's death the two men acted together to counter the growing anarchy in the kingdom. Stephen died in October 1154, and was buried beside his Queen and his son.

THE PLANTAGENETS

Henry II (b.1133 r.1154–1189)
Fontevraud Abbey Church, Anjou, France.

The first of the long line of Plantagenet kings of England. On the death of Stephen in 1154 he succeeded peacefully to the English throne and immediately began to curb the lawlessness, a consequence of the previous reign. He introduced sweeping and lasting changes in the exercise of the laws of England. In 1171 he invaded Ireland. His controversy with the Church brought him into conflict with the Archbishop of Canterbury, Thomas à Becket, for whose murder on 29 December 1170 Henry was indirectly held responsible, through his impatient words, 'Will no one avenge me of this turbulent priest?' His marriage to Eleanor of Aquitaine, divorced wife of Louis VII of France, gave him, with his own inherited French domains, control of the larger part of what is now France and brought him into conflict with the French King. His sons, stirred up by their jealous mother, openly rebelled against Henry, and the latter part of his reign was spent in warring with them. He died on 6 July 1189 at Chinon.

Richard I, Coeur de Lion or Lionheart (b.1157 r.1189–1199)
Fontevraud Abbey Church, Anjou, France. His effigy may still be seen.

Third son of Henry II and Eleanor of Aquitaine. He succeeded peacefully at the death of his father but spent the majority of his reign out of the kingdom. In 1191 he went on the Crusade, winning a great victory over Saladin at Arsuf that same year. He left the Holy Land in 1192 after concluding a treaty with Saladin. During the return journey he was captured and imprisoned by Leopold of Austria in Durnstein Castle. There, rumour has it, he was found by a troubadour, Blondel de Nesle. Ransomed, he returned to England in 1194 but stayed in the realm only a few weeks before leaving for his French domains. He left the government of England in the care of Hubert Walter, whose skill as an administrator mitigated the effects of Richard's harsh tax demands. Whilst besieging the Castle of Chälus he was struck by an arrow and died on 6 April 1199.

John, Lackland (b.1167 r.1199–1216)
Worcester Cathedal, Worcester, in the Presbytery.

The youngest son of Henry II and Eleanor of Aquitaine. During his elder brother's absence on the Crusade he tried to wrest the administration of England from the Chancellor, William Longchamp, and succeeded with the help of the nobles and the Londoners in expelling him. John, however, was prevented from heading the administration in Longchamp's place and, when it was known that Richard was imprisoned, he worked with his allies, including the French King, to prevent the release of the King. When Richard I returned to England in 1194 he forgave his brother though it was not until on his deathbed that the King reversed his previous decision to acknowledge Arthur of Brittany as his heir and made John his successor. On Richard's death his wishes were carried out and John was acknowledged King, despite the superior claims of the young Prince Arthur, who was captured in 1202 and imprisoned on John's orders, dying mysteriously a year later. John's misgovernment alienated all classes and he was forced by the baronage to sign the Magna Carta at Runnymede in June 1215. This did not bring peace and John's fight against the barons with the help of the French prince, Louis, is today seen as one of the most creditable episodes in an otherwise calamitous career in which the King lost all his continental domains. He died at Newark on 19 October 1216.

Henry III (b.1207 r.1216–1272)
Chapel of St Edward the Confessor, Westminster Abbey, London. His heart was sent to France and buried in the Abbey Church of Fontevraud, Anjou.

Eldest son of King John and Isabella of Angoulême. He was nine when his father died and during his minority the country was governed by the aged William Marshal, Earl of Pembroke. At his accession his cause was in dire straits, the rebel barons and Prince Louis of France being in control of much of eastern England. As a consequence of this Henry was crowned at Gloucester, the western capital, his coronation at Westminster not taking place until 1220. During the ensuing year Henry's cause gradually triumphed, the French prince being defeated on both land and sea until he finally renounced all his claims and retired to France. Henry's personal rule began in 1227, although he

Tomb of Henry III, Chapel of St Edward the Confessor, Westminster Abbey, London

remained for some time under the influence of the Justiciar, Hubert de Burgh, who had succeeded William Marshal, who had died in 1219, as the chief administrator of the realm. In 1236 he married Eleanor of Provence and sought to regain the traditional Plantagenet lands in France which his father had lost. His continental ambitions meant harsh taxation which led to dissension with the English barons. The Provisions of Oxford in 1258 placed the government in the hands of a feudal oligarchy, and the King's defeat by Simon de Montfort at Lewes in 1264 meant that all effective power passed from the King to the barons. The following year, the King's cause triumphed when Prince Edward, later Edward I, defeated and killed de Montfort at the Battle of Evesham. Thereafter, the King remained under the influence of his eldest son who, by the Statute of Marlborough in 1267, brought peace to the land. Henry died at Westminster on 16 November 1272.

Edward I, Longshanks (b.1239 r.1272–1307)
Chapel of St Edward the Confessor, Westminster Abbey, London.

When his father, Henry III, died Edward was in Sicily, returning to England from the Crusade. Crowned at Westminster on 18 August 1274 he is chiefly remembered as the 'Hammer of the Scots' and for his defeat of the Welsh. He reorganized the laws of England by numerous statutes in an attempt to eliminate feudalism from political life. In 1295, he convoked a representative parliament of the three estates, which has since been called the Model Parliament, because it first illustrated the type which was to be perpetuated in all subsequent parliaments. The parliamentary constitution of England was established as the result of Edward's action. His continual wars against the Scottish nation did not effect long-term English rule and the only lasting result was the removal of the coronation stone from Scone to Westminster. His subjugation of the Welsh was in reality merely a subjugation of the territories of Llewellyn but he had established his hold on the principality by 1284 during which year he presented his son, Edward, to the Welsh as their prince and, in the Statute of Wales, provided the scheme for the future government of the country. On 7 July 1307, whilst on another Scottish campaign, Edward died at Burgh-on-Sands near Carlisle, and, despite his wishes that his heart be buried in the Holy Land and his bones carried by the army for inspiration, his body was taken to London on the orders of the new King for burial.

Tomb of Edward I, Chapel of St Edward the Confessor, Westminster Abbey, London

Edward II (b.1284 r.1307–1327)
Gloucester Cathedral, Gloucester: a beautiful tomb.

Fourth son of Edward I and his first wife, Eleanor of Castile. At his succession he immediately abandoned the Scottish campaign, leaving the way clear for Robert the Bruce to establish his rule and for his ultimate defeat of Edward and his English forces at the Battle of Bannockburn on 24 June 1314, thereby confirming the independence of Scotland. Edward was a weak king, 'destitute of any serious purpose', and under the influence of his favourites. Nevertheless, he was responsible for one of the most momentous stages in English constitutional history. His parliament held at York in 1322 revoked ordinances formerly granted by the baronage because 'they trenched on the rights of the crown and were drawn up by the barons only'. From this time on no statutes were technically valid unless the Commons had agreed to them. A rising against the Despensers, the royal favourites, inspired by the Queen, Isabella of France, and her lover, Roger Mortimer, in September 1326 brought about the death of the favourites and the capture of the King. On 20 January 1327 Edward was forced to abdicate in favour of his son, Edward III, and he was murdered in Berkeley Castle on 21 September 1327 and his body interred in the Cathedral.

Edward III (b.1312 r.1327–1377)
Chapel of St Edward the Confessor, Westminster Abbey, London.

Succeeded to the throne after the deposition of his father in January 1327. He was fourteen and effective rule remained in the hands of his mother, Queen Isabella, and her lover, Roger Mortimer. In October 1330 he took Mortimer prisoner at Nottingham Castle, executing him at Tyburn the following month. Henceforth, the government was under his control. His long reign saw the outbreak of the Black Death, which intensified social and economic disturbances through its decimation of the population; the institution of the Order of the Garter; and the beginning of the Hundred Years War with France, in which Edward laid claim to the French crown. Sir Winston Churchill in his *History of the English Speaking Peoples* said that the Battle of Crécy in 1346 ranked with Blenheim, Waterloo and the final advance in the last summer of the Great War 'as one of the four supreme achievements of the British army', for the power and accuracy of the English longbow was infinitely superior to the crossbow used by the French and Genoese archers. During his reign the King fostered the woollen industry. Towards the end of his life his faculties were impaired and he fell under the influence of a greedy mistress, Alice Perrers, while his son, John of Gaunt, Duke of Lancaster, controlled the machinery of government. Edward died on 21 June 1377.

Richard II (b.1367 r.1377–1399)
Chapel of St Edward the Confessor, Westminster Abbey, London.

Son of Edward, the Black Prince, and Joan of Kent, he was the grandson of Edward III whom he succeeded whilst still a boy of ten years. In 1381, he showed courage in confronting the rebels during the Peasants' Revolt. Able and gifted, Richard's policies grew increasingly erratic during the later years of his reign. A rebellion led by his cousin Henry, Duke of Lancaster, son of John of Gaunt, brought his abdication and death in Pontefract Castle. After his death his body

Tomb of Edward III, Chapel of St Edward the Confessor, Westminster Abbey, London

was brought to London and lay in state in Old St Paul's and was then taken to Langley in Hertfordshire for burial. It was transferred to Westminster in 1413 on the orders of Henry V and re-interred in the same tomb as that of Queen Anne, Richard's beloved first wife.

THE LANCASTRIANS

Henry IV (b.1367 r.1399–1413)
Trinity Chapel, Canterbury Cathedral, Canterbury, Kent.

Eldest son of John of Gaunt, Duke of Lancaster, and Blanche, his first wife. He was first cousin to Richard II. He headed the rebellion which overthrew King Richard, forcing his abdication in September 1399. Henry then laid claim to the throne by 'right line of blood from Henry III' which was accepted by Parliament. He therefore became king, according to Capgrave, 'not so much by title of blood as by popular election', and was the first of the Lancastrian dynasty of Plantagenets to sit on the throne. His position was soon consolidated by the pursuit of sound practical policies.

Henry V (b.1387 r.1413–1422)
Chapel of St Edward the Confessor, Westminster Abbey, London. A casket, believed to contain the internal organs of the King, was discovered at Fosses, just outside Paris, in 1978.

Son of Henry IV and Mary de Bohun, he succeeded his father after an erratic youth. He renewed the Hundred Years War with France, started by his great-grandfather, Edward III, and showed brilliant generalship, defeating the French decisively at the Battle of Agincourt on 25 October 1415 with the loss of only 113 English soldiers as opposed to the loss of 5,000 French 'gentlemen of quality'. Following the Treaty of Troyes in 1420 he married Catherine de Valois, daughter of the French King Charles VI, who acknowledged his son-in-law as his heir to the French throne. But before he could succeed Henry died of dysentery at Vincennes on 31 August 1422.

Tomb of Richard II and his Queen, Anne of Bohemia, Chapel of St Edward the Confessor, Westminster Abbey, London

King Henry V, by an unknown artist

Henry VI (b.1421 r.1422–1461 restored 1470–1471)
St George's Chapel, Windsor Castle, Windsor, Berkshire, in the second bay of the choir, south side.

Succeeded his father, Henry V, as King of England when only nine months old, and, a few weeks later on the death of his grandfather Charles VI of France, he also became King of France. He was crowned King of England at Westminster on 6 November 1429 and King of France in Paris on 16 December 1431. A peaceful man, Henry supported pacific policies which gradually led to the loss of his French domains. Married to the warlike Margaret of Anjou who produced an heir, Edward Prince of Wales, in 1453, Henry increasingly withdrew from politics leaving the reins of government in the hands of his wife and Edmund Beaufort, Duke of Somerset. When Henry's mind gave way in 1453, the realm was placed under the protectorship of Richard Duke of York, who was heir to the throne after the Prince of Wales. With the King's return to sanity the following year power once more reverted to the Queen and Somerset which shortly thereafter produced a conflict between the King's party and that of the Duke of York, thus initiating the wars which became known as the Wars of the Roses. York was killed at Wakefield on 29 December 1460 but his son, Edward Earl of March, reversed the defeat at the Battle of Towton on 29 March 1461, and forced Henry and his family into exile. Edward was proclaimed King and for the next three years Henry was a fugitive in Scotland. In 1465 he was captured in the north of England after an abortive attempt to regain the throne and was taken to the Tower of London as a prisoner. For six months, during 1470 and 1471, he emerged to hold a shadowy kingship as a puppet of Warwick, the Kingmaker, but the defeat of Warwick at Barnet, and his wife and son at Tewkesbury, in 1471, brought an end to his liberty and life.

THE YORKISTS

Edward IV (b.1442 r.1461–1470 restored 1471–1483)
St George's Chapel, Windsor Castle, Windsor, Berkshire, between the High Altar and the north choir aisle.

Son of Richard Duke of York and great-great-grandson of Edward III. After the death of his father at the Battle of Wakefield on 29 December 1460 Edward became the leader of the Yorkist faction.

After his victory over the forces of Henry VI at Towton on 29 March 1461 he was proclaimed King as Edward IV. He antagonized his supporters by his marriage to Elizabeth Woodville and this led ultimately to a severance of his relations with the Earl of Warwick, the Kingmaker. During the years 1470 and 1471 he spent six months in exile in Burgundy following Warwick's successful campaign to restore Henry VI. He returned to England and with a force of loyal supporters defeated Warwick at Barnet and Queen Margaret at Tewkesbury in May 1471. Firmly established once more on the throne, the complete annihilation of the main Lancastrian claims brought peace and stability to the realm and with it increased foreign trade and the rise of the mercantile classes. Edward died in 1483.

Edward V (b.1470 r.briefly 1483)
Henry VII's Chapel, Westminster Abbey, London, 'Innocents' Corner'.

Elder son of Edward IV and Elizabeth Woodville, he was twelve when his father died. His uncle, Richard Duke of Gloucester, succeeded in ousting the young King's maternal relatives and gained possession of the boy's person. Declared illegitimate, he and his brother were kept in the Tower of London where they died, reputedly smothered, by whom or on whose responsibility is unclear, although legend has it that it was on the orders of their uncle, Richard III. Bones unearthed in the Tower in 1674 were believed to have been those of Edward and his brother, known as the Princes in the Tower, and the then King, Charles II, had them reinterred in Henry VII's Chapel at the eastern end of the aisle in what was described by Dean Stanley as 'The Innocents' Corner'.

Richard III (b.1452 r.1483–1485)
Leicester Abbey, Leicester; a tomb erected by Henry VII was destroyed at the Suppression. Plaque on Bow Bridge over River Soar in which his body was thrown at Suppression.

Younger brother of Edward IV. After the proclamation of the illegitimacy of his brother's children, Richard succeeded as the natural heir. 'An earnest and hardworking ruler', he introduced many new laws, including the bail law. He was defeated at the Battle of Bosworth Field in 1485, the last battle of the Wars of the Roses, by the Lancastrian pretender, Henry Tudor, Earl of Richmond. Richard III was the last of the direct Plantagenet line of English kings.

Funeral effigy of Henry VII, Henry VII's Chapel, Westminster Abbey, London

Henry VII (b.1457 r.1485–1509)

Henry VII's Chapel, Westminster Abbey, London, in the Nave.

Although known as the Lancastrian Pretender to the throne, Henry Tudor, Earl of Richmond, had no legitimate claim to the throne, for the Beauforts, through whom he was descended from John of Gaunt, fourth son of Edward III, were specifically barred from inheriting the crown. On his father's side he was descended from the Valois Kings of France through his grandmother, Catherine de Valois, widow of Henry V, who, after her husband's death, had secretly married the young and handsome Welsh squire, Owen Tudor. After the Battle of Bosworth Field Henry was careful to claim the throne by right of conquest although he cemented his hold on it by marrying Elizabeth of York, eldest daughter of Edward IV, thus uniting the two houses of York and Lancaster. He successfully ended the baronial wars, curbed the power of the baronage, and, through his fiscal and economic policies, prepared the way for England's period of stability and expansion under the Tudors.

Henry VIII (b.1491 r.1509–1547)

St George's Chapel, Windsor Castle, Windsor, Berkshire, in the centre of the choir with his third wife, Jane Seymour.

Second son of Henry VII and Elizabeth of York, he became the first head of the Church of England after his break with the papacy over the question of his divorce from his first wife, Catherine of Aragon, the widow of his brother, Arthur Prince of Wales. The break began the ascendancy of the Protestant Church in England, although Henry never liked the reformed religion and remained a Catholic all his life. He was married six times: firstly to Catherine of Aragon, the mother of Mary I, whose inability to provide a male heir led to her divorce; secondly to Anne Boleyn, mother of Elizabeth I, whom he both divorced and beheaded; thirdly to Jane Seymour, the mother of Edward VI, who died in childbirth; fourthly to Anne of Cleves, 'the Flanders Mare', whom he speedily divorced; fifthly to the young Catherine Howard, who was beheaded for adultery; and lastly to Katharine Parr, who survived him. During Henry's reign the parliamentary system was developed, and the powers of Parliament were exercised more widely than hitherto. Royal supremacy over the Church, despite its harsh and violent enforcement, and although forced on Henry by private rather than public consideration, saved England from a serious civil war.

Edward VI (b.1537 r.1547–1553)
Henry VII's Chapel, Westminster Abbey, London, beneath the altar in the nave.

Son of Henry VIII and his third wife, Jane Seymour, he was only nine when he ascended the throne. His maternal uncle, Edward Seymour, Duke of Somerset, was appointed Regent. The issue of religion was of paramount importance during his reign, and the Catholic bishops, Gardiner and Bonner, maintained that the royal supremacy over the Church was, or should be, in abeyance owing to the King's minority. The execution of the Protector Somerset gave power to John Dudley, Duke of Northumberland, who, as the King's health declined throughout 1552 and early 1553, sought to maintain his own position and the Protestant ascendancy by ensuring the succession of a pliant Protestant sovereign. Edward was persuaded to leave the crown to his cousin, Lady Jane Grey, 'and her heirs male', effectively disbarring Edward's half-sisters, Mary and Elizabeth. Edward's last recorded words were vehement injunctions to Archbishop Cranmer to sign the will. He died at Greenwich on 6 July 1553.

Jane, Lady Jane Grey (b.1537 r.10–19 July 1553 d.1554)
St Peter ad Vincula, Tower of London, London.

Her cousin, Edward VI, had been persuaded by the all-powerful John Dudley, Duke of Northumberland, to break his father's will and to make a new settlement of the crown by deed, which was witnessed by members of the Council, many under duress. This left the crown to the Lady Jane Grey, an avowed Protestant, great-grand-daughter of Henry VII, who was also married to Northumberland's fourth son, Lord Guildford Dudley. Edward's death was kept secret for a few days, the Lady Jane being proclaimed Queen in the City on 10 July 1553; she was sixteen, and had only accepted the crown after much entreaty. Her reign lasted but nine days, Jane's own father, the Duke of Suffolk, proclaiming Mary, Henry VIII's eldest daughter, Queen on 19 July, informing his own daughter that she must return to private life, a request she told him she had no hesitation in accepting. Despite being found guilty of treason, Queen Mary allowed Jane and her husband a semblance of freedom and it was widely believed that she would have been pardoned had it not been for her father's involvement in the uprising led by Sir Thomas Wyat in January and February 1554. Jane and her husband were both executed on 12 February 1554 on Tower Hill.

Mary I (b.1516 r.1553–1558)
Henry VII's Chapel, Westminster Abbey, London, in the north aisle.

Eldest surviving daughter of Henry VIII and his first wife, Catherine of Aragon. Her accession was interrupted by the brief nine-days reign of her cousin, Lady Jane Grey. Her marriage to her cousin, Philip II of Spain, was unpopular and its announcement led to an immediate rebellion in January 1554 by Sir Thomas Wyat, in which he was joined by the Duke of Suffolk, Lady Jane Grey's father. Wyat's defeat led to the execution of Lady Jane Grey and to the imprisonment in the Tower of London of Mary's half-sister, the Princess Elizabeth. Mary restored the realm to the ecclesiastical control of the papacy, recalling her cousin, Cardinal Reginald Pole, whom she made Archbishop of Canterbury. Her persecution of the Protestants during her five-year reign earned her the epithet 'Bloody'. The loss of Calais, the last English possession in France, shortly before her death, was a severe blow to her.

Elizabeth I (b.1553 r.1558–1603)
Henry VII's Chapel, Westminster Abbey, London, in the north aisle.

Younger daughter of Henry VIII by his second wife, Anne Boleyn. No sovereign since Saxon times had been so purely English in blood; her nearest foreign ancestor being Catherine de Valois, widow of Henry V. No English king or queen was more insular in character or policy. Her reign has long been regarded as the Golden Age and one of the greatest periods in English history. Politically and intellectually able she was shrewd and lucky in the choice of her advisers among whom were Lord Burghley, Sir Francis Walsingham and the Earl of Leicester. She valued uniformity in religion and her reign saw the establishment of the Church of England. The reformation of the coinage and her fiscal policies gave the country a secure economic base whilst the defeat of the Spanish Armada in 1588 gave England the command of the seas and security from invasion. Her reign also saw the flowering of literature with such eminent figures as Sir Philip Sidney, Christopher Marlowe and William Shakespeare, much of whose work was written during Elizabeth's reign.

Queen Mary I, by Master John

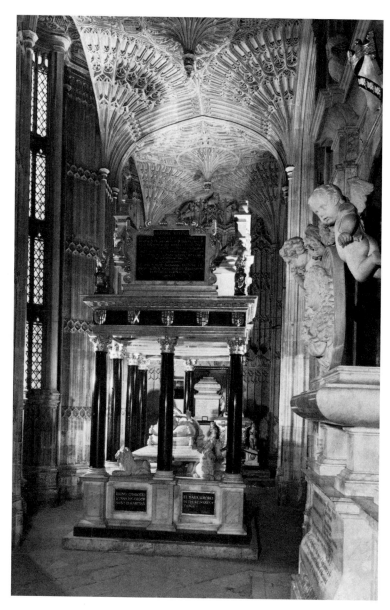

Tomb of Elizabeth I, Henry VII's Chapel, Westminster Abbey, London

THE STUARTS

James I (b.1566 r.1603–1625)
Henry VII's Chapel, Westminster Abbey, London, in the nave.

Son of Mary, Queen of Scots, and Henry, Lord Darnley, he succeeded his mother to the Scottish throne after her abdication in 1566. In 1603, on the death of his remote cousin, Elizabeth I of England, he succeeded to the English throne, his claim stemming from his descent from Margaret of England, elder daughter of Henry VII, who married his great-grandfather, James IV of Scotland. During his reign he commissioned the Authorized Version of the Bible which was published in 1611; but his religious policies brought a growing confrontation between the Established Church and the Puritans. He continued the colonial adventures of Elizabeth, encouraging settlements in North America and Ireland. A scholar, not a practical man, he was commonly known as 'the wisest fool in Christendom'.

Charles I (b.1600 r.1625–1649)
St George's Chapel, Windsor Castle, Windsor, Berkshire, in the centre of the choir.

The second son of James I and Anne of Denmark. A sincere but inept monarch, his autocratic policies soon led to a confrontation with the House of Commons and he attempted to rule without Parliament. He supported the strict Anglicanism of Archbishop Laud and this drove a number of moderate Protestants out of the Church into Presbyterianism, and created an intense feeling of hostility to the government throughout the realm. The resulting Civil War brought the King's final defeat and execution for treason at Whitehall on 30 January 1649, the only English sovereign to be so executed.

THE COMMONWEALTH

Cromwell, Oliver (1599–1658)
Henry VII's Chapel, Westminster Abbey, London, in the small east chapel, now known as the RAF Chapel, where a stone in the pavement records his burial there together with members of his family and some of the regicides. St Nicholas's Church, Chiswick Mall, London W also lays claim to his body.

Entered Parliament as Member for Huntingdon in 1628. When the

Civil War broke out he served under the Earl of Essex. His own military ability proved itself when he reorganized the Parliamentary army, winning the battles of Marston Moor and Naseby. Following the execution of Charles I on 30 January 1649 Cromwell became the head of the government and in 1653 Lord Protector of the Commonwealth of England, Scotland and Ireland. He defeated a Scottish uprising at Dunbar and his harsh treatment of the Irish enhanced his government's difficulties there. He died in 1658 and was buried in Westminster Abbey. At the Restoration, however, his body together with those of other regicides was disinterred and hung on Tyburn gallows until 30 January 1661, the anniversary of Charles I's execution, his head being stuck on a pole on top of Westminster Hall. *The Times* of July 1969 reported that according to letters from Captain E. L. Dale, the son of the Reverend Lawford Dale, Vicar of St Nicholas's Church, Chiswick Mall in West London, in 1882, the Protector's remains had been switched at burial on the Protector's own orders and were later buried in the vaults of St Nicholas's Church. If this is true, they are now sealed under a thick cement floor. A letter to *The Times*, 31 August 1989, from Phillida Grantham, stated that she once held Cromwell's head, 'then in the possession of the Wilkinson family', and that it is now buried at his old Cambridge college, Sidney Sussex.

Cromwell, Richard (1626–1712)
Hursley Church, Hampshire, in the chancel; the original church being replaced by the present All Saints' Church built for John Keble during 1846–8.
    Son of Oliver Cromwell, who succeeded his father as Lord Protector in 1658. He resigned on 25 May 1659 and went into exile on the continent using the name of John Clarke. He returned to England about 1680, living in the house of Sergeant Pengelly at Cheshunt, where he died on 12 July 1712.

THE STUARTS RESTORED

Charles II (b.1630 r.1660–1685)
Henry VII's Chapel, Westminster Abbey, London, in the Royal Vault below the south aisle.
    Eldest son of Charles I and his French queen, Henrietta Maria, he

returned to England and was restored to the throne in May 1660 after a long exile on the Continent during the Commonwealth under Oliver Cromwell and his son Richard. An able and astute politician, he was instrumental in re-establishing the monarchy as the pivot of the British constitution.

James II (b.1633 r.1685–1688)

Church of St Germains, France. Partial remains re-interred on orders of George IV after their re-discovery in 1824.

Second son of Charles I and Queen Henrietta Maria. He succeeded his brother, Charles II, peacefully despite earlier attempts to bar him from the throne because of his Catholicism. His religion played an important rôle during his brief reign but it was his lack of political insight rather than his religious bigotry which led to the Glorious Revolution of 1688, for, far from trying to impose Catholicism on the realm, he had merely tried to obtain concessions for his co-religionists. Allowed to escape to France by his daughter, Mary, and her Dutch husband, William of Orange, who had been offered the crowns of England and Scotland to safeguard the Protestant succession, James lived the remainder of his life in exile at the Palace of St Germains in France, his one attempt to re-gain the throne by an invasion of Ireland being defeated by his son-in-law at the Battle of the Boyne in 1690.

Mary II (b.1662 r.1689–1694)

Henry VII's Chapel, Westminster Abbey, London, in the Royal Vault below the south aisle.

The eldest of James II's two daughters by Anne Hyde, she was proclaimed Queen jointly with her husband, William of Orange, after the flight of her father following the Glorious Revolution, in which not a shot was fired. She died of smallpox at Hampton Court in 1694.

William III, of Orange (b.1650 r.1689–1702)

Henry VII's Chapel, Westminster Abbey, London, in the Royal Vault below the south aisle.

He accepted the crowns of England and Scotland jointly with his wife, Mary, eldest of James II's two daughters by the Protestant Anne Hyde, following the flight of his father-in-law in December 1688 during the Glorious Revolution. In 1689 the Bill of Rights defined the liberties established by the revolution of the previous year. William defeated James's attempts to re-gain his throne at the Battle of the

Boyne in 1690. Much of the King's political concern was his war with Louis XIV of France which was finally brought to an end with the Peace of Ryswick in 1697. He died from the combined effects of a fall from his horse and a chill on 8 March 1702.

Anne (b.1665 r.1702–1714)
Henry VII's Chapel, Westminster Abbey, London, in the Royal Vault below the south aisle.

Sister of Mary II and younger daughter of James II and his Protestant wife, Anne Hyde. She was the first sovereign to reign over the united kingdom of England and Scotland, the two kingdoms having been united under the Act of Union of 1707. Guided by Tory and high church principles her reign was notable for the achievements of others: the Duke of Marlborough's victorious campaigns against the French; the scientific developments of Newton; the architecture of Christopher Wren and John Vanbrugh; and the literary works of Swift, Pope, Steele, Defoe and Addison. She established Queen Anne's bounty to improve the finances of the Church. By her consort, Prince George of Denmark, she had seventeen children, all of whom died in infancy, only the young Duke of Gloucester surviving to his eleventh year.

THE HANOVERIANS

George I (b.1660 r.1714–1727)
Hanover, Germany, in the vaults of the palace.

A great-grandson of James I through his daughter, Elizabeth of Bohemia, the Winter Queen. The Act of Settlement of 1701 settled the succession on the Electress Sophia of Hanover, George's mother, to guarantee the Protestant succession, debarring all closer claimants including the exiled son of James II, the Old Pretender, who adhered to the Catholic religion. Unable to speak English, George left the affairs of the country in the hands of ministers and the system of Cabinet government under a Prime Minister evolved, the first such being Sir Robert Walpole who was the chief minister of this and the succeeding reign of twenty-one years. The first of the two Jacobite rebellions, led by James the Old Pretender, known as James III, was defeated at Preston and Sheriffmuir in 1715. George collapsed in his carriage during a journey to Osnabruck and died there on Wednesday

12 June 1727, his remains being taken to his palace at Hanover for interment.

George II (b.1683 r.1727–1760)
Henry VII's Chapel, Westminster Abbey, London, in the nave.

The son of George I and his divorced wife, Sophia Dorothea of Celle, George II continued the rôle of Sir Robert Walpole as his Prime Minister until Sir Robert fell from power in 1742. George II was the last British monarch to lead his troops personally, doing so at the Battle of Dettingen in 1743. The second Jacobite uprising, this time under Bonnie Prince Charlie the Young Pretender, was, after some initial success, defeated at Culloden in 1746 and put down with great severity by the King's son, William Duke of Cumberland, thereafter known as Butcher Cumberland. In his will the King left instructions that he be buried with his wife, Caroline of Anspach, and that the sides of their coffins should be struck away in order that their ashes might mingle.

George III (b.1738 r.1760–1820)
St George's Chapel, Windsor Castle, Windsor, Berkshire, in the Royal Vault below the Albert Memorial Chapel.

Eldest son of Frederick Prince of Wales, 'Poor Fred', he succeeded his grandfather, George II, his father having died in 1751. His reign was notable for the loss of the American colonies; but it also saw the expansion of British power in India. During his sixty years on the throne the country underwent the upheavals of the great agrarian and industrial revolutions. It was also an age of developments in other fields: science, exploration, chemistry, philosophy and invention under such great figures as Henry Cavendish who discovered hydrogen and the chemical composition of water, James Cook whose voyages of discovery took him to Australia and New Zealand, Joseph Priestley who shared with Carl Scheele the discovery of oxygen, Adam Smith the Scottish political economist who wrote the *Wealth of Nations* and Sir Humphry Davy who invented the miner's safety lamp which still bears his name. The King was a sufferer from intermittent porphyria which caused him to have two severe mental breakdowns and gave the royal power into the hands of his detested elder son, George, the Prince Regent; the first occurring in November 1788 and lasting until February 1789, the second in 1811 after the death of his favourite child, the Princess Amelia, and which lasted the remaining nine years of his life during which he also went blind.

George IV (b.1762 r.1820–1830)

St George's Chapel, Windsor Castle, Windsor, Berkshire, in the Royal Vault below the Albert Memorial Chapel.

Elder son of George III and Charlotte of Mecklenburg-Strelitz, he became Regent for the last nine years of his father's reign, from 1811 to 1820. Whilst Prince of Wales and without effective political power he had courted the Whig party in opposition, but when he gained power in 1811 he gave his support, after some hesitation, to the Tories, who remained in office during the Regency and throughout his reign. He was generally unpopular for his licentious and extravagant way of life, the general condemnation being inflamed by his treatment of his indiscreet wife, Caroline of Brunswick.

William IV (b.1765 r.1830–1837)

St George's Chapel, Windsor Castle, Windsor, Berkshire, in the Royal Vault below the Albert Memorial Chapel.

Third son of George III and Queen Charlotte, he succeeded his brother, George IV, in 1830. His reign saw a number of reforming statutes passed through Parliament, the most notable being the Reform Bill of 1832 which extended the franchise and did away with many corrupt electoral practices.

Victoria (b.1819 r.1837–1901)

Royal Mausoleum, Frogmore, Windsor, Berkshire.

Grand-daughter of George III and daughter of Edward, Duke of Kent, and his wife Victoria of Saxe-Coburg, she succeeded her uncle, William IV, when she was but seventeen. Her accession meant the separation of the crowns of Great Britain and Hanover, for under Salic Law a woman could not succeed in Hanover. Her uncle, Ernest, Duke of Cumberland, therefore succeeded his brother William IV as King of Hanover. During the Queen's reign there was a general growth in many areas – industrial, humanitarian, the arts – as well as abroad; in 1877 Victoria was proclaimed Empress of India, a title her descendants held until the independence of India and Pakistan in 1947. Her devoted husband, Prince Albert of Saxe-Coburg-Gotha, the Prince Consort, and she set a high and strict moral standard for the age by their hard work and conscientiousness. After his death in

1861 of typhoid fever the Queen withdrew from public life for a number of years until she was persuaded back into public affairs by her friend and Prime Minister, Benjamin Disraeli, Earl of Beaconsfield, and in so doing firmly established the rôle of the constitutional monarch in British political life.

THE HOUSE OF SAXE–COBURG–GOTHA

Edward VII (b.1841 r.1901–1910)
St George's Chapel, Windsor Castle, Windsor, Berkshire, his tomb being on the south side of the High Altar.

Eldest son of Queen Victoria and Albert of Saxe-Coburg-Gotha, he was 59 when he came to the throne. His natural charm and political sagacity cleared the way for an end to the prolonged period of estrangement between Britain and France with the Entente Cordiale, as well as helping to establish harmonious relations with other European powers. It was left to him to consolidate the rôle of the constitutional monarch established by his mother.

THE WINDSORS

George V (b.1865 r.1910–1936)
St George's Chapel, Windsor Castle, Windsor, Berkshire, in a tomb designed by Sir Edwin Lutyens in the second bay of the north side of the nave.

Second son of Edward VII and Alexandra of Denmark, his accession was marred by the political controversy over the Parliament Act of 1911 which decisively reduced the powers of the House of Lords. His reign saw the duration of the first world war, 1914–1918; the formation of the Irish Free State on 6 December 1921; and the first Labour Government under Ramsay Macdonald in 1924.

Edward VIII, Duke of Windsor (b.1894 r.January–December 1936 d.1972)
Royal cemetery in Windsor Home Park, Berkshire. The gardens and mausoleum of Queen Victoria are open only on May 14, 15 and 21.

Eldest son of George V and Mary of Teck, he reigned for only 325 days before abdicating over the issue of his marriage to an American divorcee, Mrs Wallis Warfield Simpson. He took the title of Duke of Windsor and lived abroad. During the second world war he became Governor of the Bahamas.

George VI (b.1895 r.1936–1952)
St George's Chapel, Windsor Castle, Windsor, Berkshire, in a specially constructed side chapel adjoining the north choir aisle.

Brother of Edward VIII and second son of George V and Queen Mary, he succeeded after his brother's abdication on 12 December 1936. With the help of his wife, Elizabeth, the present Queen Mother, he overcame his natural shyness and nervous stammer. During the second world war he and his family led the way in maintaining a high morale in a beleaguered Britain. The Labour administration of Clement Attlee immediately after the war brought independence to many former colonies, including India.

[2] Royal Consorts and Nobles

Albert of Saxe-Coburg-Gotha, the Prince Consort (1819–1861)
Royal Mausoleum, Frogmore, Windsor, Berkshire.

   Second son of the Duke of Saxe-Coburg-Gotha, he married his cousin, Queen Victoria, in 1840. He was a constant support to his wife in her political duties and in 1861 managed to avert war with the United States by advising a conciliatory course. He was responsible for the Great Exhibition of 1851. Ten years later he died of typhoid fever, and he is commemorated by the Albert Memorial in Kensington Gardens, London.

Anne Boleyn (1507–1536)
St Peter ad Vincula, Tower of London, London. She is also reputed to be buried in the Boleyn church at Salle, Norfolk; whilst two other churches claim to have her heart buried within their precincts: All Saints Church, East Horndon, near Billericay, Essex, in the altar tomb in the south transept wall; and SSs Andrew and Patrick Church, Elveden Park, near Thetford, Norfolk, which claims that the heart was discovered in the south wall in 1836 and reburied under the organ.

   The second wife of Henry VIII and mother of Elizabeth I. It was her marriage to Henry VIII which brought about the break with Rome. In 1536 she was accused of adultery and incest with her brother, George Boleyn Viscount Rochford, found guilty and executed on Tower Green, the first English Queen to be so executed.

Anne of Cleves (1515–1557)
Westminster Abbey, London, on the south side of the Presbytery.

   Fourth wife of Henry VIII. She was the daughter of John Duke of Cleves, the leader of the German Protestant princes. Sought in marriage for the King by Thomas Cromwell, when he saw her in December 1540 Henry was so abashed at her appearance that he forgot to present her with the gift he had brought her. The following day he openly expressed his dissatisfaction with her looks: 'she was no better than a Flanders mare'. Forced to continue with the marriage on 6 January 1540 he refused to consummate it and, with Anne's consent, the marriage was declared null and void by convocation and an act of

Parliament on 9 July 1540. She agreed to live permanently in England and spent the rest of her life quietly at Richmond or Bletchingley, occasionally visiting the court. She died in Chelsea on 28 July 1557.

Caroline of Anspach (1683–1737)

Henry VII's Chapel, Westminster Abbey, London, in the nave.

Consort of George II. During her husband's reign she exercised her considerable influence in support of Sir Robert Walpole, maintaining him in power. She was also responsible for appointing many learned rather than orthodox bishops, being extremely tolerant by nature. She retained her good influence over her husband until her death, and when he died he instructed that the sides of their coffins be removed so that their ashes might mingle.

Catherine Howard (c.1521–1542)

St Peter ad Vincula, Tower of London, London.

Fifth wife of Henry VIII she was the daughter of Lord Edmund Howard, the son of the Duke of Norfolk. She caught the eye of the King and, supported by the Catholic party, his attentions were encouraged. They were married privately at Oatlands in July 1540 and soon afterwards she was publicly acknowledged as Queen. In November 1541 Archbishop Cranmer informed the King that his wife had not been chaste before her marriage. Imprisoned, she was later released on her confession and forgiven by the King. But not long afterwards fresh evidence was procured that she had committed adultery and she was beheaded on 13 February 1542.

Catherine of Aragon (1485–1536)

Peterborough Cathedral, Peterborough. The tomb was destroyed during the Civil War.

First wife of Henry VIII, she was the daughter of Ferdinand of Aragon and Isabella of Castile. First married to Henry's elder brother, Arthur Prince of Wales, who died in April 1502. She was betrothed a year later to the young Prince Henry but the marriage was not celebrated for six years, despite papal dispensation for it having been obtained. However, immediately after Henry's accession the marriage took place, on 11 June 1509, and fourteen days later they were both crowned. During Henry's invasion of France in 1513 Catherine was made Regent and she successfully organized the defence of the realm against the invading Scottish forces under James IV, and was riding north to put herself at the head of the English troops when news was received of the rout of King James and his army at Flodden Field, the King and much of the Scottish nobility being slain. Between January 1510 and November 1518 Catherine gave birth to six children, including two princes, all of whom were stillborn or died in infancy with the exception of the Princess Mary, and rumour did not fail to ascribe the Queen's failure to produce an heir to the curse pronounced in *Deuteronomy* on incestuous unions. By 1526 it was apparent the Queen would bear no more children, and, as no woman had yet held the throne in her own right, a male heir was vital if a civil war was to be avoided. The Queen refused to accept the annulment of her marriage which was pronounced after the King's break with Rome. She was treated harshly, her daughter being taken from her, but her spirit was not broken and she continued to enjoy great popularity with the people of England until her death.

Catherine Parr (1512–1548)
Sudeley Castle, near Winchcombe, Gloucestershire, where a nineteenth-century tomb has replaced the original destroyed in the Civil War.

Henry VIII's sixth and last wife, she surviving him. She later married the Lord High Admiral, Thomas Seymour, the brother of Protector Somerset and uncle to Edward VI. She died of puerperal fever after giving birth to a daughter in 1548.

Cleveland, Barbara Villiers, Duchess of (1641–1709)
St Nicholas's Church, Chiswick Mall, Chiswick, London.

Mistress of Charles II, to whom she bore at least five children. She was the daughter of Viscount Grandison and married Roger Palmer, created Earl of Castlemaine in 1661, in April 1659. Shortly after her marriage her intimacy with Charles II began and she was made Lady of the Bedchamber to Charles's Queen, Catherine of Braganza, much to that lady's displeasure. She meddled in politics and was an opponent of Edward Hyde, Earl of Clarendon, at whose fall she was said to have 'exhibited a wild paroxysm of delight'. Her relations with the King declined because of her amorous exploits with others but by 1667 she was once again supreme at court. In 1670 she was made Countess of Southampton and Duchess of Cleveland with remainders to her first and third sons, the King denying he was the father of Henry, the second son. In 1670 her influence once again declined and

Catherine Parr, attributed to W. Scrots

The Duchess of Cleveland, after Lely

by 1674 she was entirely supplanted in the King's affections by Louise de Kéroualle, Duchess of Portsmouth. She went to live in Paris but returned to London just before Charles's death in 1685. Samuel Pepys wrote of her in his diary that she was 'one of England's most high-placed whores'.

Diana, Princess of Wales, Lady Diana Frances Spencer (1961–1997)
In consecrated ground on an island in a small lake on the Althorp estate of Earl Spencer, near Great Brington*, Northamptonshire. The grave may be viewed at certain times of the year. Admission is by ticket only.

Princess Diana was the third daughter of the 8th Earl of Spencer, Edward John. Her mother was Frances Roche (now, after divorce, the Hon Mrs Peter Shand Kydd) the daughter of Lady Fermoy who had descended from a wealthy American family, one of whom had married the 3rd Baron Fermoy in New York. Born at Sandringham, Diana went to several private schools in England and a Swiss finishing school. Her stepmother Raine was Countess of Dartmouth and the daughter of novelist Barbara Cartland. Diana's marriage to Charles, Prince of Wales, heir to the British throne, brought world-wide approval. Although they had met in childhood, Diana as an eligible young woman met Prince Charles on the royal yacht Britannia during Cowes Week, I.O.W. in 1980. They were married in 1981 at St Paul's Cathedral in a 'fairy tale' royal wedding. Their two sons, Prince William Arthur Phillip Louis ('Wills') and Prince Harry (Henry Charles Albert David) were born in 1982 and 1984 respectively.

She was divorced in 1996 – the title Her Royal Highness was stripped from her by the Queen. Diana met Emad Fayed ('Dodi') in July 1997. He was the son of an Egyptian millionaire, owner of Harrods department store in London. They met first at Cannes then at St Tropez. She and her children were guests at Fayed senior's estate there. Photographers constantly followed them even at sea. They had been the bane of her life since before and after she was married to Prince Charles. It has been suggested that in an attempt to escape photographers in Paris, the car carrying Diana and Fayed was being driven too fast. It crashed while returning to his apartment from the Ritz hotel, killing Diana, Dodi and the chauffeur.

* George Washington's ancestors were buried in the church at Great Brington, on the edge of the Spencer estate. They moved in the 1600s from nearby Sulgrave where the Washington Museum was established

earlier in the 20th century. It is on land where Laurence Washington's (7th ancestor in direct ascent from the first U.S. President) manor house stood.

Edward Prince of Wales, The Black Prince (1330–1376)
Trinity Chapel, Canterbury Cathedral, Canterbury, Kent, in a magnificent tomb on the south side.

Eldest son of Edward III and Philippa of Hainault he distinguished himself at the age of fifteen at the Battle of Crécy in 1346. Thereafter he gained a wide reputation as a general. He was the father of the ill-fated Richard II who succeeded Edward III whilst still a child. Edward was the first Prince of Wales to adopt the motto, *Ich Dien*, and the crest of three ostrich feathers, reputedly having taken them from the blind King of Bohemia who was slain at the Battle of Crécy.

Eleanor of Castile (1245–1290)
Chapel of St Edward the Confessor, Westminster Abbey, London.

Consort of Edward I. She accompanied her husband on his Crusade and is reputed to have sucked the poison from a wound inflicted by a poisoned dagger in an assassination attempt on her husband. When she died at Harby in Nottinghamshire the King had her body embalmed and taken to London. At each resting place a cross was erected in her memory, the most famous of which being the cross at Charing, now Charing Cross.

Elizabeth, Princess (1635–1650)
St Thomas's Church, Newport, Isle of Wight; small vault near the communion table.

Second daughter of Charles I, she was born at St James's Palace. She showed a remarkable talent for languages, being able to read and write Greek, Latin, Hebrew, French and Italian before she was eight years old. Confined at Carisbrooke Castle, she was horrified at being where her father had been imprisoned, pleading not to be sent there. Within a week of her arrival she caught pneumonia as a result of getting wet through one day. Parliament was on the point of allowing her to go to Holland when she died, with her cheek, it was said, on her Bible and a tear on her cheek. A white marble monument was placed near her grave by Queen Victoria. For two centuries all that commemorated this tragic princess in the church were the initials E.S. cut into the wall nearest to her burial vault.

Gaveston, Piers, Earl of Cornwall (d.1312)
Dominican Friary (ruins), King's Langley, Hertfordshire.

The son of a Gascon knight favoured by Edward I, Piers Gaveston was brought up in the royal household where he became a close friend of the King's son, Edward Prince of Wales, later Edward II. Exiled by Edward I he was immediately recalled when his friend became King on his father's death and created Earl of Cornwall and given Edward's niece, Margaret, daughter of Gilbert de Clare, Earl of Gloucester. He was Regent of England during the King's absence in France in 1308 and played a prominent part at the King's coronation. His arrogance and haughty behaviour angered the nobles who called for his banishment, to which the King was forced to agree in 1311. At the end of that year he returned secretly to England and was publicly restored by Edward. The barons took up arms and Gaveston was captured, after being deserted by the King, and executed on Blacklow Hill near Warwick on 19 June 1312.

Godwin, Earl of the West Saxons (d.1053)
Old Minster, Winchester, Hampshire; some of his remains may be in the mortuary chests over the cathedral choir screen.

Father of King Harold, Godwin's origins are obscure. The Anglo-Saxon Canterbury Chronicle has him as the son of Wulfnoth, a South Saxon who plundered the south coast in 1009. Later writings make him the son of a wealthy farmer of Sherston, Wiltshire. After a battle there he sheltered Earl Ulf who took him to Canute, who made him an earl. Marrying Ulf's sister, Godwin gained vast wealth and power but never became overbearing, always displaying good temper. He became the most powerful man in the kingdom, after the king, representing Canute when he was in Denmark.

Guinevere (c.500)
Glastonbury Abbey (ruins), Glastonbury, Somerset.

Historically believed to be the wife of the Romano-British general known as 'King' Arthur. After his death she is reputed to have retired to a convent.

Gundrada de Warenne (d.1085)
St John's Church, Lewes, Sussex. The black marble tomb now inside the church was originally in Lewes Priory.

The daughter of Matilda of Flanders by either William the Conqueror or a previous husband. She was the wife of William de Warenne, the first Earl of Surrey, by whom she had several children. She and her husband founded the first Cluniac priory in England, that of St Pancras at Lewes. She died in childbirth on 27 May 1085 and was buried in the chapter house at Lewes. Her tombstone was found at Ifield Church at the end of the eighteenth century, presumably having been removed there at the Dissolution. Her remains, enclosed in a chest with her name on the lid, were found side by side with those of her husband on the site of Lewes Priory in October 1845.

Isabella of France (1292–1358)

Church of the Franciscan Greyfriars, Newgate, which was destroyed, being replaced by the Wren church, Christ Church, Newgate Street, London, which itself was destroyed by bombs in 1940. The burial ground is now a garden. An effigy of the Queen is among the figures which adorn the tomb of her son, John of Eltham, in Westminster Abbey.

Consort of Edward II whom she married in January 1308, she was the daughter of Philip IV, the Fair, of France. The Queen took her son, Edward of Windsor, later Edward III, to France to do homage to her brother, Charles IV, for Aquitaine in 1325, using the occasion to voice her antipathy to her husband's favourites, the Despensers. Whilst in France she met and became the mistress of one of the baronial exiles, Roger Mortimer, Lord of Wigmore. The scandal caused by their relationship soon reached England and, in September 1326, Isabella together with Mortimer and a force of mercenaries invaded England determined to rid the country of the despised favourites. Her husband fled but he was captured by Mortimer in November and forced to abdicate in favour of his son, Edward III. She and Mortimer ruled the kingdom until October 1330, when the young King overthrew his mother and her lover, forcing her retirement to Hertford and Mortimer's execution.

Jane Seymour (c.1509–1537)

St George's Chapel, Windsor Castle, Windsor, Berkshire, in the centre of the choir with Henry VIII.

Third wife of Henry VIII and mother of Edward VI after whose birth she died in 1537.

Joan of Navarre (c.1370–1437)
Trinity Chapel, Canterbury Cathedral, Canterbury, Kent.

The second wife of Henry IV whom she married on 7 February 1403. Her first husband had been John IV Duke of Brittany and after his death in 1399 she had become Regent of Brittany for her young son, John V. Relations with her step-son, Henry V, were strained over the war with France, one of her sons, Arthur, being captured at Agincourt and brought a prisoner to England. For a time she was kept under restraint but shortly before Henry's death in 1422 he relented and she spent the remainder of her life peacefully in England.

John of Gaunt, Duke of Lancaster (1340–1399)
'Old' St Paul's Cathedral, London.

Fourth son of Edward III and Philippa of Hainault. Through his second marriage to Constance, daughter of Pedro the Cruel King of Castile and Leon, he became titular King of Castile, but never succeeded in establishing his claim. Eventually, his daughter Catherine was granted her mother's rights in Castile and, on her marriage to Henry III of Castile, reigned in her parents' place. During the latter years of Edward III's life, owing to his growing weakness and the decline in the health of Edward, the Black Prince, John of Gaunt took over the reins of government. His ambitions on the succession were frustrated by the Good Parliament which confirmed the succession to the young son of the Black Prince, later Richard II. Unpopular with the public, John of Gaunt was a firm supporter of John Wycliffe, although politically he was forced to renounce Lollard opinions.

Mary Queen of Scots (1542–1587)
Henry VII's Chapel, Westminster Abbey, London, in the south aisle.

Grand-daughter of Margaret Tudor, elder daughter of Henry VII and Elizabeth of York, Mary had the strongest legitimate claim to the English throne after the children of Henry VIII. She acceded to the throne of Scotland whilst still a baby but was forced to abdicate in favour of her son James after her marriage to Lord Bothwell, the alleged murderer of her second husband Lord Darnley. She escaped from imprisonment and fled to England where she was kept in custody for nineteen years. Numerous plots, of which she may or may not have been aware, to place her on the English throne and to restore the Catholic religion, finally but reluctantly forced her cousin,

Queen Elizabeth I, to sign her death warrant and she was beheaded at Fotheringay Castle in February 1587. She was first buried in Peterborough Cathedral but when her son, James, acceded to the English throne as James I, he had her body translated to Henry VII's Chapel in Westminster Abbey where he erected her monument beside that of her mother-in-law and his grandmother, the Countess of Lennox.

Monmouth, James Duke of (1649–1685)
St Peter ad Vincula, Tower of London, London, under the Communion table.

An acknowledged illegitimate son of Charles II by his mistress, Lucy Walter. During his father's lifetime he had been exiled to the Netherlands for his implication in the Rye House Plot but on Charles's death in 1685 he claimed the throne and invaded the realm landing at Lyme Regis in Dorset. His ragged West Country troops were defeated at the Battle of Sedgemoor and the uprising was put down with great severity by Judge Jefferies. The Duke was taken to London and beheaded, his uncle, James II, refusing to reprieve him.

Montfort, Simon of, Earl of Leicester (1208?–1265)
Evesham Abbey ruins, Evesham, Worcestershire; stone in Abbey Gardens erected in 1965 where Montfort was buried at the site of the high altar.

Credited by some writers as being the creator of the House of Commons, but in fact he only summoned together a parliament of churchmen, peers and two citizens from all English boroughs in an effort to develop the cause of justice and righteousness; not a representative democracy per se. Born in Normandy, he came to England in 1229 expecting to gain the earldom of Leicester in exchange for his continental patrimony, but he was not formally invested as the earl until a year after his marriage in 1238 to Eleanor, Henry III's sister. He went on crusade in 1240 and, after returning to Gascony, was accused of oppression and violence as its governor, and became embroiled with Henry III. Parliament, however, denounced Henry and brought Montfort back to England. Montfort captured Henry at the Battle of Lewes, becoming virtually governor of the kingdom, but Montfort was later killed in the Battle of Evesham when his nephew Prince Edward (later Edward I) fought him to become real ruler of the country through his subservient father King Henry

The Duke of Monmouth, after Wissing

III. Henry of Montfort, Simon's elder son, was also killed at Evesham and buried in the Abbey.

Napoleon III, Emperor of the French (1808–1873)
Abbey Church of St Michael, Farnborough, Hampshire.

A nephew of Napoleon I, being the son of his brother, Louis King of Holland, and Hortense Beauharnais, daughter of the Empress Josephine. He assumed power in 1851 and proclaimed himself Emperor of the French on 1 December 1852, reigning until the overthrow of his Empire on 4 September 1870, two days after the Emperor's defeat and surrender at Sedan to the Prussian troops. He and his wife, the Empress Eugénie, and their son, the Prince Imperial, went into exile in England where the Emperor died two years later.

Robert II, Curthose, Duke of Normandy (c.1054–1134)
Gloucester Cathedral, Gloucester, before the High Altar.

Eldest son of William I, the Conqueror, and Matilda of Flanders, he succeded his father as Duke of Normandy in 1087, his second brother, William II, ruling in England. Conflict with his brothers eventually lost him Normandy and after his capture by Henry I, his younger brother, at Tinchebrai on 28 September 1106 he was brought to England and imprisoned for twenty-eight years, first in the Tower of London and then in the castles of Devizes and Cardiff, dying at Cardiff in February 1134. Although a weak character he showed skill and ability as a warrior.

Rupert, Prince, Count Palatine of the Rhine and Duke of
Cumberland (1619–1682)
Henry VII's Chapel, Westminster Abbey, London, in the south aisle.

Born at Prague, the son of Elizabeth the Winter Queen, daughter of James I, and Frederick the Elector Palatine and King of Bohemia, he was a nephew of Charles I. He actively supported his uncle during the Civil War and played a dominant rôle. A cavalry leader, his strategy was bold as well as skilful and in November 1644 he was appointed general of the King's army, an appointment which was obnoxious to the King's counsellors who resented the Prince's independent line. Following his surrender of Bristol to General Fairfax of the Parliamentary forces the King's counsellors prevailed upon him to dismiss the Prince, and he and his brother, Maurice, were told to seek

Prince Rupert, attributed to Honthorst

their fortunes overseas. Convinced not only that the King's cause was lost but that it was bad, he tried to persuade the King to make peace with Parliament to no avail and reluctantly he and his brother went to France where he sought service in the French army, commanding a troop of English exiles. Later, his uncle relented and understood something of the Prince's feelings, giving him command of the royalist navy. The Prince however was still in conflict with the King's Council and once more relinquished his offices and for six years, from 1654–1660, was in Germany where little was known of his exploits. At the Restoration he returned to England where he was made a privy councillor by Charles II and, during the Dutch wars, bore a brilliant part as admiral. The Prince's scientific skill led to improved gunpowder and cannon-making, the invention of the alloy 'Prince's metal,' and a variety of scientific toys, including 'Prince Rupert's Drops', which are elongated glass drops that shatter when the tail is broken.

William Marshal, Earl of Pembroke (c.1146–1219)
The Temple Church, Temple, Fleet Street, London.
   Served Henry II, Richard I who appointed him one of the council of regency during the King's absence on the Third Crusade, and King John, being one of the few barons who clung to the King's cause during the Barons' War. John appointed him his executor and after the King's death the barons elected him Regent for the young Henry III. In spite of his advanced age, he prosecuted the war against Prince Louis and the rebels, heading the King's army at the Battle of Lincoln in 1217. Self-restraint and compromise were the keynotes of his policy and he brought stability to the realm and confirmed Magna Carta. He died on 14 May 1219.

Windsor. Bessie Wallis Warfield, Duchess of (1896–1986)
Frogmore, royal cemetery in Windsor Home Park, Berkshire, beside Edward VIII's grave. The gardens and mausoleum of Queen Victoria are open only on 14, 15 and 21 May, each year; the Duke and Duchess of Windsor's graves can be seen from pathway.
   American-born wife of the former Edward VIII, who abdicated the throne upon his marriage to her. She had previously been married, first to an American naval lieutenant, secondly to an American businessman, Ernest Aldrich Simpson.

[3] Statesmen, Politicians and Warriors

Alexander, Sir Harold Rupert Leofric George, 1st Earl Alexander of
Tunis (1891–1969)
St Margaret's Church, Ridge, Hertfordshire.

Field Marshal who served with distinction in both world wars, being
born in Co. Tyrone, Ireland and educated at Harrow and Sandhurst.
Winning the DSO and MC, among many other mentions and awards,
he served for three years in the trenches in France, where he
commanded a battalion at age 24. He later held commands in north
England and the North West Frontier of India. At Dunkirk in World
War II he was the last officer to leave the beaches. After originating
battle training schools in England he became General Officer Commanding in Burma in 1942 and then Commander-in-Chief, Middle
East. By 1944 he was Supreme Commander in the Mediterranean
theatre of war. The capture of Rome saw him promoted to Field
Marshal. He became Governor General of Canada from 1946 to
1952, being recalled as Minister of Defence by Churchill. The
Americans had earlier wanted him to command the British invasion
forces of Normandy but Montgomery got the job because Alexander
could not be spared from Italy. He received the Order of Merit in
1959 after a viscountcy in 1946 and an earldom in 1952. He is
considered to have been the most outstanding British officer of the
war.

Allenby, Edmund Henry Hynman, 1st Viscount Allenby of Megiddo
(1861–1936)
St George's Chapel, known as The Warriors' Chapel, Westminster
Abbey, London.

Field Marshal who on 9 December 1917 captured Jerusalem.
Earlier he had commanded cavalry units on the Western front and,
later, the new 3rd Army. His most notable achievements in Europe
was the Battle of Arras in 1917 when his army advanced three and a
half miles, believed to be the longest advance carried out by any
belligerent on the Western front since trench warfare had set in.
Created a viscount in 1919 he was appointed a special high commissioner for Egypt and the Sudan from 1919 to 1925 and during his
period in office he persuaded the British government to abolish the

protectorate and to recognize Egypt as a sovereign state. Strained relations between him and Mr Austen Chamberlain, then Foreign Secretary, brought his resignation.

André, Major John (1751–1780)
Westminster Abbey, London, south aisle of the Nave.

English soldier who negotiated with Benedict Arnold for the betrayal of West Point, of which Arnold was commander, during the American War of Independence. Captured at Tarrytown by three militiamen he was tried by a court martial and condemned to death as a spy. He was hanged on 2 October 1780 at Tappan, despite Washington having admitted that he was 'more unfortunate than criminal'. His death excited much sympathy both in America and in Europe and in 1821 his remains were exhumed and brought to Westminster Abbey where a mural sculptured monument was erected to him. In America, a monument to his memory was also erected on the spot where he was taken.

Arnold, Benedict (1741–1801)
St Mary's Church, Battersea, London.

American soldier. A general in George Washington's army of independence he was appointed to command West Point, the key to the Hudson River Valley. He agreed to betray his post to the British forces and met with Major John André on 21 September 1780 to perfect the plan. Major André was captured whilst returning to the British lines and, unsuspecting, his captors informed Arnold, giving him time to escape. He then openly joined the British and led an expedition into Virginia and burned Richmond. In December 1781 he went to London and was consulted by the King and his ministers on American affairs. He spent some years in St John, New Brunswick, engaging in the West India trade, but, when the war broke out between Britain and France, he returned to London and was active in fitting out privateers.

Asquith, Herbert Henry, 1st Earl of Oxford and Asquith (1852–1928)
All Saints' Churchyard, Sutton Courtenay, Oxfordshire.

Statesman elected to Parliament as a Liberal in 1886; he became Home Secretary in Gladstone's last ministry. In 1908 he succeeded

Grave of Henry Herbert Asquith, All Saints' Churchyard, Sutton Courtenay, Oxfordshire

Sir Henry Campbell-Bannerman as Prime Minister and his government introduced an avalanche of social reforms including old-age pensions in 1908 and unemployment insurance in 1911. During the first world war he was forced to resign over criticism of his leadership and Lloyd George became Prime Minister in his stead. He resigned the leadership of the Liberal Party in 1926.

Attlee, Clement Richard, 1st Earl Attlee (1883–1967)
Westminster Abbey, London, in the north aisle of the Nave.
Statesman. A former Mayor of Stepney he became Prime Minister following the landslide victory of the Labour Party in 1945 at the end of the second world war. Previously he had been Churchill's deputy during the war having, since 1935, been the leader of the Labour opposition in the Commons. His government introduced legislation which created the welfare state and was also instrumental in granting independence to India and Pakistan.

Baldwin, Stanley, 1st Earl Baldwin of Bewdley (1867–1947)
Worcester Cathedral, Worcester, west entrance.
Statesman. Stanley Baldwin followed his father as Conservative Member of Parliament for Bewdley West when he was returned unopposed in 1908. In 1916 he became a member of Lloyd George's

war cabinet and in 1923 became Prime Minister for the first time, resigning the following year to allow for the first Labour administration under Ramsay Macdonald, which lasted but a few months. He then became Prime Minister until 1929 during which term occurred the General Strike of 1926, his radio appeal at the time being credited with shortening the crisis. He became Prime Minister again from 1935 to 1937 and his handling of the issue of the King's marriage to Mrs Simpson brought about Edward VIII's abdication in December 1936. After the coronation of George VI he resigned the leadership of the party to Neville Chamberlain. His refusal to re-arm in the 1930s and his acceptance of Mussolini's annexation of Abyssinia has brought him much criticism.

Baltimore, George Calvert, 1st Baron (c.1580–1632)
St Dunstan in the West, Fleet Street, London.
   Secretary to Robert Cecil, Earl of Salisbury, and in 1609 Member of Parliament for Bossiney. Because of his conversion to Catholicism and his support for the Spanish marriage, he was distrusted by Parliament and gave up his offices of state in February 1625, accepting the barony of Baltimore and large grants of land in Ireland. In 1621 he had established a small settlement in Newfoundland which he called Avalon and visited in 1627. However, because of disputes and the unsuitable climate he left Avalon for Virginia but was refused permission to settle unless he took the oaths of allegiance and supremacy. He returned to England, dying on 15 April 1632 before a new concession was secured. It was not until 20 June 1632 that the charter of Maryland passed the Great Seal in favour of Baltimore's son Cecilius, 2nd Baron Baltimore.

Baring, Evelyn, 1st Earl of Cromer (1841–1917)
Wimborne Road Cemetery, Wimborne Road, Bournemouth, large marble cross about 50 yards from east side of chapel to the left of the path.
   Statesman and diplomatist who 'rescued, refitted and piloted Egypt into modern civilization'. Baring, who was connected with the great financial family of that name, was born at Cromer Hall, Norfolk, and brought a life of already crowded achievement with him when, in 1877, he was chosen to represent British interests in Egypt, a country virtually bankrupt because of the criminal extravagance of Khedive Ismail. Baring had served first in the army and later as a diplomat in

Evelyn Baring's Grave, Bournemouth Cemetery, Dorset

the Ionian Islands, where he 'picked up' Greek, as he put it, to add to the two languages he already knew; in Malta; in Jamaica, where he was able to spend some time with General Grant before Petersburg (1864) during the American Civil War; and in India during the Bengal famine, where he was private secretary to his cousin Lord Northbrook, Viceroy of India.

When Baring finally took the helm as consul-general in Egypt his rule was virtually absolute, since British forces were in occupation. His first aim was to make Egypt financially sound by increasing the area of taxable land through irrigation rather than raising taxes. Through many dangers, including a cholera epidemic, nationalist insurrection and the personal crisis of his first wife's death, he eventually brought forth a modern Egypt.

He was a tall man, not inclined to small-talk, but possessing 'unusually powerful and versatile talents'. During his early career he had been known as 'Overbearing', and in Cairene society he was referred to as *'le Grand Ours'*. He could, however, recognize a lost cause and was willing to compromise instead of obstinately clinging to a position for the sake of pride. He wrote *Modern Egypt* (1908), *Ancient and Modern Imperialism* (1910) and three volumes of *Political and Literary Essays* (1912 onwards), based on books he reviewed for the *Spectator*. He was twice married.

Beatty, David, 1st Earl Beatty (1871–1936)
St Paul's Cathedral, London, in the crypt.

British admiral who succeeded Lord Jellicoe as commander of the grand fleet in 1916. Whilst in command of the British battlecruisers he fought the German fleet at Heligoland Bight in 1914 and the Dogger Bank in 1915. In May 1916 in a brilliant manoeuvre he lured the German navy into the uncertain Battle of Jutland after which the German fleet remained in harbour.

Beaufort, John, first Duke of Somerset (1403–1444)
Wimborne Minster (St Cuthburga's), Wimborne, Dorset; large tomb on the south side of the presbytery.

Long-time army campaigner, he was the grandson of Edward III's son, John of Gaunt. Beaufort's father, John, had been created Earl of Somerset, and in 1409 John the younger succeeded to the title on the death of his brother Henry. After fighting for Henry V in France when only 17 years old, John was captured when attacking the

Dauphin at Anjou. In the same battle Henry V's brother the Duke of Clarence was killed. Quickly released once a ransom was paid, Beaufort stayed in France fighting for Henry VI, his nearness to the crown giving him high command. He was created duke in 1443 and became a captain-general in Aquitania and Normandy. When passed over as Regent for France, the Duke of York being preferred, Somerset became disgusted and returned to England, dying within a year by his own hand, it was said. His quarrel with the government over his slight had brought him the disgrace of banishment from the court. It was too much for him to bear as a loyal and brave commander in all his years of fighting for his sovereign.

He had married Margaret, widow of Sir Oliver St John, and his daughter, Margaret Beaufort, had a son when she was only 13 years of age. She had married Henry VI's half-brother, Edmund Tudor, Earl of Richmond, and the son became Henry VII. She it was who erected the monument to her parents in Wimborne Minster.

Bennet, Richard Bedford, 1st Viscount Bennet (1870–1947)
St Michael's Churchyard, Mickleham, Surrey.

Prime Minister of Canada 1930 to 1935, having been the Conservative leader from 1927. He was born in New Brunswick and brought about a system of trade preferences after an empire conference at Ottawa. He received his viscountcy in 1941.

Bevin, Ernest (1881–1951)
Westminster Abbey, London, in the north aisle of the Nave.

Ernest Bevin began life as a poor West Country boy. In 1911 he became assistant general secretary of the Dockers' Union which he eventually merged with others to form the powerful Transport and General Workers' Union of which he became general secretary. He was an influential member of the Trades Union Congress which called the General Strike of 1926. During the second world war he became the Minister of Labour in Churchill's war cabinet and, after the Labour victory at the polls in 1945, Foreign Secretary until his resignation in 1951, a few months before he died.

Birch, John (1616–1691)
Church of St Peter and St Paul, Weobley, Herefordshire.

A Parliamentary Colonel of Volunteers during the Civil War. He was entrusted by Parliament with the joint care of Bath and Bristol, a position of such little advantage that he was about to resign when he was ordered to 'distress' Hereford, which he took by stealth in 1645. His loyalty to the Commonwealth was dubious and he was briefly imprisoned. He supported General Monck at the Restoration and was one of the Council of State which welcomed Charles II back to England. Essentially a businessman, his affairs prospered and he remained a Member of Parliament until the year of his death.

Bligh, William (1754–1817)
St Mary's Church, Lambeth, London.

His name is remembered as the captain of HMS *Bounty* whose crew, under the leadership of Fletcher Christian, mutinied on 28 April 1789. An excellent seaman, Bligh accompanied Cook during his second voyage around the world from 1772–1774, and it was on this voyage that the bread fruit was discovered. Thereafter Bligh was known as 'Bread Fruit Bligh'. In 1805 he was appointed Captain-General and Governor of New South Wales and during his term tried to suppress the illegal trafficking of spirits. Deposed by the military because of his harsh rule he was imprisoned for two years before obtaining his release and returning to England in 1811. He was made a vice-admiral of the Blue in June 1814.

Bolingbroke, Henry St John, 1st Viscount (1678–1751)
St Mary's Church, Battersea, London, in the family vault which is no longer marked although there is a frontal bust on the north side gallery.

Politician. Entered Parliament in 1701 and held high office under Robert Harley Earl of Oxford during the reign of Queen Anne. He was created a viscount in 1712 and schemed for the return of James the Old Pretender but he was out-manoeuvred by the appointment of Lord Shrewsbury to the treasureship which ruined his plans. Dismissed by George I, he fled to France where he became secretary to the Old Pretender. He criticised the 1715 Jacobite uprising and severed his connections with James's court. Pardoned by George I, he returned to England, and although he tried to re-assert his influence any hopes he may have entertained were dashed by the death of George I, whose mistress, the Duchess of Kendal, was his chief support. In 1735 he went to live in France, his second wife being French, returning to England only occasionally. In 1744 he finally

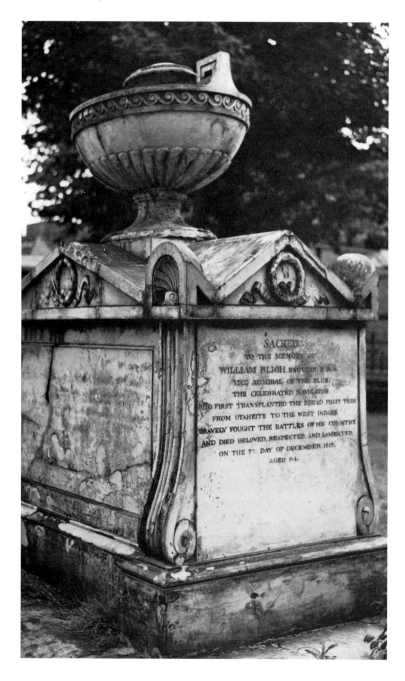

decided to settle once again in London and lived at Battersea, where he died.

Buckingham, George Villiers, 1st Duke of (1592–1628)

Henry VII's Chapel, Westminster Abbey, London, in the small chapel to the north that forms the apse.

A favourite of James I, to whom he was introduced by the anti-Spanish lobby led by the Archbishop of Canterbury, he rose rapidly to power after the eclipse of the former favourite, Robert Carr, Earl of Somerset. He played a prominent rôle in the government but veered erratically in his policies. He sided with the Spanish lobby and accompanied Prince Charles on a visit to Madrid to sue for the hand of the Spanish Infanta, but Buckingham's behaviour alienated the Spanish court and the match was called off. When Charles I came to the throne Buckingham became his principal adviser. He supported the Huguenots at La Rochelle but his intervention failed to relieve them. He was assassinated at Portsmouth before embarking for La Rochelle by John Felton, a disaffected seaman.

Buckingham, George Villiers, 2nd Duke of (1628–1687)

Henry VII's Chapel, Wesminster Abbey, London, in the small chapel to the north that forms the apse.

Son of James I's favourite. After the murder of his father he and his younger brother, Francis, born after Buckingham's assassination, were brought up with Charles I's children at court. Villiers was driven into exile with Charles II but he negotiated with Cromwell, estranging himself from the exiled Stuarts. He was imprisoned in the Tower of London by Cromwell in 1658 for suspected implication in a Presbyterian plot against the government, later being released on payment of a heavy fine. He met the returning Charles II at Dover and, despite an initial coolness in their relations, was soon back in favour. After some political setbacks he became a member of Charles II's Cabal of ministers. His affair with the Countess of Shrewsbury, whose husband he had killed in a duel, caused a public scandal, which together with his unpopular policies forced his political retirement. Later intrigue once again took him to the Tower of London as a prisoner but he was released. He died in April 1687 from a chill caught while hunting in Yorkshire.

Tomb of Admiral Bligh, St Mary's Churchyard, Lambeth, London

Buckingham and Normanby, John Sheffield, 1st Duke of
(1648–1721)
Henry VII's Chapel, Westminster Abbey, London, in the small chapel
to the north-east that forms part of the apse.

English statesman and poet who became Lord Chamberlain under
James II, whose natural daughter, Catherine, he married later. A keen
supporter of James II he nonetheless acquiesced in the Glorious
Revolution and was created Marquess of Normanby in 1694. During
Queen Anne's reign he held many high offices of state and in 1703
was created Duke of Buckingham and Normanby. After the Queen's
death in 1714 he held no further state appointments and died in
February 1721. He is credited by Sir Winston Churchill with having
said: 'Good God, how this poor nation has been governed in my time!
During the reign of King Charles the Second we were governed by a
parcel of French whores, in King James the Second's time by a parcel
of Popish priests, in King William's time by a parcel of Dutch
footmen, and now we are governed by a dirty chambermaid, a Welsh
attorney and a profligate wretch that has neither honour nor honesty.'
(*A History of the English-Speaking Peoples*, vol. III, Winston S. Churchill,
Cassell, 1957, p.81.)

Burghley, William Cecil, 1st Baron Burghley or Burleigh, K.G.
(1520–1598)
St Martin's Church, Stamford, Lincolnshire; large renaissance tomb
along with other monuments to members of his family.

Statesman born at Bourne, Lincolnshire, who rose to be chief
secretary of state under Elizabeth I, a position which he held for 40
years. He is considered to have been the power behind England's
greatness under the queen. After brilliant academic work at Cambridge he entered Gray's Inn, studying not only law but history,
genealogy and theology. His first marriage while at Gray's Inn in 1541
was to a wineseller's daughter, but his second marriage to the daughter
of Sir Anthony Cooke in 1545 brought him to the notice of Edward
Seymour the Protector, Duke of Somerset. He appointed Burghley as
his secretary. As such Burghley suffered two months' imprisonment
in the Tower of London when Somerset fell from grace. Recognition
of his talents soon brought about Burghley's release, however, and he
served as Secretary of State with a knighthood in 1551 during the
Duke of Northumberland's ascendancy.

Although conforming to Roman Catholicism under Mary I, he was not held in full favour by her but he did succeed in furthering his ideas of open trading and the abolition of some monopolies. Under Elizabeth I as her chief adviser he was responsible for the clever and bold diplomatic policies that helped England become a greatly respected power in Europe and the world. His spy network is reputed to have prevented many internecine schemes from harming England and the queen. He it was who bore the responsibility for Mary Queen of Scots' execution. In 1572, a year after awarding him a barony, Elizabeth made him a Garter Knight and Lord High Treasurer, which office he held at his death.

Burke, Edmund (1729–1797)
St Mary and All Saints Church, Beaconsfield, Buckinghamshire.

Whig statesman and political writer and one of the greatest names in the history of political literature. Born in Dublin in 1729 he moved to London in 1750 to study for the Bar after graduating from Trinity College Dublin. When the Whig Marquess of Rockingham accepted the premiership in 1765 Burke became his private secretary and in 1766 Member of Parliament for Wendover. After the fall of Rockingham in July 1766 he defended his chief in the Commons for his policies towards the colonies, advocating the emancipation of the American colonies though not their independence. He also advocated a better administration in India and whilst he had sympathy with some of the aims of the French Revolution he disapproved of it, seeing it as an attack on liberty despite the high sentiments of the revolutionaries and their English sympathisers. He did not believe that the French would be any better off under the new régime than under the old, considering that what basically required revision was the old system of government to make that work.

Chamberlain, Arthur Neville (1869–1940)
Westminster Abbey, London, south aisle of the Nave.

Prime Minister from 1937 to 1940, succeeding Stanley Baldwin as premier and leader of the Conservative Party. In September 1938 he flew to Munich to meet with Adolf Hitler, the German Führer, returning with 'a piece of paper' that promised 'peace in our time'. His appeasement policies failed with the outbreak of war on Sunday 3 September 1939 and he resigned the premiership to Winston Churchill in May 1940.

Edmund Burke, from the studio of Reynolds

Chamberlain, Joseph (1836–1914)
Birmingham General Cemetery, Key Hill, Birmingham, in the Unitarian Section, under a large stone slab.

Statesman and industrialist (Nettlefold's screw factory at Birmingham) who quickly became influential as an MP for Birmingham, becoming president of the Board of Trade and a member of the cabinet under Gladstone (whom see). He resigned in a disagreement with Gladstone on Home Rule for Ireland and became the leader of the Liberal Unionists. Secretary for the Colonies in 1895 in the Coalition government, he made his mark as a colonial administrator both during and after the Boer War. He advocated tariff reform and preferential treatment for colonial imports. He left public life in 1906 because of ill-health. His son Neville (whom see) was by a second marriage.

Churchill, Lord Randolph Henry Spencer (1849–1895)
St Martin's Churchyard, Bladon, Oxfordshire.

Conservative politician and younger son of the 7th Duke of Marlborough. He was elected to the Commons as Member for Woodstock in 1874 and soon made his mark as an exponent of independent conservatism, attacking the traditional Tory hierarchy with the vituperative invective that made him famous. An active promoter of the Primrose League he later became a controversial chairman of the National Union of Conservative Associations. He became Chancellor of the Exchequer briefly under Lord Salisbury in 1886 but resigned on 20 December 1886 over a dispute with the heads of the naval and military establishments. It was the end of his career as a leader of the Conservative Pary. In 1874 he married the American beauty, Jennie Jerome, by whom he became the father of Sir Winston Churchill.

Churchill, Sir Winston (c1620–1688)
St Martin-in-the-Fields, St Martin's Place, London.

Politician and historian who was elected to Parliament in 1661. He held influential positions at court during the reigns of both Charles II and James II. He was the father of John Churchill, 1st Duke of Marlborough, and of Arabella Churchill, the mistress of James II, to whom she bore four children, the most famous of which was James FitzJames, the Duke of Berwick.

Graves of Sir Winston Churchill and his mother, Lady Randolph Churchill, St Martin's Churchyard, Bladon, Oxfordshire

Churchill, Sir Winston Leonard Spencer, K.G. (1874–1965)
St Martin's Churchyard, Bladon, Oxfordshire.

Son of Lord Randoph Churchill and his American wife Jennie Jerome. He entered Parliament in 1900 and held many of the high offices of state. During the Boer War he was a correspondent and was captured but escaped. He became Prime Minister and leader of the Conservative Party after the resignation of Neville Chamberlain in 1940 and his leadership symbolized the courage of the British peoples during the second world war. Defeated at the General Election of 1945 he returned to 10 Downing Street as Prime Minister from 1951 to 1955, when he retired. He was a gifted amateur painter, exhibiting at the Royal Academy, as well as historian and writer.

Clarendon, Edward Hyde, 1st Earl of (1609–1674)
Westminster Abbey, London, in the North Ambulatory.

Statesman and historian. Initially a supporter of the anti-royalist party he served in both the Short and Long Parliaments. However, by 1642 he was one of the King's ablest supporters in the Commons and was expelled from the House in August 1642. He followed the Queen and Prince of Wales into exile where he became Charles II's principal adviser. At the Restoration he continued his influence over the new King and was a prominent member of Charles's Cabal of ministers. The unpopularity of Charles's administration was unjustly laid at Clarendon's door, although the narrowness of Clarendon's political views and his lack of control over the country's foreign policy were partly to blame. To avoid impeachment he fled to France and spent his remaining years until his death in 1674 in exile. He was the father of Anne Hyde, the first wife of James II, and mother of Queen Mary II and Queen Anne. He wrote the celebrated *True Historical Narrative of the Rebellion and Civil Wars in England*.

Clive, Robert, 1st Baron Clive (1725–1774)
St Margaret's Church, Moreton Say, Shrewsbury.

General, whose military successes against the French helped to lay the foundations of British power in India. Originally a clerk in the East India Company, his dislike of his work nearly drove him to suicide. When the Seven Years War broke out in 1756 Clive soon proved his military genius and the following year he conquered Bengal with his victory at Plassey, becoming the first British governor, in which rôle he proved his administrative ability. He later returned to

Robert Clive, by Dance

England and sat in the House of Commons as the member for Shrewsbury, for, being an Irish peer, he was able to do so. General John Burgoyne tried to get the House to impeach Clive for corruption but the motion was defeated by 155 votes to 55. Nonetheless it was a bitter blow to a man who had rendered his country 'great and meritorious services'. He committed suicide on 22 November 1774.

Cobden, Richard (1804–1865)
St Mary Magdelene Churchyard, West Lavington, W. Sussex; large granite slab with only his surname cut in it. (He had not wished to be buried in Westminster Abbey 'among all those men of war'.)

An economist and politician, born at Heyshott, Sussex, he was sent to a poor boys' school in Yorkshire, 'Dotheboys Hall', because of his father's failure as a farmer. After becoming a clerk and extremely capable commercial traveller he went into business with two friends in London. Four years later they had a profitable calico-printing mill in Manchester, to where he then moved. After success had sent him to America and other places he started pamphleteering: *England, Ireland and America* (1835) and *Russia* (1836) both supported the causes he now favoured, namely free trade and non-intervention in Russian affairs.

Cobden became the foremost proponent of anti-corn-laws, his 1841 election as a Stockport MP now giving him the Commons as an influential platform. His speeches were considered by Peel to have helped greatly in the abolition of the Corn Laws in 1846. His cause had seen his financial downfall with its high costs, but private subscription let him purchase Durnford, the Sussex farmhouse in which he had been born. He was now able to travel in Europe and Russia again and threw his weight against the Crimean War, also strongly opposing Palmerston's policy on China. Cobden also visited America again, supporting the North in the Civil War there. He was offered the Board of Trace presidency by Palmerston after failing in his bid for election as MP for Huddersfield but declined the offer. He still was, nevertheless, able to arrange a commercial treaty with France in 1859, though he was in ill health. He died in London.

Collingwood, Cuthbert, 1st Baron Collingwood (1750–1810)
St Paul's Cathedral, London, in the crypt near to Lord Nelson's tomb.

Admiral who assumed command of the British fleet at the Battle of Trafalgar after Nelson's death. His ship, the *Royal Sovereign*, led the fleet into battle and he is alleged to have replied to Nelson's famous signal, 'England expects . . .', that all knew well enough what to do. He died at sea.

Cromwell, Henry (1628–1674)
St Laurence's Church, Wicken Fen, Cambridgeshire.
Fourth son of Oliver Cromwell. He spent most of his active political life in Ireland where he worked hard to ameliorate the poverty of the country. He became Lord Deputy in 1657. He urged his father not to accept the office of King and, when his brother fell from office in June 1659, he returned to England and resigned. After the Restoration he was unmolested by the government and died on 23 March 1674. Carlyle referred to him as 'the best of Cromwell's sons,' and this is inscribed on a brass plate in the church where he is buried.

Curzon, George Nathaniel, 1st Marquess Curzon of Kedleston (1859–1925)
All Saints' Church, Kedleston, Derbyshire; the north aisle was added from 1906 to 1913 as a memorial chapel for Lord Curzon.
Statesman. As Viceroy of India from 1898 to 1905 he initiated important currency, education and administrative reforms, though his partition of Bengal in 1905 angered the Hindus. After a quarrel with Lord Kitchener, then commanding the Indian Army, Curzon resigned. During the first world war he was a member of Lloyd George's war cabinet from 1916–1918. From 1919 to 1924 he was Foreign Secretary and at the European Conference in Lausanne he dominated the proceedings, disapproving of the French occupation of the Ruhr, whilst his consummate diplomatic skill restored British prestige in Turkey. He was deeply disappointed when the King finally chose Stanley Baldwin to succeed to the premiership after the resignation of Bonar Law in May 1923, having confidently believed he would be called. Following his death his coffin was taken to Westminster Abbey and after a funeral service there it was removed to lie beside that of his wife in Kedleston.

Disraeli, Benjamin, 1st Earl of Beaconsfield (1804–1881)
St Michael's Churchyard, Hughenden, Buckinghamshire, with a monument erected by Queen Victoria with a profile portrait by R. C. Belt in the church.
Statesman and novelist. He entered Parliament in 1837 and became

Lord Curzon, by Cooke after Sargent

Conservative Prime Minister in 1868 and from 1874 to 1880. He arranged the purchase of the Suez Canal shares and had Queen Victoria proclaimed Empress of India. He is regarded as the founder of the modern Conservative Party. He was a considerable novelist, his novels *Coningsby* and *Sybil* rousing the social consciences of his readership.

Dowding, Hugh Caswall Tremenheere, 1st Baron Dowding (1882–1970)
Henry VII's Chapel, Westminster Abbey, London, in the small east chapel, now known as the RAF Chapel, that forms part of the apse.
Air Chief Marshal. During the second world war he was Air Officer Commanding-in-Chief of Fighter Command at the time of the Battle of Britain. His foresight in building up Fighter Command during the period between the two world wars together with his strategy and firmness during the battle was instrumental in the successful defence of Great Britain in 1940.

Eden, Sir Robert Anthony, 1st Earl of Avon (1897–1977)
St Mary's Church, Alvediston, Wiltshire, on edge of graveyard near car-parking area.
Statesman who, prior to succeeding Churchill as Prime Minister in 1955, had been Foreign Secretary for the third time in Conservative governments. After Eton and Christ Church, Oxford, he won the MC in the first world war, later becoming an MP for Leamington in 1923, holding the seat until he resigned in 1957. In the previous year he had involved Britain and France in a controversial occupation of the Suez Canal Zone. In failing health he resigned from politics in 1957, still a debonair but now somewhat crestfallen figure.

Fox, Charles James (1749–1806)
Westminster Abbey, London, in the North Transept; a monument stands in the Belfry Tower.
Whig statesman and orator. Entered Parliament at nineteen as Member for Midhurst; at twenty-one he became a junior Lord of the Admiralty under Lord North, a post he threw up to oppose the Royal Marriage Act which, along with his gambling habits, earned him the animosity of George III which was to last throughout his life. Edmund Burke drew Fox into association with the Whigs under Lord Rockingham and his great political career stems from the famous speech

he made in the House on 2 February 1775 on the disputes with the colonies. However, he only held office for a few months in 1783, 1784 and shortly before his death in 1806. Nonetheless he was a major force in the politics of the time. He upheld the liberal causes of the day: American independence; the French Revolution; he pressed for the abolition of slavery and actually effected it during his brief term in office in 1806 although he died before the Act was passed through both Houses in 1807; the repeal of the Test Acts; and concessions to the Roman Catholics in Britain and Ireland. He planted the seed of the modern Liberal Party.

Fox, Sir Stephen (1627–1716)
All Saints' Church, Farley, Wiltshire; in vault in the north transept.

Statesman who served through the reigns of six rulers of England. From being an ordinary choirboy at Salisbury Cathedral he became not only respected and honoured for his dignity, ability and honesty, but, with the fortune he made, built or contributed to the improvement of churches and various public buildings. He fought in Charles II's ill-fated Battle of Worcester (1651) and assisted his escape to France. During the Commonwealth Fox was sent to England by Charles II as a trusted agent. After the Restoration Fox was given the post of Paymaster-General to the Forces, which brought him an immense fortune. With his riches he built a church at Farley, his birthplace, and also almshouses and a school there. In addition he built almshouses, charity schools and churches in Suffolk and Northamptonshire and carried out improvements to Salisbury Cathedral. He also persuaded Charles II to found the Chelsea Hospital in 1681, the credit for which is generally ascribed to Nell Gwynne. Fox put £13,000 of his own money into its building. When James II became king he offered Fox a peerage if he would become a Roman Catholic, but Fox refused. He also refused to take an active part against James II when the Prince of Orange was brought to England, and waited until James had left the country before paying his compliments to William III. Upon Anne's accession he wished to retire but the queen asked him to lead the Commons at her coronation procession. When he was 76 he married 26-year-old Christian, the co-heiress daughter of rector Francis Hopes. He wanted an heir and had four more children by her, one of them, Henry, becoming the first Lord Holland and father of the Whig statesman and orator Charles James Fox. Sir Stephen was knighted in 1665.

Fraser, Simon, 12th Baron Lovat (c.1667–1747)
St Peter ad Vincula, Tower of London, London.

Jacobite intriguer who reputedly acted as traitor to both sides. During the rebellion of 1745 he acted with characteristic duplicity. But, following the defeat of Bonnie Prince Charlie's army at Culloden in 1746, the Hanoverian army moved against Lord Lovat whose professions of loyalty to George II did not deceive them. Arrested on an island in Loch Morar he was brought to London and executed on 9 April 1747, the last peer to be executed for treason.

Freyberg, Bernard Cyril, 1st Baron Freyberg (1889–1963)
St Paul's Cathedral, London, in the crypt.

During the first world war he distinguished himself for bravery, particularly for his exploit in swimming ashore at Gallipoli ahead of the troops and lighting flares on the peninsula in the Gulf of Xeros to draw enemy tanks away from the true landing place. In the second world war he commanded the New Zealand Expeditionary Force.

Gladstone, William Ewart (1809–1888)
Westminster Abbey, London, in the North Transept.

Liberal statesman. He entered Parliament in 1832 as a Conservative. He held office under Sir Robert Peel and was a convinced Free Trader. It was as a Peelite that he joined the coalition government of Whigs and Peelites under Lord Aberdeen, becoming Chancellor of the Exchequer and introducing his first budget on 18 April 1853. He became Liberal Prime Minister for the first time in 1868, his administration lasting until 1872 during which time it introduced the 1870 Education Act. He was Prime Minister again from 1880 to 1885, in 1886 and from 1892 to 1894, but he was never able to carry Home Rule for Ireland which he strongly advocated.

Gordon, General Charles George (1833–1885)
Recumbent effigy only in St Paul's Cathedral, London.

A Scotsman who, after distinguished service in the Crimea and in China, where he was instrumental in suppressing the Taiping rebellion, entered the service of the Khedive in Egypt. In 1877 he was made Governor of the Sudan but he resigned after three years owing to exhaustion. In 1884, following the rising of the Mahdi in the Sudan, he was asked by the British government to oversee the evacuation of the Egyptians from the Sudan, and he proceeded to Khartoum. Before he could complete the evacuation, the Mahdi's forces besieged the city and Gordon was murdered by the rebels on 26 January 1885 before the British relief force under Lord Wolseley could save him. His death was followed by an outburst of grief in Britain and in other countries. His body was not recovered.

Gorges, Sir Ferdinando (c.1566–1647)
St Budiana Church, Victoria Road, St Budeaux, Plymouth, Devon.
English colonial pioneer and founder of Maine, receiving the Royal Charter in 1639. He was an advocate, especially in later life, of the feudal type of colony. He wrote the *Briefe Narration of the Originall Undertakings of the Advancement of Plantations into the Parts of America*.

Gorst, Sir John Eldon (1835–1916)
St Andrew's Churchyard, Castle Combe, Wiltshire.
Founder of the Primrose League, the Conservative Party's organization for supporters. Born in Preston, Lancashire, he went to St John's College, Cambridge. In New Zealand he became popular with the Maoris but he and his wife barely escaped death in a Maori rebellion. Back in England he was called to the bar at the Inner Temple and, as MP for Cambridge, he became friendly with Benjamin Disraeli the prime minister, whose favourite flower was believed to be the primrose. He became solicitor-general in 1875, afterwards holding several other ministerial offices. He wrote *Children of the Nation* (1906) and switched to the Liberal Party in 1909. Unsuccessful as its Preston candidate a year later, he retired from public office.

Hampden, John (1594–1643)
St Mary Magdalene's Church, Great Hampden, Buckinghamshire, with a large hanging monument erected by Sir Henry Cheere in 1743.
A cousin of Oliver Cromwell, he was a prominent parliamentarian and refused to pay Charles I's 'ship money', an illegal tax, in 1636. At the outbreak of the Civil War he raised a regiment for Parliament but was killed at Chalgrove Field whilst trying to hold the advance of the royalist forces under the King's nephew, Prince Rupert.

Hardy, Sir Thomas Masterman (1769–1839)
In the mausoleum of the Greenwich Naval Hospital cemetery, between the present National Maritime Museum and Davenport Home for nurses. The cemetery is not at present accessible to visitors.

Vice-Admiral at the Battle of Trafalgar aboard HMS Victory with Nelson at the latter's death. Hardy had been born at Long Bredy, Dorset and was twelve years old when he joined the navy, leaving it shortly for school, then the merchant service. He returned to naval service in 1790 and first served with Nelson in 1796. He was on the *Victory*'s quarter-deck when Nelson received his mortal musket-shot wound in 1805 at Trafalgar. With his dying breath Nelson probably whispered to Hardy, 'Kismet (fate), Hardy', his words later being misinterpreted as 'Kiss me, Hardy'. Hardy served in the North and South American Stations after being created a baronet in 1806; he was later made KCB (1815) and GCB (1831). He was promoted to rear-admiral in 1825 and vice-admiral in 1837 while serving as Governor of Greenwich Naval Hospital, during which service he died. There is a large memorial to him on Black Down, near his Dorset birthplace.

Note: Also buried in the mausoleum were Admiral Sir Richard Goodwin **Keats** (1757–1834), Vice-Admiral Sir Thomas Boulden **Thompson** (1766?–1828), Admiral Sir John **Colpoys** (1724?–1821) and Admiral Samuel Hood, 1st Viscount **Hood** (1724–1816), who served under Admiral Lord Rodney (whom see); Keats and Thompson both served with or under Nelson.

Harvey, Sir Eliab (1758–1830)
St Andrew's Church, Hempstead, Essex.

English sailor who commanded the *Fighting Téméraire* at the Battle of Trafalgar where his skill and valour earned him promotion to rear-admiral. Later he was court-martialled and dismissed the service for the public manner in which he showed his disapproval of the promotion of Lord Cochrane to a special command; but in March 1810 he was reinstated with full rank and seniority 'in consideration of his long and meritorious services'. However, he was never employed again and in 1820 and 1826 he served as a Member of Parliament for Essex.

Hastings, Warren (1732–1818)
St Peter's Church, Daylesford, Gloucestershire.

Governor-General of British India for the East India Company. He reformed the finances and the administration and suppressed discontent. When he returned to England he was impeached before Parliament for corruption and though acquitted his defence impoverished

Warren Hastings by Lawrence

him. However, the East India Company gave him an annuity and later he became a member of the Privy Council.

Jellicoe, John Rushworth, 1st Earl Jellicoe (1859–1935)
St Paul's Cathedral, London, in the crypt.

Commander-in-Chief of the Grand Fleet in World War I, who planned the strategy of the Battle of Jutland in 1916. As the victory was inconclusive he was censured by many and dismissed by the Prime Minister, David Lloyd George. From 1920 to 1924 he was Governor-General of New Zealand.

Kempthorne, Sir John (1621–1679)
St Thomas's Cathedral, Portsmouth, Hampshire.

Vice-Admiral and the son of a Devonshire attorney, he first went to sea in trading ships sailing from Exeter. He seems to have become rich, probably from booty, on Levant Company ships in the Mediterranean, and married a 'young person belonging to the Turkish ambassador's lady'. He was taken prisoner when his ship *Eastland Merchant* was captured by a notorious Spanish cruiser, but he was soon released and sent home. When the captain of the Spanish cruiser was captured by an English squadron and imprisoned in the Tower of London, Kempthorne is said to have arranged his release through an exchange of prisoners. In 1664 he joined the king's service as captain, was in battle the next year aboard the *Royal James* and, within another year, after a four-day action off the North Foreland aboard the *Royal Charles*, was promoted from flag-captain to Rear-Admiral of the Blue by Prince Rupert. After several more battles, during which a false report came that the French had burnt English ships in the Medway and entered the Channel, Kempthorne in 1669 hoisted his flag on the *Mary Rose* (IV). In this ship, after taking the English ambassador to Tangiers, he retook an English vessel from some Algerian pirates. Off Cadiz on his way back and after being driven north by a violent gale, he was attacked by six Algerian ships, but a lucky shot 'between the wind and the water' struck the Algerian admiral's ship. He hauled off, followed by the others. The *Mary Rose*, her rigging badly cut and with 11 men killed and 17 wounded, put into Cadiz the next day. On his return to England, Kempthorne was knighted for great valour 'against the pirates of Algiers'. After another fierce engagement in 1673 he was made Vice-Admiral.

Since the raising of the *Mary Rose* (I) of Henry VIII's reign from the Solent in 1982 generated great interest we should recapitulate the others: *Mary Rose* (II) saw action against the Spanish Armada and carried Sir Walter Raleigh to the Azores; *Mary Rose* (III) was wrecked off the coast of Flanders in 1650; *Mary Rose* (IV) was Kempthorne's; *Mary Rose* (V) was sunk during action in 1917.

Law, Andrew Bonar (1858–1923)
Westminster Abbey, London, in the centre of the Nave.
Conservative politician who was born in Canada. He held high office in Lloyd George's governments and succeeded him as Prime Minister from 23 October 1922 to 22 May 1923. He was a firm opponent of Irish Home Rule.

Macmillan, Maurice Harold, 1st Earl of Stockton (1894–1986)
St Giles's Church, Horstead Keynes, East Sussex, in family plot with surrounding hedge.
A Conservative Prime Minister who first became an MP in 1924 for Stockton-on-Tees, becoming successively Minister of Housing, Minister of Defence and Foreign Secretary in the 1951–55 period under Churchill, and succeeding Sir Anthony Eden (whom see) as Prime Minister in 1957. After the Vassal spy case and the 'Profumo scandal' he resigned in 1963 because of ill-health. A classical scholar at Balliol College, Oxford, he served in the Grenadier Guards during the first world war and was seriously wounded. After the war he became ADC to the Governor-General of Canada, the Duke of Devonshire, marrying his daughter Dorothy (d.1966). During World War II he was Minister of Supply under Churchill and later Colonial Under-secretary. In his 'winds of change' speech at Cape Town in 1960 he accepted that African colonies would have to be given their independence. He wrote six autobiographical works.

Marlborough, John Churchill, 1st Duke of (1650–1722)
Chapel of Blenheim Palace, Woodstock, Oxfordshire. The coffins of the Duke and his Duchess are in the vaults behind glass, those of their descendants stacked on shelves nearby.
Brilliant general who won the famous battles of Blenheim (1704), Ramillies (1706), Oudenarde (1708) and Malplaquet (1709), against the French for which he was created a duke and granted a pension by a grateful Parliament. His wife, Sarah Jennings, was a close friend

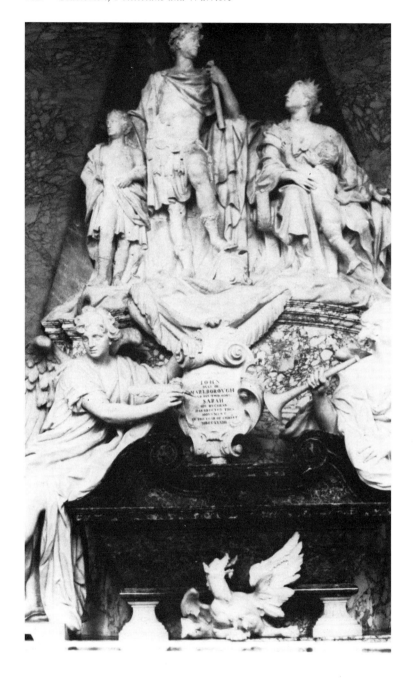

and favourite of Queen Anne. He was the ancestor of Sir Winston Churchill.

Methuen, Paul Sanford, 3rd Baron Methuen of Corsham
(1845–1932)
St Bartholomew's Churchyard, Corsham, Wiltshire; by the east path, large square grave.

Called the 'father of the British army' at a time when he was one of its oldest living officers. During the Boer War he was widely criticized for not pressing the enemy and following up some victories in his attempt to relieve the besieged Mafeking. The truth was that the force of 10,000 under his command was far too small and suffered, through no fault of their own, from lack of communications and supplies. Lord Roberts, the Commander-in-Chief of British forces there, with Lord Kitchener, Chief of Staff, retained Methuen, who later had considerable success in the Western Transvaal when most officers of his seniority had gone home. Towards the end of the war bad discipline and misconduct of half-trained irregular troops caused him to be defeated in a critical battle, wounded and taken prisoner at 57 years of age. After the war he became Commander-in-Chief in South Africa, and after that, even though he was in his seventieth year, Governor of Malta for another four years. There, his foresight saw well-equipped hospitals available when needed in the disastrous Dardanelles expedition. He had always shown three great attributes: chivalry, great personal bravery in battle and dignified endurance against baseless criticism. He was twice married, first in 1878, secondly in 1884 to his cousin. In 1919 he was appointed GCMG, having been promoted to the rank of Field-Marshal in 1911 while in South Africa.

Milner. Lord Alfred Milner, K.G., 1st Viscount (1854–1925)
St Mary's Church, Salehurst, East Sussex, at far east edge of graveyard; large, cambered, white-stone block designed by Sir Edwin Lutyens.

Statesman who became a powerful influence in British and South African affairs after a brilliant scholastic career at New College, Oxford. He was born at Geissen, West Germany, the only son of a

Memorial to John, 1st Duke of Marlborough, and his wife, Sarah, Duchess of Marlborough, in the chapel of Blenheim Palace, Woodstock, Oxfordshire

Lancashire doctor. After a time as assistant editor for the Pall Mall Gazette, in 1889 he became under-secretary of finance in Egypt on the recommendation of Lord Goschen, whose private secretary he had been. In 1885 Milner had stood as Liberal candidate at Harrow but lost this first and only attempt to become an MP.

In Egypt, under Sir Evelyn Baring (later Earl of Cromer), he was to be praised by Baring as 'one of the most able Englishmen who had served the Egyptian government'. After three years he was recalled in 1892 by Lord Goschen to become chairman of the Board of Inland Revenue. Sent by Joseph Chamberlain to Egypt again, as governor of the Cape Colony and the Transvaal, and later high commissioner for South Africa, Milner was there from 1897 to 1905, receiving his barony in 1901 and viscountcy in 1902 for services prior to and during the Boer War.

During the first world war he had, at a critical stage, brought about harmony and co-operation between French and British forces at an Allied Conference in 1918; it marked the turning-point of the war. After his resignation owing to exhaustion, in 1921, he married and devoted himself to work in the City and to writing. His *Questions of the Hour* appeared in 1923, after which he paid a final visit to S. Africa, where it is thought he caught the sleeping sickness from which he died after a brief illness at his home Sturry Court, near Canterbury.

Monck, George, 1st Duke of Albemarle (1608–1670)
Henry VII's Chapel, Westminster Abbey, London, in the south aisle; his funeral armour is now in the Undercroft Museum.

General and admiral who, following the resignation of Richard Cromwell in 1659, was largely responsible for the restoration of Charles II to the throne. Created a duke by a grateful sovereign, he was made Lord of the Admiralty in 1665, remained in charge of the government in London during the plague of 1665, and fought with the fleet in the Anglo-Dutch naval war of 1666. He died on 3 January 1670, standing, it is said, 'upright in his chair like a Roman soldier, his chamber like a tent, open with all the soldiers about him.'

Monckton, Robert (1726–1782)
St Mary Abbots Church, Kensington, London.

Second-in-command to General Wolfe during the Siege of Quebec in 1759 where Wolfe lost his life and Monckton was wounded. Later, Monckton became Governor of New York and conquered Martinique,

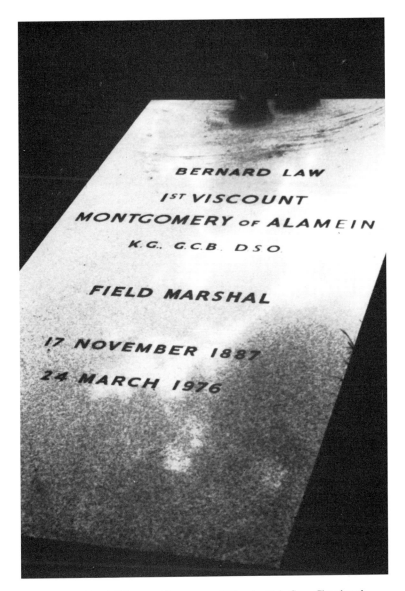

Grave of Field-Marshal Viscount Montgomery of Alamein, Holy Cross Churchyard, Binsted, Hampshire

Grenada, St Lucia and St Vincent. In 1763 he returned to England and was later made Governor of Portsmouth, which he also represented in Parliament.

Montgomery, Bernard Law, 1st Viscount of Alamein (1887–1976)
Holy Cross Churchyard, Binsted, Hampshire.

Field-Marshal Montgomery was best known for his North Africa campaigns during the second world war, when his 8th Army won the Battle of Alamein and drove the German Afrika Corps under Field-Marshal Rommel back to Tunisia. The 8th Army then went on to invade Sicily and Italy. After helping to plan the Normandy invasion he became Commander-in-Chief of the British Group of Armies and Allied Armies in Northern France in 1944. From 1951 to 1958 he served as Deputy Supreme Allied Commander Europe (NATO).

Mountbatten, Lord Francis Albert Victor Nicholas, 1st Earl Mountbatten of Burma (1900–1979)
Romsey Abbey Church, Romsey, Hampshire, in the south transept.

Great-grandson of Queen Victoria, he joined the British navy and fought at the Battle of Jutland in 1916. During the second world war he became chief of combined operations in 1942. As the last Viceroy of India he transferred power to the hands of the Indian government in 1947, becoming the first Governor-General of the Dominion of India. In 1955 he became the First Sea Lord and from 1959 to 1965 he was Chief of the Defence Staff. He was assassinated by the Irish Republican Army in 1979 whilst on holiday in County Sligo, Eire.

Napier, Sir Charles (1786–1860)
All Saints' Churchyard, Catherington, Hampshire; table-tomb hidden behind undergrowth on east side.

Admiral of the illustrious family that produced sailors, soldiers and a mathematician who invented logarithms – John Napier (1550–1617). Sir Charles was born at Merchiston Hall, Stirlingshire, and entered the navy in 1799. After service in the Miguelist Wars, for which he was made a count in the Portuguese peerage, he took Beirut from the Egyptians. He next took Acre and Sidon with his 84-gun ship *Powerful*. He received a KCB and in 1853 sailed to the Baltic in case of war with Russia. He had promised to be 'in Kronstadt or heaven within a month', a boast similar to one he had made before Portugal. But this time (after the Crimean War had begun), the land forts proved impregnable to warship bombardment. He became an MP for South-wark in 1855, and had bought an estate near Catherington in 1836, writing two books about his Portuguese and Syrian experiences.

Napier, Sir Charles James (1782–1853)
Royal Garrison Church, Portsmouth, Hampshire; tomb outside the west entrance.

Known as 'the conqueror of Sind', the vast area of south-east Pakistan north of the Indus river, he was cousin to Admiral Sir Charles. He joined the army when he was 13 years of age, the son of a colonel, and with two soldier brothers, both of whom he once met being carried away wounded from a battlefield in Spain. Charles himself, as a captain in an earlier battle during the Peninsular War, was five times wounded and listed as dead, but a French drummer-boy saved his life. Taken to the French Marshal Soult's headquarters he received medical help, being then 'paroled' by Marshal Ney not to serve until exchanged. A year later he was able to rejoin his regiment and, after two horses had been killed under him, was again wounded by a shot through the face that broke his jaw. He then took part in minor operations against the Americans in the War of 1812. In 1819 he went to Greece and had 'the happiest days of his life', helping them to build roads and attempting to protect the people from feudal oppression. Here he made a deep impression on Byron, who had also gone to Greece to help. In 1834 the colonists of South Australia asked him to become their governor, but his terms were not accepted.

The taking of Sind was to free its people from the Baluchis under Amir Shir Mohamed, who were oppressing the people 'who lived in a larder and yet starved' and were robbed by taxes and by hill-tribe brigands. In March 1843, after six months of incredible fighting, cholera, courage in desperate situations against hordes of stubborn enemy forces, not to mention the temperatures of 110°F. and sun-stroke, Napier finally achieved victory at Dubba. He still remained to fight in other campaigns, including the Sikh War of 1845, but finally retired to Oaklands near Portsmouth. Apart from his military ability he was also a prolific writer on military and social subjects, even writing a historical romance called *William the Conqueror*. He died of a liver disease he had caught during his many military privations.

Nelson, Horatio, 1st Viscount Nelson (and Duke of Bronte)
(1758–1805)
St Paul's Cathedral, London, in the crypt directly below the dome.

Went to sea at twelve and was made a captain in 1793. He lost both his right eye (1794) and his right arm (1797) during active service. He was made a rear-admiral in 1797 and the following year gained his notable victory over the French at Aboukir Bay. In 1805 he defeated the combined French and Spanish fleets at the Battle of Trafalgar, where he was himself killed. His body was preserved in rum during its return to England, hence the expression 'Nelson's blood'. He had no legitimate children, his sole child, Horatia, being the daughter that his notorious mistress, the beautiful Emma Lady Hamilton, bore him.

North, Frederick, 2nd Earl of Guildford, 'Lord North' (1732–1792)
All Saints Church, Wroxton, Oxfordshire.

Generally known as Lord North, although he was Earl of Guildford, he was Prime Minister from 1770 to 1782 during the important years of the War of American Independence. A man of undoubted ability he nonetheless allowed himself to be influenced wholly by the King, George III, a circumstance which gave rise to speculation about their relationship, some claiming that North was an illegitimate half-brother of the King. Although not a successful politician he was unique in winning the esteem, and almost the love, of his most bitter opponents for, as a man, he was extremely good tempered and humorous.

Palmerston, Henry John Temple, 3rd Viscount (1784–1865)
Westminster Abbey, London, North Transept central aisle.

Whig statesman who entered Parliament originally as a Tory in 1807; his title, being Irish, did not bar him from the House of Commons. His vigorous foreign policy whilst Foreign Secretary offended many including Queen Victoria, but it made him popular with the people. He became Prime Minister on 5 February 1855, a position he held with one short interval in 1858 until his death in October 1865.

Peel, Sir Robert (1788–1850)
St Peter's Church, Drayton Bassett, Staffordshire; there is a monument with an inscription in black letter and a florid Gothic canopy over.

Conservative statesman who first entered Parliament in 1809, holding office the following year in Lord Liverpool's government. In 1812 he was made Secretary for Ireland, a post he held until 1818. In 1821 he became Home Secretary and during his term he reformed and humanized the criminal law and reorganized the London police along the lines he had introduced in Ireland. With the support of the Duke of Wellington he managed to obtain the King's consent to the bill for Catholic Emancipation and in 1834, on the dismissal of Lord Melbourne, reluctantly accepted the office of Prime Minister, but he dissolved Parliament the following year. The Bedchamber Crisis of 1840 led him to test his majority in Parliament and, in 1841, in the country when he was returned with a commanding majority. The repeal of the Corn Laws, of which he was an ardent supporter, though successful, nonetheless alienated a considerable and powerful section of his Parliamentary party and he resigned in 1846.

Penn, William (1644–1718)
Jordans, Quaker Meeting House, Chalfont St Giles, Buckinghamshire.

Quaker and founder of Pennsylvania, the grant to which he received from Charles II on 14 March 1681, in repayment of a debt of £16,000 lent by his father, Admiral Sir William Penn, to Charles II. Philadelphia was founded and the 'Great Law of Pennsylvania' passed in which Pennsylvania was to be a Christian state on a Quaker model. His ardent support of non-conformity led him to several clashes with the administration in Britain and he spent brief spells in prison, which did not deter him from preaching. He was the author of several works, the most important of which was *No Cross, No Crown*.

Pitt, William (the Elder), 1st Earl of Chatham (1708–1778)
Westminster Abbey, London, North Transept central aisle.

Statesman. He entered Parliament in 1735 as Member for Old Sarum. Though disliked by the King, George II, he was invited to join the Pelham administration, and in 1757 'The Great Commoner' as he was known, was *de facto* head of the government which was nominally led by the Duke of Newcastle in the Lords. His vigorous lead in the conduct of the Seven Years' War was instrumental in the British gains in Canada and India. Out of office in 1761 following his difference with the new King's favourite, Lord Bute, he was recalled in 1766 by George III and asked to form a government, but chose to

Grave of William Penn, Jordans, Quaker Meeting House, Chalfont St Giles, Buckinghamshire

become Lord Privy Seal and accept the earldom of Chatham, remaining in that office until October 1768. Dr Johnson said of Chatham that 'Walpole was a minister given by the King to the people, but Pitt was a minister given by the people to the King.'

Pitt, William, the Younger (1759–1806)

Westminster Abbey, London, North Transept central aisle in his father's tomb; his monument is at the west end of the Nave.

Statesman. Second son of William Pitt, the Elder, Earl of Chatham. He entered Parliament at twenty-one as Member for Appleby, becoming Chancellor of the Exchequer two years later in 1782. The following year he was Prime Minister at the age of twenty-four. His first administration lasted seventeen years, until March 1801. For three years he remained in opposition until May 1804 when he once again became Prime Minister, holding that office until his death from exhaustion on 23 January 1806. He was an able minister of considerable talents, 'honest intentions and liberal opinions'.

Powell, (John) Enoch, MBE (1912–1998)
Royal Warwick Regimental Cemetery, Warwick, in his wartime uniform, after funeral service in St Mary's Collegiate Church there.

Politician and classical scholar, he will be remembered for his perceived racism as a parliamentarian who pointed out that serious problems of national unity may be caused by excessive immigration of coloured, former Commonwealth and colonial persons.

Educated at King Edward's School, Birmingham (he was born at Stechford) and at Trinity College, Cambridge, he was a brilliant classical student and linguist. He became Professor of Greek at Sydney University, Australia from 1937 to 1939, when he enlisted as a private soldier in World War II, rising to the rank of brigadier, being the youngest of that rank in the British Army. Elected as Member of Parliament in 1950 for Wolverhampton, after serving as parliamentary secretary to the Ministry of Housing, then as financial secretary to the Treasury, he resigned that post, later to become Minister of Health and a Privy Councillor. In the 1974 election he decided not to stand as a Conservative, resigning from that Party in 1983, but was later returned as an Ulster Unionist member. Awarded the MBE in 1943, he married Pamela Wilson in 1952.

It has been said that it was not the public who condemned him for his racism but the 'opinion formers', and where Churchill pointed out that genius can spring from every class and from every part of the land and come to fame, Powell perhaps forgot that such a fact of human existence is dangerous to be perceived of as cutting down. He supported a truly free world market and exposed the true cause of inflation, where excess government spending is the reason, long before such became generally accepted by both government and most voters. He was concerned that without the union of the British Isles devolution would lead to a dissolution of the monarchy and the total absorption of sundered areas of Britain into a European mega-state.

Raffles, Sir Thomas Stamford (1781–1826)
St Mary's Church, Hendon, Greater London.

Governor in Sumatra and Java and founder by name of Raffles Hotel, Singapore. Born at sea off Jamaica, he was the son of a sea captain in the West India trade. At 14 he was a clerk in the East India Company and, showing great proficiency in languages with fluency in Malay dialects, he was appointed by Sir Hugh Inglis as assistant secretary in Penang in 1805, becoming a full secretary two years later.

He stopped slave trading and did much to make Singapore a prosperous free-port. On his return home to retirement in Barnet he lost all his papers and valuable belongings when his ship caught fire because of a steward's carelessness. The survivors were in an open boat for many days before being rescued. His knighthood came in 1817. He also had two botanical species named after him that he had discovered in his East India travels.

Roberts, Frederick Sleigh, 1st Earl Roberts of Kandahar, Pretoria and Waterford (1832–1914)
St Paul's Cathedral, London, in the crypt.

Field-Marshal who first entered the service of the East India Company and took part in the suppression of the Indian Mutiny in 1857 and in the war with Afghanistan where he relieved Kandahar. In 1858 he won the Victoria Cross for saving the life of an Indian. During the Boer War he commanded the British forces in South Africa, relieving Kimberley and advancing on Pretoria. At 82 he was in France with the British Expeditionary Force at the beginning of the first world war when he caught a chill and died three days later. He was the author of *Forty Years in India*.

Rodney, George Brydges Rodney, 1st Baron (1719–1792)
St Mary's Church, Old Alresford, Hampshire.

Admiral who in 1762, during the Seven Years' War, captured the island of Martinique from the French. In 1780 he defeated the Spanish fleet and relieved Gibraltar. During the American War of Independence he once again defeated the French fleet under de Grasse.

Scott, John, first Earl of Eldon (1751–1838)
Old Church graveyard, Kingston, Dorset; monument in new church of St James (old church became church hall).

Lord Chancellor for 26 years; longer than any other holder of this office. He was the third son of a Newcastle-upon-Tyne coal merchant, who owned several barges and a public house. A fair scholar, John was sent to Oxford. On the way there a Latin motto painted on the coach, *Sat cito si sat bene* (quickly enough if well enough), so impressed him that for the rest of his life he invariably cited it as a reason for his apparent procrastination. In 1796 he had been called to the bar as a member of the Middle Temple, and his maxim was that he should 'live like a hermit and work like a horse'. He became expert in common law and equity. As a Tory Member of Parliament, he supported many Acts said to be oppressive by some, including the suspension of Habeas Corpus. But those French revolutionary days were dangerously radical, even in England. He also supported a bill that would have prohibited the marriage of a divorced adulteress and her lover. In 1793 he became Attorney-General and Lord Chief Justice in 1799. He was Lord Chancellor for five years (1801–6) under William Pitt the Younger until Pitt's death in 1806. A year later he resumed the Great Seal and held it for another 21 years. He was an implacable enemy of Napoleon and a great friend and influencer of George III, with whom he dealt even during the king's lunacy in 1804. Created Baron of Eldon in 1799, he received the titles of Viscount Encombe and Earl of Eldon in 1821 from George IV, and lived to take the oath in 1837 to Queen Victoria. He died of old age, a man who was at once respected and, perhaps unfairly, reviled by many for his extreme conservatism. His wife had died in 1831 and he was laid to rest beside her remains in the Old Church graveyard at Kingston, near his seat at Encombe.

Seymour, Thomas 1st Baron Seymour of Sudeley (c.1508–1549)
St Peter ad Vincula, Tower of London, London.

Younger brother of Edward, Duke of Somerset and Jane Seymour, Henry VIII's third wife. After the death of Henry VIII he married his widow, Catherine Parr, who died of fever following the birth of their daughter. According to King Henry's will he was to be made a peer of the realm and Lord High Admiral, and both orders were carried out by his nephew, Edward VI. An intriguer, he plotted against his brother, the Protector, and was executed in 1549.

Shaftesbury. Anthony Ashley Cooper, 7th Earl of (1801–1885)
St Giles's Church, Wimborne St Giles, Dorset, in the chancel.

Known as the 'philanthropic' earl, he worked to bring about the amelioration of the grim conditions of factory workers. Schools, health and other reforms came under his aegis. Florence Nightingale said that as a Crimea health commissioner he 'saved the British army'. The statue in Piccadilly Circus, popularly known as Eros, is the Shaftesbury Memorial Fountain commemorating him.

Also buried here were his predecessors, the 1st 'Protestant' Earl (1621–83) and the 3rd 'Philosopher' Earl (1671–1713), who both had the same Christian and surnames. Their forebear Sir Anthony Ashley (1551–1628), who is credited with being the first to introduce the cabbage to England, has a stylized sculpture of the vegetable on his tomb here.

Sidney, Sir Philip (1554–1586)
'Old' St Paul's Cathedral, London.

Soldier and considerable poet, he is famous for his remark as he lay wounded at the Battle of Zutphen on 22 September 1586. He had received a bullet wound in the thigh and called for some water but, seeing a dying soldier nearby whom he felt to be in greater need than himself, he offered the water to him saying, 'Thy need is greater than mine'. He died at Arnhem on 17 October 1586. As a poet he is chiefly remembered for the series of sonnets addressed to Stella, known as *Astrophel and Stella* (Stella being the Lady Penelope Devereux, sister of Elizabeth's ill-fated Earl of Essex), and *Arcadia*.

Sikorski, Wladyslaw (1881–1943)
Newark Cemetery, Newark-on-Trent, Nottinghamshire.

Polish general who was commander-in-chief in the second world war until 1943 of the Polish forces. He was born in Galicia and studied engineering. A Polish patriot, he was imprisoned by the Austrians after the Treaty of Brest-Litovsk. In 1920 as commander of a Polish Infantry Division he defended Warsaw during the Russian–Polish war, becoming Poland's Prime Minister in 1922. He became leader of the Free Polish forces during the second world war and led the government-in-exile from 1940 in London. He broke off relations with Russia in 1943 when graves of Polish officers were discovered in Katyn. He died in an air accident at Gibraltar.

Smith, Captain John (1580–1631)
Church of the Holy Sepulchre without Newgate, Holborn, London.

Adventurer and soldier who was saved from death by the Red Indian Princess Pocahontas after he was captured by the Powhatan Indians in December 1607 during an expedition to Virginia. On later expeditions he was captured by both the French and pirates, but escaped from each. A history of his adventures is recorded on a brass plate (a copy of the original which is no longer identifiable) on the south wall of the choir.

Somerset, Edward Seymour, 1st Duke of (c.1506–1552)
St Peter ad Vincula, Tower of London, London.

Brother of Jane Seymour, Henry VIII's third wife, and uncle to the boy King Edward VI, he headed the Council of Regency after the death of Henry VIII and became Lord Protector of the Realm. He repealed the heresy laws and nearly all the treason laws passed since Edward III and introduced the first Book of Common Prayer in 1549 which was a studious compromise between the old and new learning. His ideas of liberty were in striking contrast with those of most Tudor statesmen and the main cause of his ruin was the divergence between him and the majority of the Council over the question of constitutional liberty and the enclosure of the Commons. The majority scouted his notions of liberty and deeply resented his championship of the poor against greedy landlords and others. He was executed on the strength of an allegedly forged warrant of his nephew, the young Edward VI, on 22 January 1552.

Suffolk, William de la Pole, 1st Duke of (1396–1450)
St Andrew's Church, Wingfield, Suffolk. There is also a fine tomb and monument to his parents, the Earl and Countess of Suffolk, as well as one to his son, John, 2nd Duke of Suffolk and his wife Elizabeth, a sister of Edward IV.

'The Englishman who surrendered to Joan of Arc' at Jargeau in 1431. Henry V made him Admiral of Normandy and he served in France for fourteen years without returning to England. After his surrender to Joan of Arc he returned to English politics and set himself in opposition to the young Henry VI's uncle, the Duke of Gloucester. He arranged for the King's marriage to Margaret of Anjou, accompanying the bride to England in 1445. His earldom of Suffolk was raised first to a marquessate and then to a dukedom in 1448. Virtually the ruler of England after the death of Gloucester and Cardinal Beaufort, his peace policy gradually lost England much of her French territory. In 1450 he was arrested and sent to the Tower of London and the King, to save him from his enemies, banished him for five years. He sailed from Ipswich on May Day, 1450 but before he could enter Calais his ship was intercepted and his head was hacked from his body with 'six strokes of a rusty sword'.

Throckmorton, Sir Nicholas (1515–1571)
Laud Memorial Chapel, St Katharine Cree Church, Leadenhall Street, City of London.

Diplomatist who, during the nine-days reign of Lady Jane Grey, played the friend to both sides. He secured the favour of Queen Mary but was suspected of being implicated in Sir Thomas Wyat's rebellion and though acquitted was sent to the Tower of London. Restored to favour by Mary shortly after, he rose rapidly when Elizabeth ascended the throne, becoming first her Chamberlain of the Exchequer and, from May 1559 to April 1564, her ambassador to France where he became acquainted with Mary Queen of Scots whilst she was Queen of France. In May 1565 he was sent as ambassador to Mary, who had returned to Scotland, the first of many such missions he undertook for Elizabeth to the Scottish Queen, whom he greatly admired. In 1569, during the Duke of Norfolk's conspiracy to secure the release of Mary, who was by now imprisoned in England, Throckmorton fell under suspicion but was not proceeded against. He died on 12 February 1571. His daughter, Elizabeth, married Sir Walter Raleigh.

Trenchard, Hugh Montague, 1st Viscount Trenchard (1873–1956)
Henry VII's Chapel, Westminster Abbey, London, in the small east chapel, now known as the RAF Chapel, that forms part of the apse.

Served in the Boer War and in the Royal Flying Corps during the first world war. As Chief of Air Staff from 1919 to 1930 he shaped offensive strategy. He became the first air marshal of the RAF and was largely responsible for the RAF College at Cranwell. When he became Commissioner of the Metropolitan Police in 1931 he was concerned in establishing the police college at Hendon.

Unknown Warrior
Westminster Abbey, London, at the west end of the Nave.

At the suggestion of an army chaplain, the body buried in a simple grave in an Armentières garden and marked with a wooden cross on which were the words, 'An Unknown British Soldier', was brought to England and re-interred with full honours in Westminster Abbey on Armistice Day, 11 November 1920, as a symbol of the thousands of British servicemen who died during the first world war. Soil was specially brought from France for the grave and it was covered by a slab of black Belgian marble bearing an inscription written by Dean

Ryle. The Congressional Medal of Honour laid on the grave by General Pershing in 1921 is affixed to a nearby pillar.

Vane, Sir Henry, the Elder (1589–1655)
St Giles's Church, Shipbourne, Kent. The original church was rebuilt by James Gibbs in 1721 to 1722 and again in 1880 to 1881.

A courtier at the court of James I who knighted him on 3 March 1611. In 1630 he became chief adviser and a Privy Councillor to Charles I and thereafter held many high offices of state, ultimately, through the influence of the Queen, Henrietta Maria, becoming Secretary of State. He played an important part in Strafford's downfall. The King was suspicious of his loyalty during the early controversy with Parliament and dismissed him from his appointments in 1641. He joined the Parliamentary faction and remained with the Parliament after the King's execution in 1649.

Vane, Sir Henry, the Younger (1613–1662)
St Giles's Church, Shipbourne, Kent. The original church was rebuilt by James Gibbs in 1721 to 1722 and again in 1880 to 1881.

A strong Puritan, son of Sir Henry Vane, the Elder. In 1635 he emigrated to Massachusetts to obtain free exercise of his religion and was made Governor of that province in 1636. He returned to England the following year and supported Parliament in its struggle with the King, being a close associate of Oliver Cromwell, addressing each other as Brother Fountain (Cromwell) and Brother Heron (Vane). In 1650 he and Cromwell quarrelled over the structure of Parliament, Cromwell seeking an entirely new Parliament with the supremacy of the army representation. It was a permanent breach. He was arrested in 1656 and for three months imprisoned in Carisbrooke Castle. He opposed Richard Cromwell and after his abdication Vane was restored to power. At the Restoration he was arrested but his life was at first spared. Subsequently he was accused of high treason and executed on Tower Hill on 14 June 1662, Pepys describing him at his execution as being 'rather a looker-on than the person concerned in the execution'.

Vernon, or Pembruge, Sir Richard de (d.1451)
St Bartholomew's Church, Tong, Shropshire.

Knighted in 1418 he probably served with Henry V in France. He represented Derbyshire in the first Parliament of Henry VI and became Speaker of the 'Bats' Parliament of Henry VI held at

Leicester. In 1450 he was made treasurer of Calais and died the following year.

His son, Sir William, succeeded him as a treasurer of Calais and was also the last person who held for life the title of Constable of England. He died in 1467 and was buried in Tong Church.

Sir William's grandson, Sir Henry, was the great friend of, as well as governor and treasurer to, Arthur, Prince of Wales, son of Henry VII, whose marriage contract he signed in 1500. A room at Hadden Hall, the Vernon family home, is called the 'Prince's Chamber' and commemorates their intimacy. Sir Henry died in 1515 and was also buried at Tong Church.

Waller, Edmund (1606–1687)
St Mary and All Saints Church, Beaconsfield, Buckinghamshire.

As a poet and politician he was the leader of a plot to seize London for Charles I, but to save his life he revealed his conspirators. First imprisoned in the Tower of London, he was released and banished from the country. He went to Paris where he published his *Poems* in 1645. Pardoned by Cromwell, he returned to England where he published works that praised Cromwell, but upon his death wrote poems rejoicing in Charles II's Restoration. Waller returned to parliament until his death and in 1685 his *Divine Poems* appeared; a *Second Part* was published three years after his death.

Walpole, Sir Robert, 1st Earl of Orford (1676–1745)
St Martin's Church, Houghton Hall, near King's Lynn, Norfolk.

Whig statesman who from 1721 to 1742 was the chief minister of George I and George II. Considered to be Britain's first Prime Minister, he was known as a 'House of Commons man'. During his tenure of office he strove to keep England free from war and in so doing brought stability and prosperity to the realm.

Walsingham, Sir Francis (c.1530–1590)
'Old' St Paul's Cathedral, London, his body being placed in the same tomb as that of Sir Philip Sidney.

Elected Member of Parliament for Banbury in the first Parliament of Queen Elizabeth I, which sat from January to May 1559. He was largely responsible for the efficient secret service network during Elizabeth's reign which uncovered the plots aimed at unseating Elizabeth and placing Mary Queen of Scots on the throne and also

Robert Walpole, from the studio of Van Loo

gathered exact details of Spain's intended armada against England. He undertook many diplomatic missions where he was known for his devotion to Protestantism.

Wavell, Archibald Percival, 1st Earl of Wavell (1883–1950)
Chapel of Winchester College, Winchester, Hampshire.

General who served initially in the Boer War in South Africa. During the first world war he served on Allenby's staff in Palestine, earlier having been blinded in one eye on the Western front. As Commander-in-Chief of the allied forces in the Middle East in the second world war from 1939–1941 he defeated the Italians in North Africa but was forced back by General Rommel. After being relieved by Sir Claude Auchinleck, Wavell became Commander-in-Chief in India from 1941 to 1943, when he became Viceroy, a post he held until 1947. A writer of history, biography and poetry, he published many books.

Wellington, Arthur Wellesley, 1st Duke of (1769–1852)
St Paul's Cathedral, London, in the crypt.

Field-Marshal who was born in Ireland, son of the Earl of Mornington. He gained his military experience in India and during the Napoleonic Wars was responsible for driving the French from the Iberian peninsula. His defeat of Napoleon at Waterloo in 1815 brought an end to the French emperor's career and his permanent exile. Wellington entered politics as a Tory, holding the office of Prime Minister from 1828 to 1830, piloting the Catholic Emancipation Bill through Parliament in 1829. He fell from office over the issue of Parliamentary reform which he did not support. When Sir Robert Peel became Prime Minister Wellington supported the repeal of the Corn Laws.

Westmorland, Ralph Neville, 1st Earl of (1364–1425)
St Mary's Church, Staindrop, Durham, magnificent memorial in church.

A supporter of Henry IV against Richard II, he later helped the King put down the revolt of the Percies of Northumberland, the rivals to the Nevilles for supremacy in the northern counties. He later married the King's half-sister, Joan Beaufort, daughter of John of Gaunt and Katharine Swynford. In May 1405 the Percies were once again in revolt and Westmorland faced a superior force at Shipton

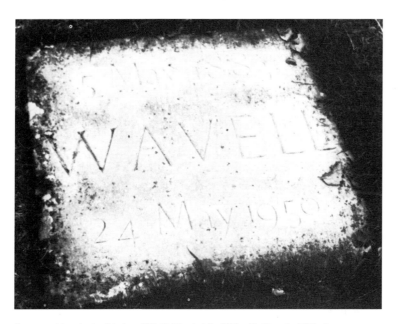

Stone marking the burial site of Field-Marshal Earl Wavell, Chapel of Winchester College, Hampshire

Moor led by Archbishop Scrope of York and Thomas Mowbray. By a trick Scrope disbanded his forces and Westmorland arrested him, but he is not held responsible for the Archbishop's hasty execution.

Whittington, Sir Richard (c.1358–1423)
St Michael Paternoster Royal Church, Cannon Street, City of London. Sir Richard's body was more than once disturbed after his burial and now cannot be found. Efforts in 1949 to locate his tomb only produced a mummified cat which, however, was unlikely to have been Whittington's.

Four times Lord Mayor of London, briefly in 1397, 1398, 1406 and 1419. Despite the legend Richard Whittington was the son of a knight of Gloucestershire or Herefordshire. He became a London mercer and was wealthy enough to make large loans to the King, Henry IV, and later his son, Henry V, in return for which he obtained valuable trading concessions. The famous legend of 'Dick Whittington' was not attached to his name until after 200 years later and seems to bear little relation to the reality of his career.

Wilberforce, William (1759–1833)

Westminster Abbey, London, buried in the North Transept. His monument is in the north choir aisle of the Nave.

Parliamentary leader of the campaign to abolish the slave trade. Elected to Parliament in 1780 he worked tirelessly against slavery and was known as 'the authorized interpreter of the national conscience'. He finally succeeded when slave trading was abolished in 1807. Thereafter he worked against slavery itself but that was not abolished until 1833, the year of his death.

Wilson, Sir Henry Hughes (1864–1922)

St Paul's Cathedral, London, in the crypt.

Field-marshal who in 1914 was responsible for the preparedness of the British Expeditionary Force at the outset of the Great War. He was elected to Parliament on a Conservative ticket for North Down in Northern Ireland in February 1921 but was assassinated by two Sinn Feiners on the doorstep of his London house the following year.

Wilson, Sir James Harold, K.G., 1st Baron of Rievaulx (1926–1995)

St Mary the Virgin churchyard, St Mary's, Isles of Scilly.

Labour prime minister of Britain, he was elected in 1964, 1966 and 1970 during the years of contentious Common Market negotiations, Rhodesian sanctions and balance-of-payments crises. Born at Huddersfield, he completed his education at Oxford, where he also became a lecturer in economics. After serving in the wartime Ministry of Fuel and Power he eventually became the youngest cabinet minister since Pitt. He was first elected in Ormskirk as a member of parliament.

Wolfe, James (1727–1759)

St Alfege's Church, Greenwich, London, in the crypt under 'Canadian Corner'; large statue on Observatory Hill.

British general who, defeating the French at the Plains of Abraham, Quebec, won Canada for the British but was mortally wounded on the battlefield. Born in Kent, he was the son of a general and served as an ensign at the age of 16 at the Battle of Dettingen – the last battle in which a British monarch (George II) personally led his troops. After further battle service in Scotland against the Jacobites, during which he was wounded, Wolfe commanded troops at Cape Breton as a colonel in 1758, capturing Louisburg. In 1759, after training 9000 men at Hambledon Hill in Dorset, he sailed with them to Canada,

James Wolfe, by an unknown artist

where at dawn his force successfully scaled a poorly guarded part of the cliffs below Quebec city to defeat the French General Montcalm, who was killed in the action. Wolfe himself lived to know that his troops had been victorious before he died on the battlefield.

Wyatt, Sir Francis (c.1575–1644)
Boxley Abbey, Boxley, Kent, in the family vault.

Appointed Governor of Virginia in 1620, he arrived in the colony the following year. In one year more than 1300 colonists arrived in Virginia and Wyatt introduced many legal reforms which aided the prosperity of the colony. In 1622 an Indian uprising caused a massacre of more than 300 settlers. In 1626 Sir Francis returned to England but, thirteen years later, in November 1639 he once again accepted the governorship of Virginia. However, his rule was unpopular and he returned to England in 1643.

Wyat, Sir Thomas (1503–1542)
Abbey Church, Sherborne, Dorset; the stone in the north transept marks his grave.

Statesman and poet who was reputedly in love with Anne Boleyn before her marriage to Henry VIII. In 1509 he was made a Knight of the Bath on the accession of Henry VIII and he held various court offices. In 1536 he was arrested and imprisoned in the Tower of London, perhaps to incriminate Queen Anne Boleyn, but was released after a month. Knighted in 1537 he was sent as the King's ambassador to the Emperor Charles V. Subsequently he fell from Henry's favour but was later restored. He died of a fever at Sherborne on 11 October 1542 whilst escorting the Emperor's ambassadors from Falmouth to London. Henry Howard, Earl of Surrey, celebrated his death in these lines: 'Wyat resteth here, that quick could never rest.'

[4] Churchmen, Philosophers, Lawyers and Scholars

Alban, Saint (d.c.303)
St Alban's Cathedral, St Albans, Hertfordshire, shrine reconstructed from fragments after original destroyed at the Reformation.

Usually styled the protomartyr of Britain, he is reputed to have been born at Verulamium (the modern St Albans) and to have served seven years in Rome as a soldier in the army of the Emperor Diocletian. On his return to Britain he settled in his native town and was put to death as a Christian during Diocletian's persecutions of the sect. About 793, King Offa of Mercia erected a church on the spot where he was alleged to have been killed, and later a monastery was added. He is commemorated in the Roman martyrology on 22 June.

Anselm, Saint (1033–1109)
St Anselm's Chapel, Canterbury Cathedral, Canterbury, Kent.

Archbishop of Canterbury who was born at Aosta in Piedmont into a noble family. At 27, after a disagreement with his father, he became a monk in the monastery of Bec, whose prior was the celebrated Lanfranc. When Lanfranc became Abbot of Caen in about 1063 Anselm was elected prior and, in 1078, Abbot of Bec. Under his rule Bec became the first seat of learning in Europe, due more to the great moral influence of his noble character and kindly discipline than to his intellectual powers. Anselm travelled often to England to supervize the monastery's possessions there and during these journeys he impressed the English greatly, so that on the death of Lanfranc he was regarded as his natural successor as Archbishop of Canterbury. But the King, William II, at Lanfranc's death seized the possessions and revenues of Canterbury and refused to appoint a new archbishop. After four years, in 1092, Anselm reluctantly agreed to travel to England to accept the see and was consecrated in 1093. The King's quarrel with Rome over who was responsible for investing the Archbishop caused friction between him and Anselm, and when in 1097 Anselm was finally allowed to travel to Rome he remained abroad until after William's death, being recalled by his successor, King Henry I. Again the question of the investiture was raised and once again Anselm travelled to Rome to seek papal guidance. The threat of excommunication against Henry finally brought about a resolution to the conflict, Henry renouncing his formal rights in 1107. Thereafter, Anselm spent his remaining years of life carrying out his pastoral duties. He died on 21 April 1109 and was canonized by Pope Alexander VI in 1494.

Ascham, Roger (c.1515–1568)
Church of the Holy Sepulchre without Newgate, Holborn, London.

Scholar and writer who was born in Yorkshire and educated in the household of Sir Humphrey Wingfield, Speaker of the House of Commons. At fifteen he went to St John's College, Cambridge, where he came under the influence of John Cheke. On the presentation of his book, *Toxophilus*, 'On the art of Shooting' (the long bow) to King Henry VIII he received an annual pension of £10. Shortly after the accession of Edward VI Ascham declared himself a supporter of the Reformed religion and in 1548 was appointed tutor to the young Princess Elizabeth. After two years he quarrelled with the steward and returned to Cambridge. During Queen Mary's reign he was her Latin Secretary and in 1555 he resumed his studies with the Princess Elizabeth. A humanist, he wrote a treatise, *The Schoolmaster*, on 'the right order of teaching', which was the first definite demonstration in favour of humanity in education.

Bacon, Sir Nicholas (1509–1579)
'Old' St Paul's Cathedral, London; his damaged effigy survived the Great Fire and is now in the crypt.

A Member of Parliament in 1545, he thereafter held a succession of appointments, the most important of which was Lord Keeper of the Great Seal in December 1558, shortly after becoming a Privy Councillor and receiving a knighthood. As a Protestant he distrusted Mary Queen of Scots and was alleged to be a supporter of the claims of the Lady Catherine Grey, sister of Lady Jane Grey, to the throne in the event of Elizabeth's death without direct heirs. He opposed the projected marriage between Elizabeth and the Duke of Anjou, his fear and distrust of the Catholics being increased by the massacre of the French Protestants, the Huguenots, on St Bartholomew's Day, 24 August 1572. He died in London on 20 February 1579. His son by his second marriage was Sir Francis Bacon.

Beaufort, Henry (d.1447)
Winchester Cathedral, Winchester, Hampshire, chantry in the south retro-choir.

Cardinal bishop of Winchester who completed the building of the cathedral itself, which had been largely rebuilt from Norman times by William of Wykeham (whom see) whose tomb and chantry are also in the south nave. Beaufort was the illegitimate son of John of Gaunt and Catherine Swyneford, and Henry V forbade him to accept the cardinalate, but in 1432 he defeated an attempt to deprive him of his see, because he was a cardinal, by the Duke of Gloucester. Beaufort crowned Henry VI king of France in 1431 in Paris and, in 1439–40, tried to arrange peace with France.

Becket, Thomas à, Saint (c.1118–1170)
Canterbury Cathedral, Kent. The original shrine was destroyed in 1538 during the Dissolution and Becket's bones were scattered. His skull, however, is reputed to have been preserved in or under the Corona, also known as 'Becket's Crown', at the extreme east end of the Cathedral.

A member of the household of Theobald Archbishop of Canterbury who, because of Becket's success in dissuading the Roman Curia from sanctioning the coronation of Stephen's son Eustace, recommended him for the appointment of Archdeacon of Canterbury which Becket accepted after becoming a deacon in 1154. The following year, the new King, Henry II, made him Chancellor. In 1162 Theobald died but before doing so he advised Henry II to appoint Becket in his place as Archbishop; Theobald seeing in Becket a champion of the Church's privileges and rights which the old Archbishop felt would soon be under attack from Henry II. Henry, however, sanctioned the appointment under the misapprehension that Becket would foremost be a king's man, and soon discovered his error, for the new Archbishop proved himself anything other than the King's tool, devoting himself uncompromisingly to the service of the Church. A dispute over the land tax at the Council of Woodstock in July 1163 brought Becket and Henry into open conflict and when Becket and his churchmen were required to approve the Constitutions of Clarendon, in which the King defined the relations between Church and State, Becket refused, supported by the Pope, although some of the bishops accepted the constitutions. He fled to France in November 1164 and succeeded in getting Pope Alexander III to condemn the constitutions formally.

Pressure by the Pope effected a reconciliation at Fréteval on 22 July 1170 and Becket returned to England. However, he would not compromise his stand, taking steps to punish those bishops who had supported the King, and declared the Constitutions of Clarendon null and void. Within a month of his return to Canterbury, on 29 December 1170, he was murdered by four of Henry's knights at Canterbury. He was canonized two years later and his shrine became a place of pilgrimage.

Bede, The Venerable, Saint (c.673–735)
Durham Cathedral, Durham, County Durham, in the Galilee Porch.

Historian and theologian who, from the age of seven, spent his entire life in the monasteries of Wearmouth, founded by Benedict Biscop in 647, and Jarrow, founded about 681 or 682. He was ordained a deacon at nineteen, which was below the canonical age, and a priest at thirty. His *Ecclesiastical History of the English Nation* justly earned him the title Father of English History. There is a touching account of his death in a contemporary letter which tells us that his last hours were spent, like most of his life, in devotion and teaching, his latest work being to dictate a translation into the vernacular of the Gospel of St John.

Bentham, Jeremy (1748–1832)
University College, London, Gower Street, London, in the south cloister where his embalmed body is on display in a show case.

Utilitarian philosopher and writer on jurisprudence. His main works were *Government* and *Principles of Morals and Legislation*. Determined to find a solid foundation for both law and morality, he taught 'the greatest happiness of the greatest number' in what he described in 1802 as 'utilitarian philosophy'.

Bere, Richard (d.1524)
Glastonbury Abbey (ruins), Glastonbury, Somerset, near the Holy Sepulchre on the south side.

Abbot of Glastonbury who was known equally for his scholarship, his passion for building, and for his controversy with Archbishop Warham of Canterbury over the siting of the relics of St Dunstan; the Archbishop claiming they were at Canterbury, Abbot Bere claiming

Tomb of The Venerable Bede, Durham Cathedral, Durham

that as the shrine was at Glastonbury, the popularity of which had caused jealousy at Canterbury, the relics should be returned to Glastonbury. The quarrel was resolved at the Dissolution with the general pillage of religious houses, by which time Bere was dead.

Birinus, Saint (d.650)
Abbey Church, Dorchester, Oxfordshire. His body was later removed to Winchester and there enshrined by Bishop Ethelwold (963–984).

Bishop of Dorchester. A Benedictine monk whom Pope Honorius sent to Britain to convert the island. He landed in Wessex in 634 and the following year baptized Cynegils King of Wessex. He founded the see of Dorchester and became its first bishop. The *Anglo-Saxon Chronicle* indicates that his influence was widespread and credits him with the conversion of many princes.

Bodley, Sir Thomas (1545–1613)
Chapel of Merton College, Oxford, Oxfordshire.

Diplomat and scholar. During the reign of Queen Mary I he lived in Geneva where his father, because of his Protestant sympathies, had been obliged to move. On the accession of Elizabeth I the family returned to England and Thomas entered Magdalen College, Oxford. After a tour of Europe he returned to become Gentleman Usher to the Queen. In 1584 he entered Parliament as the Member for Portsmouth, and the following year began his diplomatic career with a mission to the Protestant princes of northern Europe to secure aid for Henry of Navarre. In 1588 he was sent as minister to the Hague, but, because of intrigues at home, he begged to be recalled, returning to England in 1604. His best remembered achievement was the endowment of the Bodleian Library at Oxford for which he left the greater part of his fortune.

Bowett, Henry (d.1423)
The Lady Chapel, York Minster, York.

Diplomat and churchman. As Chaplain to Pope Urban VI he was the only Englishman at the papal court courageous enough to remain with the Pope after the riots at Lucia in 1385. During the reign of Richard II he was made Chief Justice of the Superior Court of

Jeremy Bentham's 'Auto-Icon', his embalmed body on display in the south cloister of University College, London, Gower Street

Aquitaine, 1397, and in the following year Constable of Bordeaux. A supporter of Bolingbroke, later Henry IV, he incurred Richard's disfavour and was banished, sentence of execution being commuted. On Henry's accession he became an influential adviser to the King, being appointed one of the regents for Henry's possessions in southern France. Appointed to the see of Bath and Wells in 1400, he was, shortly after returning from a Danish embassy, made Archbishop of York, the see having been vacant for two years following the execution of Archbishop Scrope. In 1417, despite his age and the fact that he had to be carried in a litter, he accompanied the army to fight the Scots, and his example was a contributory factor in the English victory.

Cantelupe, Thomas de, Saint (c.1218–1282)
Hereford Cathedral, Hereford, north transept.

English prelate and saint. Educated at Paris and Orléans, afterwards he taught Canon Law at Oxford and became Chancellor of the University in 1262. A supporter of Simon de Montfort in the Barons' War he represented the barons before St Louis of France at Amiens in 1264. He was made Chancellor of England but lost his position after the death of de Montfort at Evesham in the same year, 1265, and went to live abroad. Returning to England he once more became Chancellor of Oxford University and in 1275 was made Bishop of Hereford and became a trusted adviser to the new King Edward I. In 1279 he revisited Italy and died at Orvieto on 25 August 1282. He was canonized in 1330 by Pope John XXII after many miracles were reputed to have occurred at his shrine.

Coke, Sir Edward, commonly called Lord Coke (1552–1634)
St Mary's Church, Tittleshall, Norfolk, where there is a fine monument.

One of England's greatest lawyers, who was successively Chief Justice of the Common Pleas (1606), and Chief Justice of the Common Bench (1613). His challenge to James I over the King's supreme prerogative brought his dismissal from all his offices in 1616. In 1620 he entered Parliament as the Member for Liskeard and was an outspoken supporter of the freedom of Parliamentary discussion and the liberty of speech of its members. Together with Pym and Sir Robert Philips he was imprisoned for entering in the journal of the House the famous petition on 18 December 1621 embodying those principles. In 1628 he re-entered Parliament for Buckinghamshire and took an important part in drawing up the great Petition of Rights. At the end of his career in Parliament he bewailed 'with tears' the ruin he declared the Duke of Buckingham was bringing on the country.

Cowper, William, 1st Earl (c.1665–1723)
St Mary's Church, Hertingfordbury, Hertfordshire.

English jurist who, as Lord Keeper of the Great Seal, conducted the negotiations between the English and Scottish commissioners in 1706 to arrange for the union between England and Scotland. When Union between the two countries came into operation in May 1707 he became the first Lord High Chancellor of Great Britain. He resigned the office in 1710 but was reinstated by George I shortly after his accession. In April 1718, a month after he was elevated to the peerage as Viscount Fordwich and Earl Cowper, he resigned, having earned the King's disfavour by espousing the cause of George, Prince of Wales, later George II, in his quarrel with his father.

Cranmer, Thomas (1489–1556)
Burned at the stake near Balliol College, Oxford; a cross on the surface of Broad Street, opposite Balliol College, Oxford, marks the spot where the burning took place.

Archbishop of Canterbury under Henry VIII and Edward VI and an ardent supporter of the Reformation. He was brought to the attention of Henry VIII when he suggested that the King's marriage to Catherine of Aragon could be declared null and void without recourse to Rome if the canonists and the universities should decide that the marriage with a deceased brother's widow was illegal. He pleaded the King's cause in Rome in 1530 and before the Emperor in Germany in 1531. Henry VIII appointed him to the see of Canterbury in 1532 and he was consecrated on 30 March 1533. He declared the King's marriage to Catherine null and void and pronounced the marriage of Henry to Anne Boleyn to be valid. On 1 June 1533 he crowned Anne as Queen and on 10 September that year stood as godfather to the baby Princess Elizabeth. At the death of Edward VI he supported the accession of Lady Jane Grey and he alone remained true to her cause. When Mary acceded Cranmer was first confined to Lambeth Palace and then in September 1553 removed to the Tower of London with the bishops Latimer and Ridley. In February 1556 he was degraded from his archbishopric and he recanted his allegiance to the Reformation. When he was asked to repeat his 'Recantations' publicly on 21 March 1556 he refused and affirmed his belief in Protestantism. He was then burned at the stake, extending his right hand to the flames as the instrument of his recantation.

Cuthbert, Saint (d.687)
Durham Cathedral, Durham, County Durham; his shrine lies behind the High Altar.

Bishop of Lindisfarne. He was probably Northumbrian by birth and is reputed to have taken monastic vows after a vision at the death of Bishop Aidan and to have entered Melrose Abbey about 651. Bede, to whom we owe our knowledge of Cuthbert's life, informs us that he became Prior of Melrose in 661 and was transferred to Lindisfarne in 664 where he was also Prior. In 671 he became an anchorite on the island of Farne and is said to have performed miracles. At the instigation of King Ecgfrith of Northumbria he gave up his solitary life and became Bishop of Hexham in 685, afterwards exchanging the

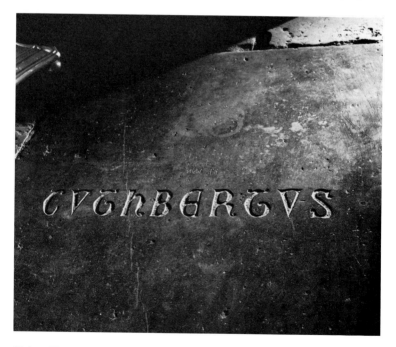

Shrine of St Cuthbert, Durham Cathedral, Durham

see for that of Lindisfarne. In 687 he retired to Farne, dying on the island on 20 March 687.

Darby, John Nelson (1800–1882)
Wimborne Road Cemetery, Bournemouth, Dorset; in the south-west section near the main path.

Founder of the Darbyites, a breakaway sect from the Plymouth Brethren. The sect rejected all forms of distinction in denominational religion, and Darby wrote voluminously and travelled widely in the furtherance of his cause. In 1838 he worked in Switzerland for two years opposing Methodism, but Jesuit intrigue put his life in jeopardy when revolution broke out in the canton of Vaud. In 1854 he made a great impact in Germany when he translated the New Testament into German, and his travels took him to the United States, Canada, New Zealand and the West Indies, as well as to Germany. Pilgrims from Germany regularly visit his grave.

De La Mare, Thomas (1309–1396)
St Alban's Cathedral, St Albans, Hertfordshire.

Abbot of St Albans and a member of Edward III's council. He resisted the attempts of Wat Tyler during the Peasants' Revolt of 1381 to 'shave the heads of the Abbot, Prior and monks' and to ransack St Albans.

Despenser, Henry le (c.1341–1406)
Norwich Cathedral, Norwich, Norfolk, before the high altar.

Became Bishop of Norwich in 1370 and was known as the 'warlike bishop' for his military prowess. He put down a rising of Norfolk peasantry during the Peasants' Revolt of 1381 with great severity. In 1382 he led the forces of Pope Urban VI on a crusade against the supporters of the anti-Pope, Clement VII, in Flanders, but his army was defeated by the French and decimated by disease. A strong supporter of Richard II, he stood by the King after his deposition and was imprisoned. Released, he made his peace with Henry IV. A fierce opponent of the Lollards, whose leader, John Wycliffe, had denounced the Bishop's Crusade in Flanders.

Dunstan, Saint (924–988)

Canterbury Cathedral, Canterbury, Kent; the diaper on the south wall above the altar steps is considered to be part of his shrine.

Archbishop of Canterbury. As a boy he entered the household of King Athelstan but was later banished. Recalled by King Edmund, he was made one of the King's counsellors. Again he was banished through the machinations of his enemies but shortly after Edmund revoked the order and made him Abbot of Glastonbury. Edmund's successor, Edred, showed him greater favour, but, at the succession of Edwy in 955, Dunstan's fortunes suffered a temporary eclipse, and he was compelled to flee to Flanders. In 957 Northumbria and Mercia chose Edgar, Edwy's younger brother, as king and he recalled Dunstan, making him Bishop of Worcester in 958 and Bishop of London in 959. That year King Edwy died and Edgar became sole king; Dunstan shared in his triumph, being made Archbishop of Canterbury. In 975 it was Dunstan's influence that secured the throne for Edgar's elder son, Edward, but with the accession of Ethelred II, the Unready, in 978, Dunstan's influence diminished and he returned to Canterbury, dying there on 19 May 988.

Etheldreda, Saint (c.630–679)

Ely Cathedral, Ely, Cambridgeshire.

Queen of Northumbria and Abbess of Ely. The third of four sainted daughters of King Anna of East Anglia. In 652 she married, reluctantly, Tonbert, Prince of Southern Gyrvii, approximately southern Cambridgeshire. Her jointure was the whole of the Isle of Ely. Tonbert died in 655 and, after five years spent in seclusion at her home on the Isle of Ely, she was married to Ecgfrith of Northumbria who, ten years later, became its king. She refused to carry out her conjugal duties and despite an appeal by the King to Saint Wilfrith, who told the King that his wife had chosen the better life, that of sanctity, the King could not persuade Etheldreda to fulfil her rôle either as Queen or wife. She was allowed to enter the monastery of Coldingham in Berwickshire, founded by her aunt, St Ebba, receiving the veil from Saint Wilfrith. When her husband tried to force her to accept public life she fled south to the Isle of Ely and there founded her own monastic house in 673. She died there in 679.

Ferrar, Nicholas (1592–1637)
St John's Church, Little Gidding, Cambridgeshire; tomb outside west door.

Theologian of high learning and influence who, after assisting as a member of parliament in the impeachment of the Earl of Middlesex, established an Anglican community at Little Gidding, Cambridgeshire. As a Fellow of Clare Hall, Cambridge, he had devoted himself to the affairs of the Virginia Company in 1619 and his community at Little Gidding later became a Royalist stronghold. A great friend of George Herbert, he was instrumental in publishing Herbert's poems.

Fisher, John, Saint (1469–1535)
St Peter ad Vincula, Tower of London, London, in the crypt of the Tower Chapel (with Sir Thomas More).

Martyr, Bishop of Rochester who refused to swear the oath to the 1534 Act of Succession, whereby Henry VIII's marriage to Catherine of Aragon was declared invalid and his secret marriage to the already pregnant Anne Boleyn valid. Committed to the Tower after appearing before Lambeth Palace commissioners, and attainted for treason, he was imprisoned in the Bell Tower near the cell of Sir Thomas More (whom see). Fourteen months later too weak to walk, he was carried in a chair to Tower Hill and executed, two weeks before More. Previously, after being educated at Cambridge and becoming Master of Michaelhouse, Fisher had been made chaplain to Henry II's mother Margaret, Countess of Richmond, in 1502 and two years later chancellor of the university. Living a life of piety, he zealously resisted Martin Luther's schismatic teachings. He was made a cardinal a month before his execution and was canonized in 1935.

Gilpin, Bernard (1517–1583)
St Michael and All Angels' Church, Houghton-le-Spring, County Durham, where he has an uncommonly large tomb chest whose sides are decorated by large panels with squares and circles.

Known as the 'Apostle of the North' for his attacks on the clerical vices of the times and for his high ideals. Towards the end of the reign of Mary I he was installed as Archdeacon at Durham and, despite attacks on him by those who felt his sermons on clerical vices were aimed at them, given the rich living of Houghton-le-Spring in refutation of his enemies' charges. Enraged at their defeat, his enemies

Nicholas Ferrar and George Herbert window in St Andrew's Church, Bemerton,
Wiltshire

appealed to Bonner and a royal warrant was made out for Gilpin's arrest. During his journey to London he broke his leg and, during the delay, Queen Mary died. He returned to Houghton where he worked unceasingly for the good of his parishioners: endowing a grammar school, remitting tithes at times of bad harvests, and feeding the poor. He died at Houghton on 4 March 1583.

Grosseteste, Robert (c.1175–1253)
Lincoln Cathedral, Lincoln, south-east transept.

Bishop of Lincoln who was reputedly one of the most learned men of his time. Of humble origin, he nonetheless was educated at Oxford and, possibly, briefly at Paris. Between 1214 and 1231 he held a succession of archdeaconries but in 1232 resigned all offices but that of Lincoln owing to illness. In 1235, however, he accepted the bishopric of Lincoln and without delay he undertook the reformation of morals and clerical discipline through his diocese, incurring the wrath of his own chapter. The dispute over his rights was eventually settled in 1245 in his favour by the Pope. He supported the independence of the Church and when in 1244 Henry III tried to separate the clergy from the baronage, Grosseteste wrote 'It is written that united we stand and divided we fall'. When it became clear that Henry and Pope Innocent IV were in alliance to crush the independence of the English clergy, the Bishop openly criticized the Pope, even attacking the Curia whom he held responsible for the evils of the Church. The question of English benefices for foreigners arose when Grosseteste was commanded to provide in his own diocese for a papal nephew. His letter of expostulation and refusal was couched in strong terms. He died on 9 October 1253.

Herbert, George (1593–1633)
St Andrew's Church, Bemerton, Wiltshire; in the chancel. There is a beautiful stained-glass window in the church's west wall, showing Herbert holding a lute and his friend Nicholas Ferrar holding one of Herbert's manuscripts.

Churchman and poet who became famous as a poet only after his death. He was the younger brother of Lord Herbert of Cherbury and early showed great classical promise in his studies at Cambridge. He also became an accomplished singer and player of the lute and viol. Upon being appointed public orator at Cambridge University, he frequently attended James I at court. Eventually, however, he had doubts about the 'painted pleasures of court life' and revived an earlier desire to go into the Church. Among his friends were John Donne, Francis Bacon, Izaak Walton and Nicholas Ferrar. Persuaded by William Laud, then Bishop of London, he took the parsonage of Fuggleston and Bemerton, which had been offered him by Charles I. He wrote a series of sacred – but certainly not dull and sombre – poems, which were published after his death by Ferrar. They became famous. *The Temple, Sacred Poems and Private Ejaculations*, containing 169 of his poems, was read by Charles I while he was in prison. Most of Herbert's unpublished writings were burnt by Cromwell's forces.

Higden, Ranulf (c.1299–1364)
Chester Cathedral, Chester, Cheshire.

Chronicler who was a Benedictine monk in the monastery of St Werburg in Chester, in which he lived, it is said, for 64 years. He was the author of a popular work of general history, styled the *Polychronicon*. The work is divided into seven books in imitation of the seven days of *Genesis*, and, with the exception of the last book, is a summary of general history, revealing the scientific, geographical and historical knowledge of the time. A translation from the Latin by John of Trevisa was printed by Caxton in 1482.

Hobbes, Thomas (1588–1679)
St John the Baptist Church, Ault Hucknall, Derbyshire.

Philosopher who favoured strong government and supported the supremacy of the state, the absolute power of the sovereign stemming from the will of the people. His most famous work, *Leviathan*, was published in 1651.

Hugh of Avalon, Saint (1135–1200)
Lincoln Cathedral, Lincolnshire, shrine in cathedral.

Bishop who was born in Burgundy of a noble family and invited to England by Henry II (c.1175) to head a Carthusian house at Witlow, Somerset. He became the king's adviser and greatly helped the poor and the lepers. He excommunicated King John in 1194 as Bishop of Lincoln, which he became in 1186 until his death. Later John sought his goodwill and Hugh pacified Richard I in a personal interview. He was canonized in 1220. He had rebuilt a major part of Lincoln cathedral, where his shrine was much visited and venerated although he had always regarded miracles with dislike.

Hugh of Lincoln, Saint (c.1246–1255)
Lincoln Cathedral, Lincoln, in the south choir aisle.

A native of Lincoln. He was about ten years old when he was found dead on premises belonging to a Jew. It was said, and then generally believed, that the boy had been scourged and crucified in imitation of the death of Jesus Christ. A disclaimer is now exhibited in Lincoln Cathedral. As a result a number of Jews were put to death. The incident is referred to by Chaucer in the *Prioress's Tale* and by Marlowe in the *Jew of Malta*.

Keble, John (1792–1866)
All Saints' Churchyard, Hursley, Hampshire; the large marble tombstone lies near the church, that of his wife being next to his.

Poet and Divine. Obtained a scholarship to Corpus Christi College, Oxford, being elected a scholar in his fifteenth year and a fellow in his nineteenth. Ordained a deacon in 1815 and a priest in 1816. In 1831 he was elected Professor of Poetry at Oxford, a position he held for ten years. On Sunday 14 July 1833 he preached his famous sermon, 'National Apostasy', of which Cardinal Newman wrote: 'I have ever considered and kept the day as the start of the religious movement of 1833'. It was the beginning of the Tractarian Movement which asserted the claim of the Church to a heavenly origin and a divine prerogative, and led to action by some leading spirits in Oxford and elsewhere to revive High Church principles and the ancient patristic theology, by these means both to defend the Church against the assaults of its enemies and also to raise to a higher tone the standard of Christian life in England. The movement derived its name from the famous *Tracts for the Times*, to which Keble contributed four: numbers 4, 13, 40 and 89. After the end of his tenure as Professor of Poetry Keble saw little of Oxford, but the defection of Newman to the Roman Catholic Church, which affected him deeply, brought Keble into the forefront of the Tractarian Movement and with Pusey he strove to maintain the High Anglican principles with which he had always been identified.

Knox, Ronald Arbuthnot (1888–1957)
St Andrew's Parish Church, Mells, Somerset, one of three low headstones in a row which includes Sassoon and Hollis (whom see).

A Roman Catholic monsignor and writer, he was the son of an Anglican bishop. His retranslation (the 'Knox Bible') of the Vulgate

Grave of John Keble, All Saints' Churchyard, Hursley, Hampshire

occupied a major part of his energies from 1939 to its appearance in 1945, but in his life he also wrote many essays and novels and engaged in theological controversy. In 1924 the *Daily Mail* called him 'the wittiest young man in England' and in 1926 he broadcast a spoof eye-witness account of an uprising of the unemployed, who were suppos-edly attacking Westminster and hanging cabinet ministers from lamp-posts and so on; a forerunner by twelve years of Orson Welles's radio 'scare' in New York about Martian landings. One of Knox's brothers, Edmund George Valpy (1881–1971), was editor of *Punch*, and another, Alfred Dillwyn (1883–1943), was a code-breaker who helped break the Zimmerman telegram and the Enigma codings in the first and second world wars respectively.

Lanfranc (c.1005–1089)
St Martin's Chapel, Canterbury Cathedral, Canterbury, Kent.

Archbishop of Canterbury. Born about 1005 at Pavia, where his father was a magistrate, he studied law and, after his father's death, crossed the Alps to found a school in France. Then he decided to move to Normandy where, in 1039, he became master of the cathedral school at Avranches. In 1042 he took monastic vows at Bec where he lived in absolute seclusion until 1045. He was then persuaded to open a school in the monastery and many prominent churchmen were pupils, including a man who later became Pope, Alexander II. While Prior of Bec he quarrelled with William I, then Duke of Normandy, over his marriage with Matilda of Flanders, but he and the Duke resolved their differences and Lanfranc successfully accomplished the difficult task of obtaining the Pope's approval for the marriage. In 1066 he became the first Abbot of St Stephen's, Caen, and thereafter he exercised a perceptible influence on William's politics. After the conquest of England he accepted the archbishopric of Canterbury after Stigand had been canonically deposed in 1070. In 1075 he detected and foiled a conspiracy against William by the earls of Hereford and Norfolk. In 1087 he secured the succession for William II (Rufus), and persuaded the English militia to resist the attempts by Robert of Normandy and Odo of Bayeux against Rufus. He died of fever on 24 May 1089.

Lang, (William) Cosmo Gordon, Baron Lang of Lambeth (1864–1945)
St Stephen's Chapel, Canterbury Cathedral, Canterbury, Kent.
  Archbishop of Canterbury from 1928 to 1942. Earlier he had been Archbishop of York, and during the Great War he travelled extensively to encourage the troops and the fleet. During the abdication crisis of 1936 his advice was sought by both the King, Edward VIII, and the Prime Minister, Stanley Baldwin. He died of a heart attack while running to catch a train.

Latimer, Hugh (c.1485–1555)
Burned at the stake 'at the ditch over against Balliol College', Oxford, and ashes scattered; a cross on the surface of Broad Street, opposite Balliol College, marks the spot where his burning took place.
  One of the chief promoters of the Reformation in England. Initially he was a punctilious observer of the minutest rites of the Roman Church, being described as 'as obstinate a Papist as any in England'. However, his sermons against the abuses of the Church earned him the wrath of his superiors but, following his two 'sermons on the cards', he was asked to preach before Henry VIII during Lent, 1530. The King was impressed and gave him the living of West Kineton in Wiltshire. Sentence of imprisonment and excommunication was passed on him by the Convocation for his 'heretical' views on his refusal to subscribe certain articles, but Henry VIII secured his

release. Disturbances in Bristol over his sermons brought a revocation from the Bishop of his right to preach but Cranmer, consecrated Archbishop of Canterbury in 1533, granted him a special licence. Following the formal break with Rome in 1534 Latimer, along with Cranmer and Cromwell, became one of Henry's chief advisers regarding the legislative powers necessary to implement the repudiation of Rome. In September 1535 he was made Bishop of Worcester but in 1539, being opposed to the 'act of six articles', he resigned. In 1546 he was arrested and sent to the Tower of London on account of his connection with the preacher Edward Crome. Henry died before he could be brought to trial and he was pardoned in the amnesty at the accession of Edward VI. He refused the offer to return to Worcester and began preaching. In May 1553, shortly after Mary I's accession, he was summoned to appear before the Council. He did so, and was removed to Oxford, where after a long and hard imprisonment he was burned with Ridley on 16 October 1555, having spoken the immortal words, 'Be of good comfort, Master Ridley, and play the man; we shall this day light such a candle by God's grace in England as shall never be put out.'

Laud, William (1573–1645)
Chapel of St John's College, Oxford.

Archbishop of Canterbury. Son of a Reading clothier, he won a scholarship to St John's College, Oxford, in 1589. In 1601 he took orders and became chaplain to Charles Blount, Earl of Devonshire. His High Church doctrines earned him the rebuke of the authorities in Oxford, but elsewhere they were welcomed and he made rapid advancement, becoming Bishop of St David's in 1621. He developed a close relationship with George Villiers, Duke of Buckingham, and, on the accession of Charles I, he provided a list of clergy, each name distinguished with an 'O' (Orthodox) or 'P' (Puritan) indicating that the orthodox should be advanced and the Puritans suppressed. By 1629 he was Bishop of London and Chancellor of Oxford University and, in August 1633, Archbishop of Canterbury. He tried to force his High Church methods on both England and Scotland and was instrumental in forcing the Scots to resort to arms to safeguard their national religion and national independence. A strong supporter of the arbitrary methods of Strafford and Charles I, he was himself impeached and imprisoned in the Tower of London. Convicted at his trial he was executed on Tower Hill on 10 January 1645.

William Laud, after Van Dyck

Leofric, (d.1072)
Exeter Cathedral, Exeter, Devon, in the crypt; the monument erected in 1568 is believed to stand on his burial place.

First Bishop of Exeter. A chaplain to Edward the Confessor, in 1046 he became Bishop of the united dioceses of Devonshire and Cornwall, the seat being at Crediton. He did much to reconstruct the diocese, repairing the ravages caused by plundering pirates. He sought the aid of Pope Leo IX to transfer the seat of the diocese to Exeter which occurred in 1050. He was confirmed in his see by William the Conqueror and died on 10 February 1072.

Malthus, Reverend Thomas Robert (1766–1834)
Abbey Church, Bath, Avon, in the porch.

Economist. In his pessimistic essay 'The Principle of Population' he contended that population tends to increase faster than the means of subsistence and that its growth could only be checked by moral restraint or by disease and war.

Marx, Karl (1818–1883)
Highgate 'new' Cemetery, Highgate, London.

Political and economic philosopher. Born in Trier in Germany of Jewish parents he studied law, philosophy and history at both Bonn and Berlin. Later he took up the study of economics. With his friend Engels he wrote the *Communist Manifesto* in 1848, for the Communist League of which he was the leader. He was forced to leave the Continent because of his political agitation in 1849 and settled in London. It was in London that he wrote *Das Kapital*, which is an analysis of the economic laws that govern society. In 1864 he helped to found the first International, and he is generally regarded as the founder of modern international communism.

Merton, Walter de (d.1277)
Rochester Cathedral, Rochester, Kent, in the north choir transept.

Bishop of Rochester and founder of Merton College, Oxford. Ordained as a sub-deacon sometime after June 1235, he became a clerk in the royal chancery. In 1261 he was appointed Chancellor and continued in that office until 12 July 1263, when the supremacy of the baronial party forced his resignation in favour of Nicholas of Ely. After Evesham in 1265 he returned to the chancery but was known as

Justiciar and on the death of Henry III in 1272 he was appointed Chancellor by the Council of Regency, holding office until the return to England of Edward I in August 1274. He was made Bishop of Rochester in July 1274 and died as a result of an accident while fording the River Medway on 27 October 1277.

More, Sir Thomas, Saint (1478–1535)
St Peter ad Vincula, Tower of London, London; his head was interred by his daughter Margaret Roper in St Dunstan's Church, Canterbury, Kent, in the Roper vault.

Writer and lawyer. In 1529 he succeeded Wolsey as Lord Chancellor but his refusal to swear the Oath of Supremacy, acknowledging the King, Henry VIII, as head of the Church in England brought about his dismissal, imprisonment, trial and execution for treason on 7 July 1535. As he mounted the scaffold he remarked to the lieutenant, 'I pray thee see me safely up, and for my coming down let me shift for myself.' His work, *Utopia*, describes an ideal state. He was canonized in 1935.

Morton, John (c.1420–1500)
Chapel of our Lady, Canterbury Cathedral, Canterbury, Kent, in the crypt.

Cardinal Archbishop of Canterbury. Graduated in law at Balliol College, Oxford, and practised ecclesiastical law in London where he attracted the attention of Archbishop Bourchier. A supporter of the Lancastrians, he was exiled after the Yorkist victory at Towton in 1461. He returned with Warwick the Kingmaker but after the complete failure of the Lancastrian cause following their defeat at Tewkesbury in 1471 he made his peace with Edward IV. He became Master of the Rolls in March 1473, and undertook several diplomatic missions. In 1479 he was made Bishop of Ely and later was an executor of the will of Edward IV. He was arrested by Richard III and imprisoned in the Tower of London but later released into the custody of the Duke of Buckingham. He urged Buckingham in his designs against Richard III, put him in touch with the Queen-Dowager, Elizabeth Woodville, and Henry Tudor, Earl of Richmond, but, after Buckingham's defeat by Richard, Morton fled to Flanders where he devoted himself to the cause of Henry Tudor. Following Henry's defeat of Richard III at Bosworth Field and his accession as Henry VII Morton became his principal adviser and, in 1486, succeeded

Sir Thomas More, after Holbein

Bourchier as Archbishop of Canterbury, a year later becoming also the Chancellor. In 1493 he was made a cardinal and in 1495 was Chancellor of the University of Oxford. He died at Knole on 12 October 1500.

Newton, John (1725–1807)
St Peter and St Paul's Church, Olney, Buckinghamshire.

Slave-trader and churchman. Son of a ship's master he was impressed on board a man-of-war, the *Harwich*, when he was about eighteen years old. He tried to escape but was caught and treated with great severity. He exchanged on to an African trader and spent many years in slave-trading ships. A growing dissatisfaction with his work and the breakdown in his health forced him to leave the sea and he became tide-surveyor at Liverpool. All his life he had striven to improve his education and whilst at Liverpool he studied Greek and Latin. He applied to the Archbishop of York for ordination, but he was refused. However, the curacy of Olney having been offered him, he was ordained by the Bishop of Lincoln. At Olney he became friendly with William Cowper and in 1779 the two men published *Olney Hymns*, of which Newton wrote 'Amazing Grace', 'How Sweet the name of Jesus sounds', and 'Glorious things of Thee are spoken'. In 1779 he went to the parish of St Mary Woolnoth in the City of London where his sermons aganst slavery inspired William Wilberforce to get slavery abolished. John Newton is commemorated in a tablet in St Mary Woolnoth near the pulpit which is inscribed: 'once an infidel and libertine', he was 'appointed to preach the faith he had long laboured to destroy'.

Osmund, Saint (d.1099)
Salisbury Cathedral, Salisbury, Wiltshire; the slab in the nave aisle is said to mark the exact spot where his remains were re-buried.

Bishop of Salisbury. Reputedly the son of Henry, Count of Séez, and Isabella, William the Conqueror's sister, he accompanied William to England as a chaplain and was made Chancellor, probably in 1072, a position he is presumed to have held until his consecration as Bishop of Salisbury by Lanfranc in 1078. He helped in the preparation of the Domesday Book. In 1095 he supported the new King, William II, against Anselm, but in May 1096 he sought and obtained absolution from the Archbishop. He died on 3 December 1099.

Poore, Richard (d.1237)

St Mary's Church, Tarrant Crawford, Dorset (his body): his heart is said to have been buried in Salisbury Cathedral at the west end of the north aisle of the nave next to William Longsword's supposed tomb. In the same aisle as Poore's heart are the tombs of Sir John de Montecute (d.1390), who fought at Crécy; Walter, Lord Hungerford (d.1449), an Agincourt hero; and Sir John Cheyney (d.1509), a giant who was bodyguard to Henry VII and fought at Bosworth.

As Bishop of Salisbury he was responsible for moving the see from Old Sarum to Salisbury, where the new cathedral was built. When he moved from Chichester to Salisbury there was general joy in Salisbury because he was much loved, and he lost no time in pressing forward with the plan for the new cathedral, which had been long contemplated. Sending special envoys to Rome, he got permission, in 1219, to choose a site, named Maryfield, and at once a wooden chapel and cemetery were provided. By Poore's efforts, including his own contributions of a manor and money (he had been an executor of King John), Henry III and many nobles supported the cathedral. On 28 April 1220 the cathedral's foundations were laid. The work went on steadily for five years, and in 1225 he consecrated a temporary high altar in the Lady Chapel. At the consecration of the entire site the next day there was an enormous audience. The first person to be buried there was William Longsword, Earl of Salisbury, in March 1226, and in June the remains of Osmund, bishop of Salisbury from 1078 to 1099, were removed to the new cathedral from the old one at Old Sarum, Poore pressing for Osmund to be made a saint. In 1220 Poore had obtained a royal charter for 'New Sarum' and laid out the town in rectangular areas, known as 'squares' or 'chequers'. In 1228 he was made Bishop of Durham, and in 1230 he refounded the Cistercian Abbey for nuns at Tarrant Crawford, which he handed over to Queen Joan of Scotland. He died and was buried there.

Ricardo, David (1772–1823)

St Nicholas's Church, Hardenhuish, Wiltshire, large and intriguing monument near south-east corner of church exterior.

Economist and founder of the Geological Society (1807), he made his fortune by the time he was 25, having been a member of the Stock Exchange only five years. He then turned to scientific interests, setting up a minerological laboratory. He wrote *Principles of Political Economy and Taxation* (1817), becoming an MP for Portarlington from 1819 to

David Ricardo's grave, Hardenhuish, Wiltshire

the year of his death. The classical school of political economy reflects his thinking as a principal founder. He derided Robert Owen's socialist theories, but contributed to nearly every London charity.

Ridley, Nicholas (c.1500–1555)
Burned at the stake 'at the ditch over against Balliol College', Oxford, and ashes scattered; a cross on the surface of Broad Street, opposite Balliol College, marks the spot where his burning took place.

Bishop of London. Educated at Pembroke College, Cambridge, and the Sorbonne, Paris, he became Chaplain to the University of Cambridge. In 1538 he was appointed Chaplain to Thomas Cranmer, Archbishop of Canterbury, and in 1541 Chaplain to Henry VIII and Canon of Canterbury. In 1543 he was accused of heresy but managed to allay the suspicions of the Commissioners. After Edward VI came to the throne he was one of the visitors appointed to establish Protestantism in the University of Cambridge and was made Bishop of Rochester. In 1548 he helped to compile the English Prayer Book and in the following year was created Bishop of London. A supporter of Lady Jane Grey, he declared the Princesses Mary and Elizabeth illegitimate. Arrested at Framlingham seeking the pardon of Queen Mary, after the failure of Lady Jane Grey's cause, he was sent to the Tower of London. Early in 1554 together with Cranmer and Latimer he was sent to Oxford to be examined where, on 16 October 1555, he and Latimer were burned at the stake.

Rotherham, Thomas, sometimes known as Thomas Scott
(1423–1500)
St Nicholas's Chapel, York Minster, York, in the north transept.

Archbishop of York. It is probable that while Chaplain to the Earl of Oxford he met Elizabeth Woodville, later Edward IV's Queen. Through her he was appointed Keeper of the Privy Seal in 1467, in 1468 Bishop of Worcester, in 1472 Bishop of Lincoln, and in 1475 Chancellor of England. He negotiated the peace between Edward IV and Louis XI of France and in 1480 became the Archbishop of York. He lost the Chancellorship after the death of Edward IV because of his support for Elizabeth Woodville, and was imprisoned. Released, he died at Cawood, near York, in 1500.

Sacheverell, Henry (c.1674–1724)

St Andrew's, Holborn, London, under the High Altar. An oval tablet of cherry wood by John Skelton, inscribed with fine white lettering, commemorates him.

Clergyman and politician. His two famous sermons against the Whig ministry, in which he urged the Church to safeguard its interests, were preached in Derby on 15 August 1709, and in St Paul's Cathedral on 5 November 1709. The Whig authorities committed him for trial, which lasted from 27 February to 23 March 1710, and he was suspended for three years and his two sermons ordered to be burned at the Royal Exchange. At the expiration of his sentence, the new Tory ministry, despite their dislike of Henry Sacheverell and their fear of his influence over the mob, appointed him to the rich living of St Andrew's, Holborn. He died at Highgate on 5 June 1724.

Scrope, Richard le (c.1350–1405)

The Lady Chapel, York Minster, York.

Archbishop of York. He was the fourth son of Henry Scrope, first Baron Scrope of Masham, and after graduating in arts at Oxford and law at Cambridge was ordained priest in March 1377. He is said to have held a canonry at York and in 1378 was made Chancellor of the University of Cambridge. By a Bull, dated 18 August 1386, Pope Urban VI appointed him Bishop of Coventry and Lichfield and in August 1387 he was installed in the presence of Richard II. He undertook missions for King Richard to Scotland and to Rome and, on 2 June 1398, against the wishes of the Chapter but at the King's request, Scrope was appointed by a Bull of the Pope to be Archbishop of York. He acquiesced in the revolution of 1399, being present when Richard II abdicated in favour of Henry IV. With the Archbishop of Canterbury he joined in the enthroning of the new King, Henry IV. He criticized Henry's government for 'its spoliation of the church proposed by the "unlearned parliament"'. He took up arms at York with Percy of Northumberland and Thomas Mowbray the Earl Marshal. At Shipton Moor in May 1405, despite his own superior forces, he agreed to treat with the Earl of Westmorland who had guaranteed favourable terms, a promise that was immediately broken. Removed to Pontefract, he was tried and executed at York where he begged the headsman to deal five blows at his neck in memory of the five sacred wounds.

Selden, John (1584–1654)
Temple Church, Temple, Fleet Street, London, beneath a glass panel in the floor near the entrance.

Jurist and scholar. Studied at Oxford and the Middle Temple and was called to the Bar in 1612. Believed to be the instigator and perhaps the draftsman of the memorable protestation on the rights and privileges of the House of Commons, of which he was not a Member, and which was affirmed by the Commons on 18 December 1621. He, together with several of the Members of the House of Commons, was imprisoned first in the Tower of London and subsequently placed in the charge of the Sheriff of London, Sir Robert Ducie. In 1623 he entered Parliament as Member for Lancaster and allied himself with Pym. In the second Parliament of Charles I in 1626 he played a prominent part in the impeachment of George Villiers, first Duke of Buckingham. Thereafter he played an influential rôle in formulating Parliamentary policies in its quarrel with the King. As a scholar and writer he was pre-eminent among his contemporaries.

Spooner, Dr William Archibald (1844–1930)
Town Cemetery (near the entrance), Pye Lane, Grasmere, Cumbria.

Historian and philosopher, he rose from a New College, Oxford, scholarship in 1862 to become Warden of the college in 1903. He was author of *The History of Tacitus* (1891), *William of Wykeham* (1909) and other historical works. His endearing lapses of speech led to them being called 'Spoonerisms'. Attributed to him are such examples as: 'You have hissed my mystery lectures . . . take the next town drain' and others that are no doubt apocryphal.

Sudbury, Simon of (d.1381)
St Gregory's Church, Sudbury, Suffolk, in the vestry.

Archbishop of Canterbury. He studied at Paris and became Chaplain to Pope Innocent VI who sent him on a mission to Edward III in 1356. In October 1361 the Pope appointed him Bishop of London and he served Edward III on several diplomatic missions. In 1375 he succeeded William Wittlesey as Archbishop of Canterbury, and, for the remainder of his life, was a partisan of John of Gaunt, Duke of Lancaster. In 1377 he crowned Richard II. In 1378, very reluctantly, he agreed to proceed against John Wycliffe, the leader of the Lollards. In 1380 he became Chancellor and, during the Peasants' Revolt of

Shrine of St Swithun, Winchester Cathedral, Hampshire

1381, he was one of their principal targets. The mob rushed the Tower of London, and, finding the Archbishop therein, captured and executed him on Tower Hill on 14 June 1381.

Swithun, Saint (d.862)
Winchester Cathedral, Winchester, Hampshire, where his golden shrine is near the Lady Chapel.

Bishop of Winchester and patron saint of Winchester Cathedral from the tenth to the sixteenth century, having been adopted by Dunstan and Ethelwold of Winchester when inaugurating their church reform. The body of St Swithun was transferred from his almost forgotten grave to the new basilica inside the restored church on 15 July 971. There many miracles are reputed to have occurred both before and after the translation of the body.

Temple, Frederick (1821–1902)
Canterbury Cathedral, Canterbury, Kent, in the cloister garth.

Archbishop of Canterbury. Whilst at Oxford he leaned towards 'the

Oxford Liberal Movement' and in 1846 entered the Church. In 1858 he became Headmaster of Rugby and, as a supporter of William Gladstone, was in 1869 offered the bishopric of Exeter. In 1885 he was translated to London and in 1896, although going blind, he became Archbishop of Canterbury. His radical views and his unfailing work amongst the poor made him a controversial figure.

Tenison, Thomas (1636–1715)
St Mary's Church, Lambeth, London.

Archbishop of Canterbury. He was educated at Cambridge, and after ordination became Vicar of St Andrew-the-Great, Cambridge. In 1680 Charles II gave him the important cure of St Martin-in-the-Fields. He opposed the religious policies of James II. The general liberality of his views brought him rapid advancement under William III and Mary II and in 1694 he was made Archbishop of Canterbury. A commissioner for the Union with Scotland in 1707, he supported the Hanoverian succession and was given power, with two others, to appoint a Regent until George I should arrive in England. He is also remembered for having preached the sermon at the funeral of Nell Gwyn in 1687.

Walter, Hubert (d.1205)
Canterbury Cathedral, Canterbury, Kent; his tomb, the oldest in the Cathedral, lies in the aisle just south of the entrance to Henry IV's Chantry.

Archbishop of Canterbury. He rose rapidly through the influence of his uncle, Ranulf de Glanville, Justiciar to Henry II. In 1186 he became Dean of York, and in October 1189 Bishop of Salisbury. He accompanied Richard I on the Third Crusade, organizing supplies and negotiating with Saladin. After Richard left the Holy Land in October 1192 he directed the return of the English army, returning to England himself in April 1193 where, on Richard's recommendation, he was elected Archbishop of Canterbury. In December of that same year he was made Justiciar. He organized the collection of Richard's ransom and suppressed the rebellion of Prince John. After the King's brief return to England in March 1194 Hubert Walter became the effective governor of the kingdom during Richard's absence. In March 1195 Pope Celestine III appointed him Papal Legate to England. He was instrumental in securing the throne for King John and was made Chancellor by the new King on 27 May 1199.

Isaac Watts, by an unknown artist

Watts, Isaac (1674–1748)
Bunhill Fields Burial Ground, City Road, Finsbury, London.

Nonconformist minister who is regarded as the father of English hymnody. His collection of hymns includes, 'O God, Our Help in Ages Past'; 'When I Survey the Wondrous Cross'; and 'Jesus Shall Reign'.

Wesley, John (1703–1791)

John Wesley Chapel, City Road, Finsbury, London.

Clergyman who became the founder of Methodism. Son of a former Nonconformist minister, he was educated at Oxford, where, on 9 September 1725, he was made deacon by the Bishop of Oxford. He joined with his brother Charles to form the Holy Club which carried out social and educational work among prisoners and the poor of Oxford. In 1736 he went to America as spiritual adviser to the new colony of Georgia, with a brief to convert the Red Indians. He did not. However, he did describe his experiences in Georgia as the 'second rise of Methodism', the first being the Holy Club. On 24 May 1738, having been strongly influenced by the Moravian, Peter Böhler, during a reading of Luther's *Preface to the Epistle to the Romans*, Wesley underwent a profound awakening. Thereafter he saw his aim as recalling the Church of England to its spiritual mission. In 1784, after trying to work within the jurisdiction of the Church of England, he declared that his societies and their work operated independently of the main Church, although to the end of his life Charles Wesley regarded himself as a loyal priest of the Church of England.

White, John (1575–1648)

Holy Trinity Church, St Peter's Chapel and All Saints Church, Dorchester, Dorset; in the porch.

Credited with being the founder of Massachusetts, White never actually went there himself. He was known as the Patriarch of Dorchester, being rector of Holy Trinity Church from 1606 until almost the end of his life. In 1624 he sent a colony of Dorset men to Massachusetts, and four years later he instigated the formation of the Massachusetts Company. Its capital cost was £1800 and Sir Richard Saltonstall was a chief shareholder, while John Endicott was sent out as the first governor of the colony. The first ministers, Francis Higginson and Samuel Skelton, sailed there on 4 May 1629 in the *George Bonaventura*, while John Winthrop, who became patriarch of the famous Winthrop family in America, landed at Salem in the *Arbella* in 1630 from Plymouth.

Wolsey, Thomas (c.1475–1530)

The Lady Chapel, Leicester Abbey, Leicester.

Cardinal and statesman. Son of an Ipswich grazier, he was educated at Magdalen College, Oxford. Ordained in 1498, he became a chaplain to Henry VII. By 1509 his obvious abilities had won him a place on the Royal Council. He attracted the notice of the young King, Henry VIII, and Wolsey's influence soon outstripped that of William Warham, Archbishop of Canterbury, whom he replaced, on 22 December 1515, as Lord Chancellor. His almost impregnable power, which lasted for fourteen years, suddenly disappeared in 1529 when he was stripped of office, the reason being his failure to secure for Henry VIII his divorce from Catherine of Aragon. The King did not proceed against Wolsey until his intention to have himself enthroned as Archbishop of York on 7 November 1530 alarmed Henry, who had him arrested. On his way to London he died at Leicester Abbey on 29 November 1530.

Wycliffe, John (c.1320–1384)
St Mary's Church, Lutterworth, Leicestershire; his body was later exhumed and his ashes scattered on the River Swift.

Ecclesiastical reformer and theologian. He inspired the Lollards and the Czech, John Huss; thus he was a major figure behind the Protestant Reformation. A protégé of John of Gaunt, Duke of Lancaster, who managed to protect Wycliffe against many of the charges brought against him for his heretical views, despite the Duke's own hostility to a number of those views. The clergy, Wycliffe argued, should be stripped of worldly offices and all surplus wealth. His Eucharistic teachings approximated closely to the later Lutheran doctrine of consubstantiation, although it is said that his views approached 'receptionism': the view that the nature of the consecrated elements depended on the spiritual state of the communicant. He died of a stroke, while saying Mass in his church at Lutterworth on 28 December 1384. In 1415 at the Council of Constance his teachings were condemned.

Wykeham, William of (1324–1404)
Chantry Chapel, Winchester Cathedral, Winchester, Hampshire. The three monkish figures at the feet of his effigy on the tomb are said to represent his master mason, master carpenter and clerk of the works.

Bishop of Winchester from 1367–1404, and twice Chancellor of England, from 1367–1372 under Edward III, and from 1389–1391 under Richard II. He was the founder of Winchester College and of New College, Oxford. He was dismissed from the Chancellorship in 1372 as a result of an anti-clerical movement among the barons. He

Tomb of William of Wykeham, Winchester Cathedral, Hampshire

had always opposed the designs of John of Gaunt, Duke of Lancaster, and as a result was tried for the conduct of affairs during his first term as Chancellor. He was convicted in November 1376 and sentenced to forfeit the temporalities of his see. But the following year saw the jubilee of Edward III and although he was exempted from the general pardon his property was returned. He was present at the coronation of Richard II in June 1377 and in July of that year Richard gave him a full pardon, restoring him to the chancellorship on 3 May 1389, a position he held for two and a half years.

[5] Scientists, Doctors, Businessmen, Engineers and Industrialists

Abel, Sir Frederick Augustus (1827–1902)
Nunhead Cemetery, Ivydale Road, London.

English military chemist who, in 1845, was one of the twenty-six original students of the Royal College of Chemistry. In March 1852 he succeeded Faraday as lecturer in chemistry at the Royal Military Academy at Woolwich and on 24 July 1854 became Ordnance Chemist, two years later being made chemist to the War Department. He developed a process for reducing gun cotton to a pulp, thus enabling it to be worked and stored in safety. Together with Sir Andrew Noble he developed new and important theories of explosives. In 1868 he developed the open-test for determining the flash point of petroleum, which, in 1879 was superseded by the Abel close-test with a flash point at 73°. Ten years later he and Sir James Dewar invented cordite. Sir Frederick Abel was also an accomplished musician.

Addison, Thomas (1793–1860)
Lanercost Priory, Lanercost, Cumbria.

Eminent physician whose contributions to the science of medicine were numerous and important. His researches into pneumonia revealed truths, novel at the time, but now generally accepted; he influenced the progress of knowledge of pulmonary phthisis; and, in 1853, produced his best-known work, his 'Essay of Disease of the Supre-renal Capsules', in which he announced that these organs, not previously known to be the seat of any definite disease, were in certain cases affected in such a way as to produce a fatal malady. It is commonly known as 'Addison's disease'. Its discovery was one of the most brilliant medical achievements of the nineteenth century.

Airy, Sir George Biddell (1801–1892)
St Mary's Churchyard, Playford, near Ipswich, Suffolk. There is a frontal bust of Sir George in an oval medallion.

Astronomer Royal who, for forty-six years, as Lucasian Professor of Mathematics at Cambridge, first drew attention to the visual defect known as astigmatism, from which he himself suffered. In 1838 he created a magnetic and metereological department at Greenwich Observatory. From 1826 to 1854 he conducted researches which led him to determine the mean density of the earth. He was consulted on a number of projects '. . . the launching of the *Great Eastern* steamship, Babbage's calculating machine, the layer of the transatlantic cable, the chimes of Westminster clock, and the smoky chimneys of Westminster Palace.'

Arkwright, Sir Richard (1732–1792)
St Mary's Church, Cromford, Derbyshire.
   Originally a Preston barber, he began experiments with cotton-spinning machines, and, in 1796, patented his water frame, so called because it was driven by water. His neighbours referred to it as the 'Devil's bagpipes' – a reference to the large number of pipes used in the experiments. Later, he adapted it for steam. Together with his partner, Jebediah Strutt, he established large cotton mills that began the movement known as the Industrial Revolution.

Babbage, Charles (1792–1871)
Kensal Green Cemetery, Kensal Green, London.
   Mathematician and engineer whose inventions and work on mechanical calculating machines laid the foundations for modern computers. He was instrumental in founding the Astronomical (1820) and Statistical (1834) Societies.

Baker, Sir Benjamin (1840–1907)
St Mary's Church, Idbury, Oxfordshire. Large memorial stone in the graveyard at the back of the church.
   Civil engineer who built the Forth Bridge, completed in seven years in 1890, for which he was awarded the KCMG and Prix Poncelet of the Institute of France. Born near Frome, Somerset he served his apprenticeship at Neath Abbey ironworks before coming to London where his major works as a consultant were the building of Victoria Station, the Underground railways such as the Inner Circle Line, and the first 'tubes', including the Baker Street–Waterloo line. In 1902 he was awarded the KCB for his building of the Aswan dams (low and high) in Egypt. For devising the float to convey Cleopatra's Needle to England (1877) he was awarded the coveted Telford Medal of the

Institute of Civil Engineers. At his death he was a Fellow of the Royal Society and one of the most respected engineers in the world.

Baring, Sir Francis (1740–1810)
St Mary's Church, Micheldever, Hampshire; in the family vault.

Founder of the financial house of Baring Brothers and Company. He could be regarded as a British Rothschild, Rockefeller or Morgan, in the sense that all four gigantic financial houses were formed round about the same time. Sir Francis was the son of a clothmaker, who had settled near Exeter and who sent the young Baring to study commerce in London. Although he was deaf as a youth, his tremendous energy and ability overcame all obstacles and, after starting an import-export agency with his brother, he went on to found the merchant bank that helped Britain's financial needs during the Napoleonic wars. He became a friend of William Pitt the Younger and, as a director of the East India Company, Sir Francis was often asked for financial advice by the government. By the time of his death he is said to have earned £7 million. He was knighted in 1793, and his descendants included Evelyn Baring, first Earl of Cromer (1841–1917), 'maker of modern Egypt' (whom see). Sir Francis also wrote several works, largely to justify his belief that the issue of Bank of England notes should be limited.

Baskerville, John (1706–1775)
Originally buried in the brick windmill he had built as a papermill alongside his house, site of the present Baskerville House in Birmingham. It was destroyed in the Riots of 1791 and later the coffin was on public display in a shop. It was secretly placed in one of the catacombs under Christ Church (Victoria Square) but, when that was closed in 1899, the coffin was moved to the vaults under the chapel in the Birmingham Church of England Cemetery, Warstone Lane. That chapel was demolished about 1955 but the vault remains. There is no visible monument.

Printer and typeface designer who about 1726 became a writing master at Birmingham where he showed an exceptional talent for calligraphy and for cutting inscriptions in stone. Whilst at Birmingham he made some important improvements in the process of japanning, and gained a considerable fortune. Around 1750 he began to make experiments in type-founding, producing types superior to any hitherto. He set up a printing house and in 1757 published his first book, a Virgil in a royal quarto, followed in 1758 by his famous edition of Milton. That same year he was appointed printer to the University of Cambridge. Baskerville's typefaces are still much used.

Bessemer, Sir Henry (1813–1898)
Norwood Cemetery, Norwood, London.
 Inventor of the process for converting cast-iron directly into steel, thus revolutionizing steel manufacture and extending its use.

Boyle, The Hon Robert (1627–1691)
St Martin-in-the-Fields, St Martin's Place, London.
 Seventh son of the Earl of Cork. A member of the 'Invisible College', a group which devoted itself to the cultivation of the 'new philosophy' and which, in 1663, became the Royal Society, of which Boyle was a member of the council. His important work in physics – the discovery of the part taken by air in the propagation of sound, and investigations into the expansive force of freezing water – and in chemistry, which was his favourite study – he advanced towards the modern view of elements as the undecomposable constituents of material bodies – laid the foundations of the modern sciences of physics and chemistry.

Brunel, Isambard Kingdom (1806–1859)
Kensal Green Cemetery, Kensal Green, London.
 Civil engineer, who was the engineer of the Great Western Railway, and who built several ocean steamships: the *Great Western*, the *Great Britain* and the *Great Eastern*. He also built the Clifton Suspension Bridge over the River Avon, and the Royal Albert Bridge over the River Tamar.

Brunel, Sir Marc Isambard (1769–1849)
Kensal Green Cemetery, Kensal Green, London.
 Fled to New York from his native Normandy in September 1793, during the French Revolution, where he began to practise as a civil engineer and architect. He constructed the Bowery Theatre, but his highly ornamental designs for the National Capitol in Washington were not accepted. In 1799 he came to England to submit to the Government his plans for the mechanical production of ships' blocks in substitution for the manual process then employed; and these were eventually accepted. He designed swing bridges, and a floating landing

stage at Liverpool in 1826; but he became famous for the use of his 'shield' in the construction of the Rotherhithe Tunnel which was finally completed and opened in 1843. He was knighted in 1841.

Cadbury, George (1893–1922)
In Friends Meeting House, Bourneville, Birmingham; ashes in urn.

Cocoa and chocolate manufacturer and philanthropist, son of a Quaker grocer, Cadbury worked for a time in Joseph Rowntree's grocery store. They both became world-wide competitors as chocolate manufacturers. Cadbury founded the town of Bourneville as a village trust in 1900 to ensure the new factory location he had selected would not become surrounded by slums as workers were attracted to the area. For a time he taught in the Adult School movement and, later, acquired several Birmingham newspapers to ensure that his liberal views were represented.

Caslon, William, 'The Elder' (1692–1766)
St Luke's, Old Street, Islington, London.

Born at Cradley in Worcestershire, he came to London and in 1716 started business as an engraver of gun locks and barrels, as well as a bookbinder's tool-cutter. He was induced, through his association with printers, to fit up a type foundry, and the distinction and legibility of his type secured him the patronage of the leading printers of the time in England and on the Continent. The use of Caslon type was discontinued at the beginning of the nineteenth century but revived about 1845 at the suggestion of Sir Henry Cole. Caslon's business was continued by his son William (1720–1798)

Cassell, John (1817–1865)
Kensal Green Cemetery, Kensal Green, London.

Publisher. The son of a Manchester publican, he was apprenticed to a joiner. Self-educated, he moved to London in 1836 where he became involved in the Temperance Movement. In 1847 he established himself as a tea and coffee merchant and soon afterwards started a publishing business with the aim of supplying good literature to the working classes. The firm, which in 1859 became Messrs Cassell, Petter, Galpin & Co., issued the *Popular Educator* (1852–1855), the *Technical Educator* (1870–1872), the *Magazine of Art* (1878–1903) and *Cassell's Magazine* (from 1852). A special feature of their popular books was the illustrations and, at the time of the

Crimean War, he procured from Paris the cuts used by *L'Illustration*, and by printing them in his *Family Paper* (begun in 1853) secured a large circulation for it. The firm became Cassell & Co. in 1883.

Cavendish, Henry (1731–1810)
Cathedral of All Saints, Derby.

Chemist and physicist who was the first scientist to recognize inflammable air, later called hydrogen. He conducted investigations which determined the specific gravity of hydrogen and carbon dioxide with reference to common air, showed the extent to which gases are absorbed by various liquids, and noted that 'common air containing one part in nine by volume of fixed air is no longer able to support combustion, and that air produced by fermentation and putrefaction has properties identical with those of fixed air obtained from marble.' He also carried out successful experiments into the chemical composition of water.

Caxton, William (c.1422–1491)
St Margaret's, Westminster, London.

Born in Kent, he was apprenticed to Robert Large, a rich silk mercer, who probably sent Caxton direct to Bruges, then the central market for the Anglo-Flemish trade. In 1463 Caxton was acting governor of the company, Merchant Adventurers, in the Low Countries, sometimes known as the 'English Nation', which was dominated by the Mercer's Company, and he undertook diplomatic missions to the Burgundian court. In about 1469 he entered the household of Margaret Duchess of Burgundy, sister to Edward IV, possibly in the rôle of commercial adviser, where he must have met her brother, the English King, during his brief exile at the Burgundian court in 1470. During Caxton's thirty-three years of residence in Bruges he would have had access to the rich libraries of the Duke of Burgundy and other Flemish nobles, and during the same time he learned the art of printing, possibly at Cologne, according to his disciple de Worde. He printed his first book, the *Recuyell*, in 1474 or 1475. In September 1476 he set up his press in the Almonry at Westminster at the sign of the Red Pale, from which many of his texts came.

Chippendale, Thomas (d.1779)
St Martin-in-the-Fields, St Martin's Place, London.

Son of a Worcester cabinet-maker, he moved to London in the reign of George I. In 1752 he describes himself as a 'cabinet-maker and upholsterer of St Martin's Lane'. His influence was so great that almost all mahogany furniture in the eighteenth century is erroneously referred to as 'Chippendale'. In 1754 he published the first edition of *The Gentleman and Cabinet Maker's Director*. Sheraton, writing of Chippendale and his work in 1793, said, 'As for the designs themselves, they are now wholly antiquated and laid aside, though possessed of great merit according to the times in which they were executed'.

Darby, Abraham (1677–1717)
All Saints' Church, Broseley, Shropshire.

Quaker ironmaster of Coalbrookdale, Shropshire, who paved the way for the Industrial Revolution by developing iron metallurgy with his employee, John Thomas. His grandson, Abraham (1750–1791), built the first cast-iron bridge, over the Severn at Coalbrookdale, in 1779.

Darwin, Charles Robert (1809–1892)
Westminster Abbey, London, in the north choir aisle of the Nave.

Naturalist who was one of the pioneers of experimental biology. His five years voyaging the world on the *Beagle*, 1831–1836, provided him with the material from which over the next twenty years he developed his controversial theory of evolution, which he published in *The Origin of Species* in 1859, arguing that the evolution of present-day morphology had been built up by the gradual and opportunistic mechanism of natural selection.

Dee, John (1527–1608)
St Mary's Church, Mortlake, Surrey.

Astrologer and mathematician. He was educated at St John's College, Cambridge, and was later elected a Fellow of Trinity College. In 1548 he was forced to leave England because of suspicions that he was a conjurer but returned in 1551 when he was awarded a pension by Edward VI. During the reign of Queen Mary I he was accused of issuing enchantments against the Queen's life and briefly imprisoned. He was released in 1555 by an order in council. When Elizabeth ascended the throne he was asked to name a propitious day for her coronation and he was introduced to the new Queen, who then took lessons from him in the mythical interpretations of his writings. Whilst he remained her favourite astrologer, she did not often carry out her promises to him, although in May 1595 he was made the Warden of Manchester College. He died in poverty and seclusion and is described by Aubrey as 'of a very fair, clear sanguine complexion, with a long beard as white as milk – a very handsome man – tall and slender. He wore a goune like an artist's goune with hanging sleeves.'

Faraday, Michael (1791–1867)
Highgate 'old' Cemetery, Highgate, London.
    Son of a Yorkshire blacksmith who had moved to Surrey, the young Michael Faraday was apprenticed to a bookbinder. He came to the attention of Sir Humphrey Davy who, in 1813, had him appointed as an assistant to the Royal Institution of Great Britain, becoming its director twelve years later, and then, in 1833, Fullerian Professor of Chemistry for life without the obligation to deliver lectures. He founded the science of electromagnetism which led to the modern developments in physics and electronics. Gladstone is reputed to have asked Faraday of what use electricity would be, to which Faraday replied, 'One day you will be able to tax it, sir.'

Ferranti, Sebastian Ziani de (1864–1930)
Hampstead Cemetery, Fortune Green Road, London.
    Electrical engineer who was born in Liverpool of an Italian father and English mother. His first job was with Siemens Brothers, where in 1881 he assisted Sir William Siemens in his experiments with an electric furnace for making steel. At the same time he attended evening classes at University College, London. He made the first Ferranti dynamo with a cordless disc in 1882, patenting it as the Ferranti alternator; it had an electrical output far greater than its rivals. In 1887 he became chief electrician to the newly formed London Electric Supply Corporation, resigning in 1892 to devote his time to private business, founding Ferranti Ltd at Hollinwood in Lancashire. A pioneer in high-voltage systems, he may be considered the originator of long-distance transmission of high-tension electric current.

Flamsteed, John (1646–1719)
St Bartholomew's Church, Burstow, Surrey, in the chancel.

Son of a Derby maltster, he left the free school of Derby because of ill health. He interested himself in astronomy and read all he could buy or borrow on the subject. He observed a partial solar eclipse on 12 September 1662 and attempted the construction of measurement instruments. Became acquainted with Isaac Newton at Cambridge in about 1670, entered the university and took the degree of MA four years later by letters patent. He was appointed 'astronomical observator' by Charles II on 4 March 1675 at a salary of £100 per annum, during which year he was also ordained. In 1684 Lord North presented him with the living of Burstow in Surrey. During the latter part of his life Flamsteed was in disagreement with Newton over the results of their observations, Flamsteed not wishing to publish his results until they could be presented in complete form. But, being a public servant, he had to make known the progress of his observations and was forced to submit. The result, *Historica coelestis*, was nonetheless denounced by him as surreptitious, and he set about producing his own monumental work, the *Historica coelestis Britannica*, which was only partially published at his death.

Fleming, Sir Alexander (1881–1955)
St Paul's Cathedral, London, in the crypt.

Bacteriologist who in 1922 discovered the antibacterial enzyme, lysozyme, and in 1928, penicillin. In 1945 he shared the Nobel Prize for Medicine with Florey and Chain.

Foyle, William Alfred Westropp (1885–1963)
Highgate 'new' Cemetery, Highgate, London.

Founder of Foyle's, the famous London bookshop in the Charing Cross Road.

Freud, Sigmund (1856–1939)
Golders Green Crematorium, Hoop Lane, London NW11. Ashes in urn in East Columbarium; receptionist desk will provide key to allow viewing.

Physician, psychopathologist, founder of psychoanalysis, Freud was born at Freiberg, Moravia. After graduating in medicine he specialized in neurology. His interest in the Viennese Dr Breuer's work, whereby hysteria could be cured by hypnosis, led the young Freud to further study under Professor Charcot in Paris. Here Freud turned exclusively to psychopathology and gradually developed his famous methods of psychoanalysis. In this technique a person relaxes with the analyst and is guided in free thought-association. Previously such thoughts were brought out under hypnotism but Freud's method obviated such a procedure. Infantile sexuality and interpreted dreams were the basic work-blocks of his theories. Repressed sexual thoughts and desires manifested themselves, he believed in dreams, which were a subconscious way of repressing painful thoughts. If the person could be made to face these hidden thoughts, and replace them with rational judgement, mental illnesses could be cured.

Freud's work caused much controversy and still does. In 1938 he was forced to escape from Hitler's Austria and fled to England. Here he lived at Hampstead, London until he died of jaw cancer.

Friese-Green, William (1855–1921)
Highgate 'new' Cemetery, Highgate, London.
English inventor of the cinematograph through the production of continuous photographs on celluloid. He died virtually penniless.

Gresham, Sir Thomas (1519–1579)
St Helen's Church, Bishopsgate, City of London, where there is a fine free-standing tomb-chest of Siena marble without effigy but large coats of arms.
Merchant and financier who gave his name to 'Gresham's Law', which states that 'Bad money drives good money out'. He advised and served four successive sovereigns, including Elizabeth I, on money matters. He also founded The Royal Exchange.

Hansard, Luke (1752–1828)
St Giles-in-the-Fields, Holborn, London.
Printer. Born in Norwich, he went to London after the expiration of his apprenticeship to Stephen White, a Norwich printer. He joined the firm of John Hughs, printer to the House of Commons, who in 1774 made him a partner. In 1800 the business came entirely into Hansard's hands and was renamed later as Luke Hansard & Sons. From 1774 until his death he printed the *Journals of the House of Commons*. It was his son, Thomas Curson Hansard, who began

Sir Thomas Gresham, by an unknown Flemish artist

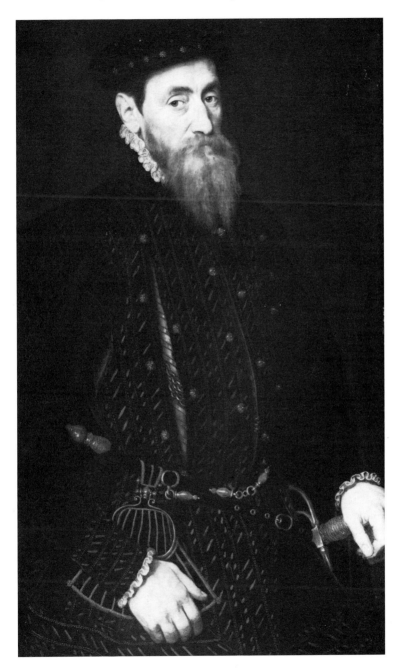

printing the *Parliamentary Debates* in 1803 from his own press in Paternoster Row.

Harvey, Sir William (1578–1657)
St Andrew's Church, Hempstead, Essex.

Physician who first demonstrated the circulatory system of blood and the function of the heart. He has been called 'the grandfather of modern medicine'. He studied at Cambridge and Padua, and in 1607 became a fellow of the Royal College of Physicians and two years later physician to St Bartholomew's Hospital. He was physician to both James I and Charles I, and carried out many reforms in the practice of medicine. His notes on the circulation of blood, the heart and other organs are still in the British Library. His treatise on circulation, *Exercitatio anatomica de motu cordis et sanguinis*, was published in 1628 in Latin.

Heaviside, Oliver (1850–1925)
Paignton Cemetery, Paignton, Devon.

A self-taught mathematical physicist and electrical engineer who discovered that when an electric current starts in a wire it begins on its boundary and works inwards. Thus, in the language of Heaviside, such a transient current is 'in layers, strong at the boundary, weak in the middle'. His work was responsible for the enrichment and clarification of the language of electro-dynamics. Also, in 1902, he remarked, with regard to 'wireless' waves, that there might possibly be a sufficiently conducting 'layer' in the atmosphere to aid their transmission. This useful conception became known as the 'Heaviside Layer'.

Herschel, Sir William (1738–1822)
St Laurence's Church, Upton, Slough, where there is a monument by J. Theakston in the form of a simple, heavy Grecian tablet. A commemorative stone lies in the north aisle of the Nave in Westminster Abbey.

German-born astronomer who joined the Hanoverian guards as an oboist and, about 1757, came to England, technically deserting his regiment for which, in 1782, he was granted a full pardon by George III. At first he made his living by training the band of the Durham Militia and, after incurring the notice of Dr Miller of Doncaster, going there to teach music. The study of harmony eventually led to an interest in astronomy and inspired his resolution 'to take nothing on trust'. He bought a small reflector with his brother's help, the better to study the heavens. On 13 March 1781 he discovered the planet Uranus and investigated the distribution of stars in the Milky Way, concluding that some of the nebulae he could see were separate star systems.

Herschel, Sir John Frederick William (1792–1871)
Westminster Abbey, London, in the north aisle of the Nave.

Astronomer. Son of Sir William, who continued with his father's researches, completing his own survey of the heavens in the southern hemisphere at the Cape of Good Hope in February 1834. His work at Feldhausen near Cape Town marked the commencement in a wide sense of southern sidereal astronomy. He was also a highly accomplished chemist and in 1819 he discovered the solvent power of hyposulphate of soda on the otherwise insoluble salts of silver, which was a prelude to its use as a fixing agent in photography. In 1839, independent of Fox Talbot, he invented the process of photography on sensitized paper and was the first person to apply the terms 'positive' and 'negative' to photographic images and to imprint them on glass prepared by the deposit of a sensitive film.

Hill, Sir Rowland (1795–1879)
Chapel of St Paul, Westminster Abbey, London.

Originally a mathematics teacher in his father's school at Hilltop, Birmingham, where when he came into its management he propagated an educational system whose principal feature was 'to leave as much as possible all power in the hands of the boys themselves'. As an educationalist he deserves to stand with Arnold of Rugby. His zeal as an administrative reformer was directed to the postal system in 1835 and five years later he suggested the 'penny postage' which was introduced on 10 January 1840. Appointed at first to the Treasury, he was later made Chief Secretary to the Postmaster General in order to implement his reforms. He was knighted in 1860.

Hoare, Sir Richard Colt (1758–1838)
St Peter's Churchyard, Stourton, Wiltshire; large mausoleum to the east of the church.

A Wiltshire historian and antiquary who, after being privately educated and joining his family's banking house in Fleet Street for a while, was given his financial independence by a large allowance from

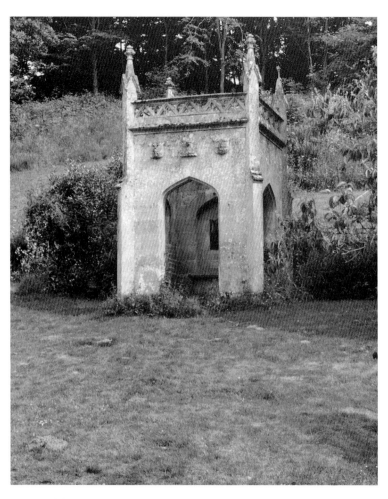

Sir Richard Colt Hoare's mausoleum, Stourton, Wiltshire

his grandfather. After travelling widely in Europe he devoted his zeal to the history and antiquities of Wiltshire, listing in his chronicles the position and contents of hundreds of barrows. One of his main works is an 'everthing-you-want-to-know' *History of Modern Wiltshire* (1822–1844) in six volumes, besides travel books on Elba, Italy and Sicily. He also wrote a description of the house and gardens of Stourhead, which his grandfather had planned and built. They are a great tourist attraction.

Hooke, Robert (1635–1703)
St Helen's Church, Bishopsgate, City of London.

Experimental philosopher whose inventions include the wheel barometer, the application of springs to the balance of watches, together with the explanation of their action by the principle *ut tensio sic vis*; he also originated the idea of using the pendulum as a measure of gravity. His scientific achievements would have been more striking if they had been less varied and while he originated much he perfected little. As an architect he constructed a model for the rebuilding of the City of London after the Great Fire of 1666, but Wren's was preferred though never realised. When rebuilding did commence Hooke was appointed Surveyor.

Hunter, John (1728–1793)
Westminster Abbey, London, in the north aisle of the Nave. His remains were removed here from their original burial site in St Martin-in-the-Fields in 1859.

Physiologist and surgeon. In 1748 he moved to London from Scotland to attend dissections at Symonds' anatomical school where his brother, William, lectured. In 1754 he became a surgeon-pupil at St George's Hospital where, in 1756, he was appointed house surgeon. In 1761 he went with Keppel's expedition to Belleisle as staff surgeon and when he returned to London two years later he set up as a surgeon. He developed several new surgical techniques. His anatomical collection is now housed in the Royal College of Surgeons.

Hunter, William (1718–1783)
St James's Church, Piccadilly, London.

Physiologist and elder brother of the more famous surgeon, John Hunter. He moved from Scotland to London about 1741 and entered St George's Hospital as a pupil surgeon. He attained considerable fame as a lecturer. In 1747 he became a member of the Corporation of Surgeons, but, by degrees, he renounced surgery in favour of obstetrics, in which he excelled. In September 1756 he became a Licentiate of the Royal College of Physicians and in 1764 he was made Physician-Extraordinary to Queen Charlotte, wife of George III.

Huxley, Thomas Henry (1825–1895)
Finchley Cemetery, Finchley, London.

Biologist who began his career as an assistant surgeon on HMS *Rattlesnake*. During the voyage of 1846 to 1850 he studied marine organisms. In 1870 he gave the first recognizably modern lecture on the origin of life to the British Association, having become an ardent evolutionist after the publication of Darwin's *The Origin of Species*. He originated the term 'Agnostic'. His writings, which include *Man's Place in Nature*, attempted to interest the public in the importance of science.

Jenner, Edward (1749–1823)
St Mary's Church, Berkeley, Gloucestershire.

Physician. A pupil of John Hunter, in 1792 he obtained the degree of doctor of medicine from St Andrew's. He practised at Berkeley in Gloucestershire, where he was born, and pursued his earlier enquiries into the relations between cowpox and smallpox. He developed a vaccine against smallpox in 1798, the use of which, with the support of the King, George III and his wife, Charlotte, and their son, George, Prince of Wales, gradually spread throughout Britain and the world. His discovery helped lay the foundations of modern immunology.

Jones, Inigo (1573–1652)
St Benet's Church, Paul's Wharf, City of London, now the Metropolitan Welsh Church. A small tablet on the east wall records the inscription raised in the original church, which was destroyed in the Great Fire of 1666 and subsequently rebuilt by Sir Christopher Wren.

Architect who studied in Venice where he became addicted to the style of Palladio. In 1604 he had acquired such a reputation that he was invited by King Christian IV to Denmark where he is reputed to have designed the two royal palaces of Rosenborg and Frederiksborg. In 1605 he was appointed architect to Anne of Denmark, Queen of James I and VI, and Henry, Prince of Wales, being largely responsible for supplying the designs and decorations of the court masques. After a second visit to Italy in 1612 he was made Surveyor-General of royal buildings by James I. He built the Queen's House at Greenwich and the Royal Banqueting House, Whitehall; designed St Paul's Church, Covent Garden; and advised on the building of Wilton House, Wiltshire, for the Earl of Pembroke.

Kelvin, William Thomson, 1st Baron Kelvin of Largs (1824–1907)
Westminster Abbey, London, in the central aisle of the Nave.

Mathematician and physicist who was born in Belfast. He is principally known for his work on heat and thermodynamics, and for his contributions to electrical science and submarine telegraphy. He introduced the Kelvin or Absolute scale of temperature. In 1902 he was awarded the Order of Merit on its institution, having been made President of the Royal Society in 1890 and created a baron in 1892.

Lane, John (1854–1925)
St Nectan's Church, Hartland, North Devon.

Publisher. Born at West Putford in Devon, the only son of a miller and corn merchant. After working for eighteen years as a clerk in the Railway Clearing House he became an antiquarian bookseller in partnership with an Exeter friend, Elkin Mathews. He then founded the Bodley Head publishing house, whose imprint honoured Sir Thomas Bodley, an illustrious Devonian and founder of the Bodleian Library at Oxford. His list included many of the most famous literary figures of the day: Max Beerbohm, Baron Corvo, Anatole France and William John Locke. He started the celebrated illustrated quarterly, *The Yellow Review*; and opened a branch of his firm in New York.

Leverhulme. William Hesketh Lever, 1st Viscount (1851–1925)
Christ Church, Port Sunlight, Cheshire, in enclosure adjoining church, two tombs: he and his wife.

Soap-maker–philanthropist who, after expanding his father's grocery business, specialized in the making of soap for which he registered the name Sunlight, in partnership with his brother James. His first soap was purchased from a manufacturer but, changing the way it was made – from tallow to vegetable oils – he began to make it in his own factory, founding Port Sunlight as his headquarters. He housed his workers in new homes, providing schools and a pleasant environment for them in a forward-thinking social philanthropy that was to mark his future efforts and earn him a baronage in 1917 and viscountcy in 1922. The school of tropical medicine at Liverpool University was one of his many endowments. He travelled widely and saw his firm grow into a world-wide enterprise after an early financial crisis.

Lister, Joseph, 1st Baron Lister of Lyme Regis (1827–1892)
Hampstead Cemetery, Fortune Green Road, London.

Surgeon. His early observation of gangrene and pyaemia at the University College Hospital, London, led him to suspect the parasitic nature of the disorders. He continued his researches as a young surgeon at Edinburgh and developed a fine spray of a watery solution of carbolic acid to destroy the germs in the atmosphere and on the surgeon's hands. The spray, which was but one of his anti-septic methods, and his arduous campaign for greater hygiene, especially in the sterilization of catgut used in suturing wounds, led to a dramatic improvement in patient recovery. While they met with ridicule and opposition in some quarters of the profession, his methods were eventually recognized as vital.

Lodge, Oliver Joseph (1851–1940)
St Michael's Church, Wilsford (Lake), Wiltshire, close to the south-east wall.

The virtual inventor of practical wireless telegraphy, he was born at Penkhull, Staffordshire, of a family of schoolmasters and clergymen. His paternal grandfather had twenty-five children, of whom Oliver's father was the twenty-third. Oliver left school when he was 14 years old and worked in his father's agency business until his aunt encouraged him to study science in London. He 'had his eyes opened' by a series of lectures on the physics of heat. He won prizes and studied under T. H. Huxley at the Royal College of Science. His discovery of the cohesion of metals under the influence of electro-magnetism earned him the Royal Society's Rumford Medal and made wireless telegraphy practical by taking away the 'disease which afflicted early transmitters' after he prescribed the remedy. Later he became interested in psychic phenomena, believing the mind lives on after death. He wrote several scientific works, but his psychical book *Raymond, or Life and Death* (1916), gained popular interest. His son Raymond had been killed in the war. Lodge was knighted in 1902, retiring in 1919 to Lake to devote his time to the 'ether of space', which he saw as a medium for the storage of mental energy.

Marks, Michael (1859–1907)
Old Jewish Cemetery, Manchester, Lancashire; small stone obelisk.

Co-founder of Marks and Spencer merchandising chain, Marks was born in Slonim, Russia and came as a penniless refugee from the

St Michael's Church, Wilsford, Wiltshire; Sir Oliver Lodge's grave here anti-Semitic pogroms there to Stockton-on-Tees in 1881. Starting with a pedlar's tray he followed fairs and markets hawking his wares until 1884 when he was lent £5 by Isaac Dewhirst that enabled him to set up a trestle stall in an open market at Leeds. Within ten years he was operating eight penny bazaars. He still used the wording he had on his pedlar's tray: 'Don't Ask the Price – It's a Penny'; a marketing phrase that he kept for many years, originated to solve his language problem. He went into partnership in 1894 with Tom Spencer, who had been Dewhirst's cashier. With continued success he was living a happy family life in Manchester when he died suddenly of a heart attack on New Year's Eve. He had married Hannah Cohen in 1886 and his son Simon, later to become Lord Marks of Broughton, fought successfully to keep the business in the family.

Maudslay, Henry (1771–1831)
St Mary Magdalene's Church, Woolwich, London.

Engineer who first produced precision-cut nuts and bolts that were completely interchangeable by designing a precision thread-cutting lathe that produced the screw-thread within close tolerances to a uniform pitch. He also designed and invented many other engineering artefacts, including the first cup valve for high-pressure steam engines, the micrometer and steamboat engines. Brunel, with whom Maudslay had worked, specified a Maudslay slide-lever engine for his *Great Western*, the first successful trans-atlantic steamship.

Maxim, Sir Hiram Stevens (1840–1916)
Norwood Cemetery, Norwood, London.

An American engineer who was born in Maine, coming to England in 1884. He invented the machine gun, known as the Maxim gun, a delayed-action fuse, smokeless powder and an aeroplane. His Maxim Gun Company merged with Vickers in 1896. He became a British citizen in 1900 and was knighted a year later.

Murray, John (1778–1843)
Kensal Green Cemetery, Kensal Green, London.

Son of John McMurray who founded the London publishing house of John Murray in Fleet Street. His father died when he was fifteen and the firm was largely run by his father's partner, Samuel Highley. In 1803 John Murray dissolved that partnership and launched into literary speculation which earned him the name given him by Lord

Byron, 'the Anak of publishers'. He was the publisher of Lord Byron, as well as of Sir Walter Scott, Jane Austen, Robert Southey and Francis Palgrave.

Newton, Sir Isaac (1642–1727)
Westminster Abbey, London, in the central aisle of the Nave.

Born in Lancashire he studied at Cambridge where in 1669 he became Lucasian Professor of Mathematics. He made three important discoveries: his theory of gravitation indicated that the universe was regulated by simple mathematical laws; that white light could be separated into a sequence of coloured components, forming the visible spectrum; and the use of the calculus, which he invented independent of Leibnitz, to investigate the forces of nature in a quantitative way. He propounded his views in his famous *Naturales Principia Mathematica* of 1687.

Northcliffe, Alfred Charles William Harmsworth, 1st Viscount
(1865–1922)
Finchley Cemetery, Finchley, London. There is a bust of Lord Northcliffe on the south front of St Dunstan in the West, facing Fleet Street.

Born in Dublin, the son of a barrister. He began *Answers* in 1888 with his brother, Harold (later Lord Rothermere). In 1894 he bought the *Evening News*, in 1896 the *Daily Mail*, and in 1908 he took over *The Times*. His real claim to fame is that he changed the whole face of English journalism, woke it up, made it come alive and also made it prosperous.

Nuffield, William Richard Morris, 1st Viscount (1877–1963)
Holy Trinity Church, Nuffield, Oxfordshire, where a plain, blue-slate slab at the south-east corner of the church marks his grave.

Motor-car manufacturer and philanthropist. He started his career in a bicycle shop but his genius for business led him to found Morris Motors which made him a multi-millionaire. He retired from the company's chairmanship in 1952. As a philanthropist he provided large sums for the advancement of medicine to Oxford University and for Nuffield College, Oxford, and, in 1943, established the Nuffield Foundation, endowing it with £10 million.

Rothschild, Nathan Mayer (1777–1836)
Jewish Burial Ground, Brady Street, Whitechapel, London.

Banker. German-born, he arrived in Manchester in 1800 to act as a purchaser of manufactured goods for his father. His boldness and skill in financial transactions, at first treated with reserve, excited the admiration and envy of the British bankers and merchants. By using carrier pigeons and fast-sailing boats for the transmission of news he was able to utilize to his greatest advantage his special information. In 1810 he staked his reputation on the downfall of Napoleon and the Allies negotiated loans through Rothschild to carry on the war against the Emperor. He effected immense profit by the purchase of stock which rose as soon as news of Napoleon's defeat at Waterloo, already transmitted to Rothschild several hours before by his own fast service, reached the public. He was the first to popularize foreign loans in Britain by fixing the rate in sterling and making dividends payable in London and not in foreign capitals.

Rowntree, Joseph (1836–1925)
Society of Friends burial ground, Skeldergate, York; alongside the River Ouse.

Cocoa and chocolate manufacturer and philanthropist, son of a Quaker. Rowntree first joined his father in the grocery business, then went into partnership with his brother Henry in a cocoa-making firm they had acquired. Joseph took care to avoid the expense of labour troubles and their wasteful disruptions of production by paying top wages for reasonable hours and providing employees with good working conditions. His social work marked him as a foremost philanthropist of the day, of 'gentle ways and strong convictions'. He strongly supported the League of Nations and the Society of Friends.

Rutherford, Ernest, 1st Baron Rutherford of Nelson (1871–1937)
Westminster Abbey, London, in the central aisle of the Nave.

Physicist. He was born in New Zealand. In 1911 he announced his theory on the structure of the atom, and in 1918 succeeded in splitting it, thus preparing the way for future nuclear research. In 1908 he received the Nobel Prize for Chemistry for his work on radioactivity and the discovery of alpha and beta radiation. He was the Cavendish Professor of Experimental Physics at Cambridge and Director of the Royal Society Mond Laboratory in Cambridge.

Grave of Lord Nuffield, Holy Trinity Churchyard, Nuffield, Oxfordshire

Selfridge, Harry Gordon (1857–1947)
St Mark's Church, Highcliffe, Hampshire; in south part of graveyard about half-way down beside the west fence.

An American-born businessman who completed the building of, and opened, his famous London department store in 1908. His father had owned a small dry-goods shop in Ripon, Wisconsin, but went away with the US cavalry in the Civil War of 1861–5, attaining the rank of major and never returning to his family. After getting a clerk's job and rising high in the Chicago mail-order firm of Marshall Field & Co., Selfridge left America with a small fortune he had accumulated. Despite contrary advice, he decided that a department store in Oxford Street, London, would do well. With a capital of £900,000 he opened 'Selfridge's' and included many innovations, such as a free information bureau for all kinds of difficult questions, a library and roof-garden, and a pioneer 'truth-in-advertising' guarantee.

The business prospered, especially during World War I and up to the mid-1930s, but, because of a series of expensive personal follies in the years before World War II, he drew too much capital from his company and was forced to resign in 1939 with the honorary title of president. The company was taken over in 1951 by Lewis's Ltd, of Liverpool. Thus did the fortunes of the 'merchant prince' rise and fall within 30 years, perhaps reflecting in some ways England's own fortunes during the same period. He rented Highcliffe Castle for a few years when it was a magnificent Gothic mansion, which had been built in the 1830s by Lord Stuart of Rothesay, some of the stones having come from a medieval castle near Rouen. Selfridge's wife and mother are buried near him.

Siemens, Sir William (1823–1883)
Kensal Green Cemetery, Kensal Green, London.

Metallurgist and electrical engineer. Born in Hanover, he visited England in 1842 to set up his electro-plating service and equipment because the British patent laws afforded him better protection. He decided to settle there in 1844 and became a British citizen in 1859. He worked in two distinct fields: the application of heat, and the application of electricity. He was responsible for numerous inventions, and his improvements of the steel furnace which led to the 'open-hearth' process introduced Siemens' steel.

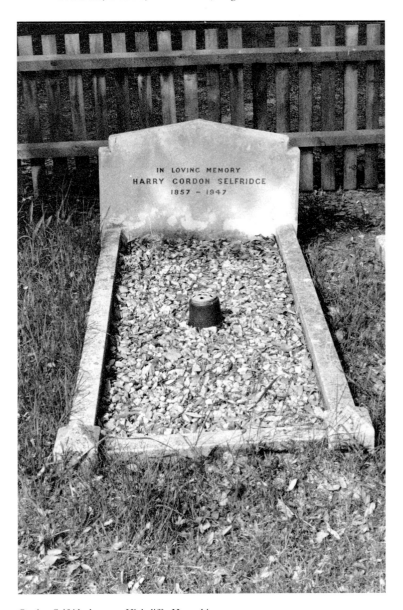

IN LOVING MEMORY
HARRY GORDON SELFRIDGE
1857 – 1947

Gordon Selfridge's grave, Highcliffe, Hampshire

Snow, John (1813–1858)
Brompton Cemetery, West Brompton, London.

During his observations of cholera Snow discovered that this disease was communicated by contaminated water. He was the first doctor to use ether as an anaesthetic in England. He gave chloroform to Queen Victoria at the birth of her son, Prince Leopold, on 7 April 1853, and again in April 1857 at the birth of Princess Beatrice. The Queen was the first royal personage to receive an anaesthetic.

Sopwith, Sir Thomas Octave Murdoch (1888–1989)
Little Somborne Redundant churchyard, near King's Somborne, Hampshire.

Aircraft designer whose name will be ever associated with the fighter planes he built during the first world war. He flew across the English Channel in 1910, winning the Baron de Forest prize for so doing. His Kingston-on-Thames aeroplane manufacturing company designed and built the famous 'Camel' and 'Pup' fighters and others of World War I. Later he became chairman of Hawker-Siddeley's and also chaired the Society of British Aircraft Constructors. He was also a keen yachtsman, competing in the 1934 America Cup race. A CBE came to him in 1918 and a knighthood in 1953.

Spencer, Thomas, 'Tom' (1842–1905)
St Giles's Churchyard, Whittingham, Lichfield, Staffordshire; well-maintained grave.

Co-founder of Marks and Spencer, he had been a cashier for Isaac Dewhirst whom Michael Marks had first sought as a partner when his 'penny bazaars' that he had started from a street vendor's basket grew to eight in number. In 1903 the two partners incorporated, dividing 30,000 shares equally. Spencer bought a chicken farm at Lichfield shortly after, leaving the running of the company to Michael Marks. Spencer's son Tom, who became a director, later had a falling-out with Simon Marks, the founder's son. Spencer was born in Skipton, North Yorkshire, but the house in which he was born is now the site of a Woolworth store. They magnanimously allowed an identification tablet of Spencer's birthplace to be put up there, where it was unveiled by directors from both companies.

Spilsbury, Sir Bernard Henry (1877–1947)
Golders Green Crematorium, Golders Green, London; ashes dispersed on Garden of Rest lawn, Book of Remembrance in Chapel of Memory.

Pathologist who became famous at the trial (1910) of Dr Crippen, who had murdered his wife with hyoscyamine, which is difficult to detect after death. This was the first time this poison had been used in a murder – so far as is known! For 35 years after that Spilsbury was famous in England as a 'detective-pathologist' whose evidence as a Crown witness frequently helped to establish either the guilt or innocence of the accused person. Spilsbury, the son of a manufacturing chemist, was born in Leamington, Warwickshire. Depressed after the loss of a sister and two sons (one killed in an air raid) and suffering from increasing coronary thrombosis and arthritis, he took his own life by administering carbon monoxide to himself in his University College laboratory.

Stephenson, George (1781–1848)
Trinity Church, Chesterfield, Derbyshire, beneath the communion table.

Engineer and locomotive designer. In 1825 he and his son, Robert, built the *Locomotion* for the Stockton and Darlington Railway; and four years later his engine the *Rocket* won the £500 prize offered by the Liverpool and Manchester Railway when it reached speeds of 30 mph. He was also responsible for discovering the method on which the miners' safety lamp was based.

Talbot, William Henry Fox (1800–1877)
Lacock Cemetery, Lacock, Wiltshire, by the path on the right-hand side.

Often called 'the inventor of photography', but in the early days he really shared the honour with the Frenchman Louis Daguerre and in England with Thomas Wedgwood (1771–1805; buried at St Mary's church, Tarrant Gunville, Dorset) and Joseph Reade. Talbot's idea of getting permanent 'sun pictures' of the projected images of a camera obscura led him to the discovery that paper was made sensitive to light by coating it with iodide and nitrate of silver. Gallic acid was used to bring out the latent image so formed. This so-called Talbotype was the basis of modern photography. His photography, however, has tended to obscure his other skill in mathematics which he early

Fox Talbot's grave in Lacock Cemetery, Wiltshire

displayed at Cambridge University. He won the Rumford Medal for his photographic discoveries. He was the first to decipher the cuneiform inscriptions on objects found in the 'Nineveh' excavations by Sir Austen Henry Layard (1817–1894).

Tate, Sir Henry (1819–1899)
Norwood Cemetery, Norwood, London.

Son of a cleric, he was born at Chorley, Lancashire. His father put him into business in Liverpool and he became a prosperous sugar broker. In 1874 he moved to London and there made Tate's Cube Sugar known all over the world. A collector of paintings which he left to the nation, paying for a new gallery to house them and others. This was the Tate Gallery which was opened on 21 July 1897. The following year he was made a baronet.

Tizard, Sir Henry Thomas (1885–1959)
Oriel College Ante-chapel, Oxford, Oxfordshire; ashes under stone bearing his initials.

Scientist and administrator who was responsible for much of the work behind the development of a series of radar stations that were ready in time to help give air victory in the Battle of Britain. A Magdalen College graduate in chemistry, he was in the Royal Flying Corps during the first world war when he worked on the early development of bomb sights. He was also among the founders of the aircraft and armament establishment at Martlesham Heath in Suffolk, later moved to Boscombe Down, Wiltshire. He was a Controller of Aeronautical Research and later Chairman of the Aeronautical Research Committee between the world wars. He was valued by Churchill for his scientific advice but he also came into notorious disagreement with Churchill's official scientific adviser Professor F. A. Lindemann (later Lord Cherwell) over the mass bombing of Germany that Lindemann had championed – Tizard did not believe in wasting valuable pilots on blind bombing of population centres but in more wisely concentrating on destroying Germany's naval capabilities. He was a Fellow of the Royal Society and a Fellow of Oriel, whose Provost married him in 1915 to Kathleen Wilson, daughter of a mining engineer; there were two sons of the marriage.

Vanbrugh, Sir John (1664–1726)
St Stephen's Church, Walbrook, City of London, in the north aisle.
There is an epitaph attributed to his fellow architect, Nicholas
Hawksmoor:

> Lie heavy on him, Earth! for he
> Laid many heavy loads on thee.

Architect and dramatist. His most famous play, the *Provok'd Wife*,
was written whilst under arrest in France as a spy during the period
1690 to 1692. But the first of his plays to be performed was *The
Relapse* in 1696 and its success was followed by a performance of the
Provok'd Wife at the theatre in Lincoln's Inn Fields in May 1697. This
led to attacks on him for immorality, and it is thought that these
attacks were partly responsible for his turning his attention to architecture. His many buildings include Blenheim Palace for the great Duke
of Marlborough; Castle Howard in Yorkshire, and Seaton-Delaval. In
1716 he was appointed architect to the Greenwich Hospital.

Verdon-Roe, Sir Edwin Alliot (1877–1958)
St Andrew's Church, Hamble, Hampshire, large white family grave
just outside porch.
   Pioneer aviator and aircraft manufacturer, born at Manchester, who
after beating 200 competitors to win a model aeroplane competition,
in 1908 designed, built and flew his own plane, the first Englishman
to so do. In partnershp with his brother Humphrey (1878–1949) he
founded the Avro aircraft company (1910), where the Avro 504 was
made in 1913. It became one of the most famous military aircraft of
the 1914–1918 war, in 1914 bombing Zeppelin sheds in the first air-
raid in history. It was still in use 25 years later. In 1928 Roe sold his
interest in Avro and formed Saunders-Roe, building flying boats.
Knighted in 1929, he prefixed in 1933 the name Verdon to his
surname in honour of his mother, Sofia Verdon.

Wallace, Alfred Russel (1823–1913)
Broadstone Cemetery, off Gravel Hill, Broadstone, Dorset; half-way
down the main path on right with petrified tree-trunk on a plinth over
his grave.
   Naturalist, born at Usk in Wales, who shares with Darwin the
honour of giving the theory of evolution to the world. Wallace,

however, believed the soul of man came directly from God. One of eight children, whose father was a 'dabbler in many things but a master of none', he first worked as a surveyor with his brother in London. Alfred developed an interest in geology, astronomy and agriculture, and after meeting a famous naturalist, Henry Walter Bates, was introduced to entomology. This meeting became the pivot-point of Alfred's career. He proposed they join forces and go on a collecting expedition in 1848 to the Amazon in South America; they would finance the trip from the sale of specimens they brought back. Wallace became fascinated with the incredible variety of birds, butterflies and plants, and by the majestic equatorial forest. After four years, when Bates had parted company with him, he set sail back to England, but all his notes and specimens were lost in a fire at sea. He and the ship's company were rescued after eleven days at sea in open boats.

Undaunted, he went next to the Malay Archipelago, where he remained for eight years, visiting every island. In 1855 he published his work on the law governing the introduction of new species of life. In 1858, while recovering from yellow fever in Ternate, the idea of natural selection as the means of evolution 'flashed' through his mind. He wrote his views and sent them to Charles Darwin, who had also been working on the same theme. Their joint paper was read before the Linnaean Society in 1858. Wallace could have been the first, technically, to announce the theory but he generously shared the honour with Darwin. After achieving many honours and world-wide fame Wallace died at Broadstone, where he had lived since 1902.

Watt, James (1736–1819)
St Mary's Church, Handsworth, Birmingham.

Scottish engineer and inventor of the modern steam engine. This resulted from his important improvements to Thomas Newcomen's steam engine by inventing a separate condenser. He perfected a rotary engine and defined one horse power as the rate at which work is done when 33,000lbs are raised one foot in one minute. The electrical unit of power, the 'watt', was named after him.

Also buried at St Mary's Church were:

Matthew Boulton (1728–1809), an engineer who was a partner to Watt and in Boulton's workshops at Soho, near Birmingham, found the way to make Watt's steam engine work efficiently.

William Murdock (1754–1839), an engineer with Boulton and

Watt whose experiment on the distillation of coal and wood first brought gas lighting to a practical stage, illuminating their factory with it in 1803. He advanced engineering by giant steps with his ability, being presented with the Rumford Medal by the Royal Society.

White, Gilbert (1720–1793)
St Mary's Churchyard, Selborne, Hampshire; small sign near path points to grave.

Naturalist and antiquary whose *The Natural History and Antiquities of Selborne*, based on letters to Daines Barrington and Thomas Pennant, was published in 1789 by White's brother Benjamin, a Fleet Street publisher. It is one of the few books on natural history to gain the rank of an English classic. Part of its secret was that White was a 'prince among observers', nearly always observing the right thing at the right time and writing of what he saw with a great economy of words. It has been said: 'open the book where you will, it takes you out of doors'.

White's father was a barrister, and his grandfather was vicar of St Mary's Church at Selborne. At Oxford White became a fellow of Oriel College in 1744, dean of the college in 1752, and was ordained as a priest between those two dates. He served as a curate at nearby parishes and at Selborne from 1751. He produced other works including *Of the House-Swallows, Swift, and Sand-Martin* but *The Natural History of Selborne* is his paramount claim to fame.

Wren, Sir Christopher (1632–1723)
St Paul's Cathedral, London.

Architect who was born in Wiltshire. His plan for the rebuilding of the City of London after the Great Fire of 1666 was unsuccessful but he was asked to rebuild St Paul's Cathedral, which he began in 1675 and completed in 1710. He also built more than fifty other churches in the City of London including St Stephen's, Walbrook and St Mary-le-Bow, Cheapside. Other buildings designed by him include the Sheldonian Theatre and the Ashmolean at Oxford, and the Chelsea Hospital in London. A founder member of the Royal Society, he became its president in 1681. He was Professor of Astronomy at Gresham College, London and Savilian Professor of Astronomy at Oxford.

Sir Christopher Wren, by Kneller

Wyatt, James (1746–1813)
Westminster Abbey, London, in the South Transept, now known as 'Poets' Corner'.

Architect of country houses and designer of London's Pantheon, which was demolished in 1937. His classical works were surpassed by his Gothic constructions: Fonthill Abbey, Wiltshire; Ashridge Park, Hertfordshire; and Lee Priory, Kent. He was Surveyor-General to the King, George III. He died in a coach accident near Marlborough on 4 September 1813.

[6] Authors, Playwrights and Poets

Addison, Joseph (1672–1719)

Henry VII's Chapel, Westminster Abbey, London, in the north aisle. His monument is in the South Transept, now known as 'Poets' Corner'.

Poet and writer. Son of a Dean of Lichfield. He was a distinguished classical scholar whose Latin verses attracted the attention of John Dryden. In 1704 he published his famous poem, 'The Campaign', in celebration of the Duke of Marlborough's victory at Blenheim. In 1706 he was appointed Under-secretary of State and from 1708 until his death he sat as a Member of Parliament. He later went to Ireland as Chief Secretary. The fall of the Whigs in 1711, however, meant that he too lost office. He was a close friend of Jonathan Swift and Richard Steele, to whose *Tatler* Addison contributed a number of papers between 1709 and 1711, and with whom during 1711 and 1712 he was associated in the production of the *Spectator*. Addison's tragedy, *Cato*, was produced successfully in 1713 but his prose comedy, *The Drummer*, failed. When the Whigs returned to office Addison once again went to Ireland as Chief Secretary. During 1715 and 1716 he started his political newspaper the *Freeholder*. He retired from office in 1718 and died the following year. His marriage to the Countess of Warwick was unhappy. Pope satirized Addison in the character of Atticus.

Amis, Sir Kingsley (1922–1995)

Cremated in Golders Green

Novelist, born in London, who was described around the time he wrote his first novel *Lucky Jim* (1953), as one of England's Angry Young Men. It had a satirical attitude to academic life but was well received. He graduated from St John's College, Oxford and was an officer in the Royal Corps of Signals during the war, after which he taught English literature at University College, Swansea. A variety of material came from his enthusiastic pen, from jazz essays to science fiction and poetry. *Lucky Jim* reflects an attitude of exasperation with the social life of the time. Later works, *That Uncertain Feeling* (1956) and *I Like It Here* (1958), have the same unruly and cynical character who appears respectively as a small-town librarian and as a small-town author away from

England. His works included *One Fat Englishman* (1963), *The Anti-Death League* (1965), *Jake's Thing* (1978) and others. As 'Robert Markham' he wrote a James Bond type novel *Colonel Sun* (1968) and *The James Bond Dossier* (1965). He had written of Bond's first novel *Casino Royale* that in an age of less literary snobbishness, it would have been 'hailed as one of the most remarkable to have been published in England in the previous thirty years.' He was knighted in 1990.

Arbuthnot, John (1667–1735)
St James's Church, Piccadilly, London.

Author, whose *History of John Bull*, a collection of pamphlets issued in 1712 advocating the termination of war with France, made him famous. This work was the origin of John Bull, the typical Englishman. Arbuthnot was also the principal author of the 'Memoirs of Martinus Scriblerus', which were published with Pope's *Works* in 1741. A doctor, who was Physician in Ordinary to Queen Anne, he published many medical writings which showed him to be in advance of his age in medical science. He was a close friend of Jonathan Swift and he was generally praised for his medical science, his wit and humour, and his kind heart. Dr Johnson referred to him as 'an unusual genius'.

Arnold, Matthew (1822–1888)
All Saints' Churchyard, Laleham, Surrey.

Poet and writer. Son of Thomas Arnold, the great reforming headmaster of Rugby School. Matthew was educated at Rugby and Oxford where, from 1857 to 1867, he was Professor of Poetry. His first volume of poems appeared in 1849, *The Strayed Reveller and other poems*, but most of his prose works did not appear until after 1860. The most important of these was *Essays in Criticism*, 1865 and 1888, in which he widened the scope of literary criticism, using it to attack the 'philistinism' or 'provinciality' he considered then prevailed in the country. Arnold, like his father, was a strong supporter of educational reform, and worked strenuously to improve education, particularly secondary education, in England.

Ashmole, Elias (1617–1692)
St Mary's Church, Lambeth, London.

Antiquarian and writer. He was born in Lichfield. In 1638 he became a lawyer and in 1644 was appointed a commissioner in excise.

Two years later he was initiated as a Freemason, the first gentleman, or amateur, to be accepted. He held various minor offices after the Restoration. He is chiefly remembered as the founder and benefactor of the Ashmolean Museum in Oxford. In 1672 he published his *Institutions, Laws and Ceremonies of the Order of the Garter.* He was a keen astrologer and alchemist.

Austen, Jane (1775–1817)
Winchester Cathedral, Winchester, Hampshire, in the north aisle of the Nave.

Novelist. Daughter of the Rector of Steventon in Hampshire, where she spent the first twenty-five years of her life. Her most famous novels were *Pride and Prejudice*, originally entitled 'First Impressions', which she began in 1796, but, when it was rejected by a publisher, she revised it before its publication in 1813; and *Sense and Sensibility* which, though it was started a year after *Pride and Prejudice* and not completed for many years, was the first to be published in 1811. In all she wrote six finished novels, the remaining four being *Mansfield Park*, 1814, *Emma*, 1816, *Northanger Abbey* and *Persuasion*, which were published posthumously in 1818. She also wrote three other unpublished works, *Lady Susan* and two fragments, *The Watsons* and *Sanditon*. She died at Winchester.

Bacon, Francis, 1st Baron Verulam and Viscount St Albans (1561–1626)
St Michael's Church, St Albans, Hertfordshire, where his monument depicts a life-size marble figure seated comfortably and asleep.

Philosopher, essayist and statesman. Younger son of Sir Nicholas Bacon, Queen Elizabeth I's Lord Keeper, he held many high offices of state under James I, ultimately becoming Lord Chancellor in 1618. In 1621 he was impeached and sent to the Tower of London accused of 'corruption and neglect', to which he confessed. He lost all his offices and a heavy fine was imposed, though this was later remitted by the King. After his release from the Tower, he devoted himself to literary and philosophical works. His literary output can be divided into three classes: the philosophical, the most important of which are the *Advancement of Learning*, 1605; *Novum Organum*, 1620, and *De*

Jane Austen, by Cassandra Austen, c. 1810

Augmentis, 1623; the literary, which include the *Essays*, 1597 and 1625, *New Atlantis*, 1626, and the *History of Henry the Seventh*, 1622; and his professional works, of which *Maxims of the Law* and *Reading on the Statute of Uses* are the most famous.

Commemorative brass to Jane Austen in the wall beside her grave in Winchester Cathedral, Hampshire

'Barbellion, W.N.P.' Bruce Frederick Cummings (1889–1919)
St Mary's churchyard, Basing, near Basingstoke, Hampshire.

An author whose name is probably unknown to all but a handful of present-day readers, but was highly praised by Arnold Bennett. In a letter to the author's widow Bennett said the book was 'first class' and that 'if any man upheld the dignity of English letters by really distinguished books written under conditions of extreme difficulty, your late husband was that man.' The author had developed multiple sclerosis, which he knew doomed him to an early death. He wrote *Journal of a Disappointed Man* (published 1919) while suffering greatly, both physically and mentally. It was hailed by such perceptive authors as Hugh Walpole and Wells (who wrote the Introduction to it); critic Professor Thomas Mallon, writing of it in 1984, thought it was one of 'the most remarkable human documents of the generation.' In his book *Last Diary*, published after his death, he had written that, as a puny, undersized child, nervously shy with a tiny white face and melancholy eyes, 'I was a little alien among my schoolfellows', of Barnstaple, Devon where he was born. In 1911 he topped university candidates by 141 marks for a post in the Kensington Natural History Museum; he left school at seventeen apprenticed to journalism for five years, his father's profession. He lived at Badsey and Camden (now a pub) Cottages, Gerrards Cross in his last three years. The Journal is indeed quite awesome to read; '. . . the greatest diary a man has written,' said Professor Mallon. The initials in his pseudonym stood for Wilhelm Nero Pilate.

Barnes, William (1801–1886)
St Peter's Churchyard, Winterborne Came, Dorset; tall Celtic cross close to church's south-west window. Village is south side of the A352, through white gate and left fork to sign to church.

Poet who is generally known as the Dorset dialect poet. The son of a tenant farmer, whose great-grandfather had been granted land by Henry VIII, he went to Dorchester as a solicitor's clerk. He then became a schoolmaster at Mere and a parson, contributing many articles to magazines of the day. It is his dialect poetry that has claimed popular memory of him, his best-known poem perhaps being *A Bit o' Sly Coorten*, which first appeared in an 1883 issue of the *County Chronicle*. One of his serious works on language was a study of fundamental roots of Teutonic speech, entitled *Tiw*, after the god

William Barnes's statue, outside St Peter's Church, Dorchester, Dorset

from whom the race derives its name. He did not like the encroachment of Latin and Greek words into the English language, preferring, for example, 'sunprint' to 'photograph' and 'wheelsaddle' to 'bicycle'. He became greatly loved, and his appearance on Dorchester market days was much looked for. There is a statue of him outside Holy Trinity Church there. At well over 80 years of age he worked as he had always done as rector of Came, the benefice bestowed upon him by Captain Seymour Dawson Damer, who sleeps almost beside the poet in the graveyard. A list of Barnes's works numbers eighteen diverse and interesting titles.

Beaumont, Francis (1548–1616)
Westminster Abbey, Westminster, London, in the South Transept now known as 'Poets' Corner'.

Poet and dramatist whose name is inseparable from that of John Fletcher with whom he collaborated closely in dramatic works from 1606 to 1616, their best-known joint productions perhaps being *The Maid's Tragedy* and *The Knight of the Burning Pestle*. He also wrote commendatory verses for several of Ben Jonson's plays, as well as for Michael Drayton. *The Woman-Hater*, a comedy which he published in 1607, shows Jonson's strong influence.

Beckford, William (1759–1844)
Walcot Cemetery, Bath, Avon.

Author and eccentric. He inherited a large fortune from his father who was twice Lord Mayor of London. In 1783, after his marriage to Lady Margaret Gordon, he travelled, having been involved in a homosexual scandal, spending the majority of his brief married life in Switzerland, his wife dying in 1786. He then moved to Spain and Porgual and wrote his *Portuguese Letters*, which rank among his best work. He returned to England and built a magnificent residence, Fonthill Abbey, on the site of his birthplace, which cost him about £273,000. He later sold it. His oriental romance, *The History of the Caliph Vathek*, is regarded as one of the finest productions of luxuriant imagination.

Beerbohm, Sir Max (1872–1956)
St Paul's Cathedral, London.

Critic, essayist and caricaturist. Known for his wit, irony and satire, and for his polished and incisive style which he directed at literary mannerisms and social pretences. He succeeded George Bernard Shaw as drama critic on the *Saturday Review*. His best-known critical work is possibly *A Christmas Garland*, 1912, which is a series of parodies of contemporary writers – Wells, Bennett, Chesterton, etc. His novel, *Zuleika Dobson*, 1911, is a humorous work about the impact of an adventuress on the youth of Oxford.

Beeton, Mrs Isabella Mary, née Mayson (1836–1865)
Norwood Cemetery, Norwood, London.
Author of *Mrs Beeton's Book of Household Management*, which was published in 1861 by her husband, the controversial publisher, Sam Beeton. It had originally been published in serial form in *The Englishwoman's Domestic Magazine*, and was a guide to 'cookery in all branches' as well as to the problems affecting 'mistress & servant, hostess & guest, menu making, sick nursing, the nursery, the home lawyer, the home doctor, marketing, trussing & carving' and the 'daily duties' of a Victorian household.

Belloc, Hilaire (Joseph Hilary Pierre) (1870–1953)
Church of Our Lady and St Francis (RC), West Grinstead, Sussex; a tablet by the church door gives the location of the grave.
Writer. Born in France but educated in England, becoming a British citizen in 1902. A versatile writer, his best-known works include *The Path to Rome*, 1902, describing his trek through France, Switzerland and northern Italy to Rome; a history of *Marie Antoinette; The Servile State*, a sociological work; his essays on *Nothing, Something,* and *Everything*. He and G. K. Chesterton founded a political weekly, *The New Witness*, which was devoted to their idea of 'distributism', a form of medieval communism. G. B. Shaw referred to the paper as 'Chesterbelloc'.

Bennett, Enoch Arnold (1867–1931)
Burslem Cemetery, Burslem, Stoke-upon-Trent, Staffordshire.
Novelist. Born at Hanley in Staffordshire, he was educated at London University, after which he became a solicitor's clerk. In 1893 he was made assistant editor of *Woman*; subsequently he became its editor. His fame as a writer derives from his Clayhanger novels, or, as they are sometimes referred to, the 'Five Towns' novels, the five towns being Tunstall, Burslem, Stoke-upon-Trent, Hanley and Long-ton, the centre of the pottery industry. They provide the grim, sordid

background to the lives and pretentions of his middle-class characters. His other successful works are *The Old Wives' Tale*, 1908, *Riceyman Steps*, 1923, *The Grand Babylon Hotel*, 1902, a play, *Milestones*, which he wrote with Edward Knoblock, and some short stories, *The Grim Smile of the Five Towns*, 1907, and *The Matador of the Five Towns*, 1912.

Betjeman, Sir John (1906–1984)
St Enodoc's Church, Trebetherick, north Cornwall, near south side of church. The church is approached across the 10th fairway of the golf course.

Poet Laureate who also used his 'impish' but strong and popular voice against ill-conceived or excessive urban development, especially where it resulted in the destruction of Victorian architecture and our cultural heritage in general. After an unhappy school life at Marlborough he left Magdalen College, Oxford, in 1928 without a degree to find himself congenial work with the *Architectural Record*. His *Ghastly Good Taste* (1933) established him as an uncompromising critic of architecture. As a press attaché for the UK in Dublin during the war his poems first began to attract attention: *New Lights for New Chancels* (1940) and *New Bats in Old Belfries* (1945) brought him much popular acclaim. His total works make a long list. He was awarded the CBE in 1960 and made a Companion of Literature by the Royal Society in 1968, after which he succeeded Clarence Day Lewis (whom see) in 1972 as Poet Laureate.

Blackmore, Richard Doddridge (1825–1900)
Teddington Cemetery, Teddington, Greater London.

Author of *Lorna Doone*, 1869, which recreated his native Exmoor during the seventeenth century, as well as of other novels including *Springhaven*, 1887, a Napoleonic romance. Originally Blackmore was a barrister at the Middle Temple, but after a breakdown in his health he moved to Teddington where he pursued his literary work, supplementing his income by opening a market garden.

Blake, William (1757–1827)
Bunhill Fields Burial Ground, City Road, Finsbury, London.

Poet. He had no education but was apprenticed to the engraver, James Basire. His earliest poems, *Poetical Sketches*, were published in 1783, followed by *Songs of Innocence* in 1789, which first indicated his mystical leanings. His most important prose work, the *Marriage of*

Heaven and Hell, 1790, took a revolutionary stance, denying the reality of matter, as well as denying eternal punishment and authority. In *The French Revolution*, 1791, *America*, 1793, and *The Visions of the Daughters of Albion*, 1793, Blake develops the theme of revolt against authority. The symbolic and imaginative qualities that pervade his literary works were also present in his illustrations and watercolours.

Bowles, Caroline Ann (Mrs Robert Southey) (1786–1854)
St Thomas the Apostle churchyard, High Street, Lymington, Hampshire.

Poet whose talents were 'rather those of a story teller' than a poet, it has been said. She was born at Lymington, Hampshire, and the parish register of St Thomas's Church records her baptism. Her father, Captain Charles Bowles, on retiring from the East India Company, had bought an old-fashioned house, surrounded by elms, called Buckland Cottage, and it was here that Caroline grew up. By all accounts she was happy enough, but she found herself virtually alone in the world when her mother died in 1816 and a dishonest guardian defrauded her out of the cottage.

When brought face-to-face with the necessity of supporting herself, she decided to see if her pen could provide for her. She had sent one of her poems to Southey, who praised it and recommended it to the publisher John Murray, who admired but did not publish it. Longman's eventually brought it out under the title *Ellen Fitzarthur: a Metrical Tale*. As with her other poems, its strength lay, it is said, in its pathos. *The Widow's Tale* (1822) 'marked an advance' in the art of poetry. She met her future husband in 1820 when he asked her if she would work with him on his new poem, *Robin Hood*. Little came of this because she was unable to master the rhymeless style in which the poem was to be written. She had gone to Southey's Keswick home, but he was busy reading his books so the poet Wordsworth undertook the job of showing her the countryside. After this she wrote the work for which she is most famous, *Chapters on Churchyards*. She followed with poems such as *Tales of Factories*, in which she protested about the ill-treatment of workmen, and *The Birthday*, for which she was called the Cowper of modern poetesses. She left 'my, our, dear New Forest' when she returned to Keswick to live as Southey's wife, after their marriage at the church in Boldre, Hampshire. The couple were congenial enough, but it was said that Southey's state of health should have forbidden the marriage, and his mental health deteriorated rapidly. After his death she said 'the last three years have done upon me the worth of twenty'. She had even forfeited her annuity upon marriage, and although Southey left her £2,000 it did not compensate for the loss of the annuity. In the last two years of her life a pension of £200 was given her by the government.

Bowles, William Lisle (1762–1850)
Salisbury Cathedral, monument east side of the south-west transept, near his grave.

Poet, who was prebendary of Salisbury cathedral and, in 1818, chaplain to the Prince Regent. His first volume, *Fourteen Sonnets* on 'picturesque spots during a journey' (1789), had an extraordinary success. His other poems and writing include *Combe Ellen* (1798), *The Battle of the Nile* (1799), *The Grave of the Last Saxon* (1822), *Ellen Gray* (1823), *Scenes and Shadows of Days Departed* (1837) and some histories, of which *Hermes Britannicus* (1828) was the most important. An eccentricity of his was a constant refusal to be measured by a tailor. He died at his home in the cathedral close.

Brontë, Anne (1820–1849)
St Mary's Churchyard, Castle Road, Scarborough, Yorkshire. A memorial tablet to the three Brontë sisters is in Westminster Abbey, London, in the South Transept now known as 'Poet's Corner'.

Novelist. Daughter of Patrick Prunty, or Brontë, perpetual curate of Howarth in Yorkshire from 1820 till his death in 1861, and sister to Charlotte and Emily. She grew up in Haworth with her sisters and brother, Patrick Branwell. She was part author with Charlotte and Emily of *Poems* by Currer, Ellis and Acton Bell, published in 1846; and it was under the pseudonym of Acton Bell that she wrote *Agnes Grey*, 1847, and *The Tenant of Wildfell Hall*, 1848.

Brontë, Charlotte (1816–1855)
St Michael and All Angels' Church, Haworth, Yorkshire. A memorial tablet to the three Brontë sisters is in Westminster Abbey, London, in the South Transept now known as 'Poets' Corner'.

Novelist. Sister to Anne and Emily Brontë. She, together with three of her sisters, attended a boarding school for the daughters of clergy after the death of her mother in 1821. This school was the basis for Lowood in her novel *Jane Eyre*. During 1831 to 1832 she attended Miss Wooler's school at Roehead, to which she returned as a teacher

The Brontë sisters, by P. B. Brontë

from 1835 to 1838. Subsequently she became a governess, then, in 1842, she accompanied her sister Emily to Brussels to study languages, and there she also taught. Following the publication of *Poems* by Currer, Ellis and Acton Bell her novel *Jane Eyre* was published by Smith, Elder in 1847, her first novel *The Professor* having been rejected and not finally published until 1857, two years after her death. *Jane Eyre* was an immediate success and was followed by *Shirley*, 1849, and *Villette* in 1853 which recalled her memories of her time in Brussels. In 1854 she married her father's curate, but died a few months later.

Brontë, Emily Jane (1818–1848)
St Michael and All Angels' Church, Haworth, Yorkshire. A memorial tablet to the three Brontë sisters is in Westminster Abbey, London, in the South Transept, now known as 'Poets' Corner'.

Novelist. Sister to Charlotte and Anne Brontë. Also part author of *Poems* by Currer, Ellis and Acton Bell. Under the pseudonym of Ellis Bell she published *Wuthering Heights* in 1848. She was also an accomplished poet, her best-known poems being 'Last Lives' and 'Remembrance'.

Browning, Robert (1812–1889)
Westminster Abbey, London, in the South Transept now known as 'Poets' Corner'.

Poet. Son of a clerk in the Bank of England, he had little formal education. In 1835 his poem 'Paracelsus', attracted the encouraging attention of Carlyle and Wordsworth. He published numerous poems but perhaps his best known is 'The Ring and the Book' which he wrote during 1868 and 1869. He also wrote plays, his tragedy *Strafford* being produced at Covent Garden in 1837, and *The Blot on the 'Scutcheon* produced by Macready at the Drury Lane Theatre in February 1843. In 1846 Browning married Elizabeth Barrett and they spent the majority of their married life in Italy, at Pisa, Florence and Rome, where Mrs Browning died in 1861. Thereafter her husband returned to England and settled in London where he continued his writing. His last volume of poems, *Asolando*, was published on the day of his death.

Buchan, John, 1st Baron Tweedsmuir (1875–1940)
St Thomas of Canterbury Churchyard, Elsfield, Oxfordshire.
   Author of the famous thriller, *The Thirty-Nine Steps*, 1915, as well
as of *Greenmantle*, 1916, and other novels. He also wrote *Montrose,
Oliver Cromwell*, 1934, and *Julius Caesar*, 1932. From 1901 to 1903 he
was private secretary to the High Commissioner of South Africa, Lord
Milner; from 1916 to 1917 he was director of information under the
Prime Minister; and from 1935 until his death he was Governor-
General of Canada.

Bulwer-Lytton, Edward George 1st Baron Lytton (1803–1873)
Westminster Abbey, Chapel of SS Edmund and Thomas The Martyr.
   Perhaps most famous for his book *The Last Days of Pompeii*, which
he wrote in 1834, he was a brilliant poet at an early age. At Cambridge
from 1822–1825 he won a gold medal for a poem and had published
Ishmael And Other Poems when he was only seventeen. Novelist, playwright, essayist and poet his prolific output of various works became
extremely popular. It is said that his unhappy marriage to Rosina
Wheeler, an Irish beauty, which ended in a separation, spurred his
literary output to the good. He was a Member of Parliament for St Ives
in 1831 for ten years, being made a baronet in 1838. He was the son of
General Earl Bulwer and the former Elizabeth Barbara Lytton, who was
heiress to the Knebworth estate in Hertfordshire to which he succeeded
in 1843, when he assumed the name Lytton. As an M.P. again in 1852,
for Hertfordshire, he was instrumental as Colonial Secretary in establishing British Columbia and Queensland. In 1866 he was raised to the
peerage. His son Edward Robert Bulwer (1831–91) 1st Earl of Lytton
wrote his father's life and Letters while his grandson the 2nd Earl of
Lytton wrote his Memoirs in 1932.

Bunyan, John (1628–1688)
Bunhill Fields Burial Ground, City Road, Finsbury, London.
   Author of *The Pilgrim's Progress*. Son of a Bedfordshire tinsmith, he
was educated at the local village school before working at his father's
trade. When he was sixteen he was drafted into the Parliamentary
army. In 1653 he joined a Nonconformist church in Bedford, where
he preached. He came into conflict with the Quakers and his first
writings, *Some Gospel Truths opened*, 1656, and *A Vindication*, 1657,
were antagonistic to them. His first wife died in 1656 leaving four
small children and three years later he married his second, Elizabeth.

The following year he was arrested for preaching without a licence and was imprisoned for twelve years for refusing to comply with the law. During his first six years in prison he wrote nine of his books including *Grace Abounding to the Chief of Sinners*, 1666, and *The Holy City, or the New Jerusalem*, which also appeared in 1666. There was a gap of five years before the publication of *A confession of my Faith, and a Reason of my Practice* in 1671. The next year he was released and appointed pastor to the same church in Bedford. Shortly afterwardshe was again imprisoned briefly, and it was during this short spell that he wrote the first part of *The Pilgrim's Progress from this World to that which is to come*. The second part, with the whole work, was published in 1678. Thereafter he preached in many places but was not molested.

Burney, Fanny, Madame d'Arblay (1752–1840)
Walcot Cemetery, Bath, Avon; but her gravesite is no longer identifiable.

Novelist. The daughter of Dr Burney, she grew up in a literary society which included Dr Johnson and Edmund Burke. Her first novel, *Evelina*, was published anonymously. When her authorship was revealed she received much acclaim and was invited by Queen Charlotte to become the Queen's second keeper of the robes, a rôle which she accepted in 1786 although her health was not good. Her *Diary and Letters 1778–1840* gives an interesting account of her period at court. However, her health was not up to the rigours of the position and, after some difficulty, she was given permission to retire. In 1793 she married General d'Arblay, a French refugee in England, whom she later accompanied to France where, from 1802 to 1812, she was interned by Napoleon. In 1782 she had published her second novel, *Cecilia*, which was followed in 1796 by *Camilla* and *The Wanderer* in 1814. Her *Early Diary 1768–1778* with its pleasant sketches of Dr Johnson and David Garrick was published in 1889. She is known as the originator of the simple novel of home life.

Butler, Samuel (1612–1680)
St Paul's Church, Covent Garden, London. A monument to his memory was erected in 1721 by John Barber, Lord Mayor of London, in Westminster Abbey, London, in the South Transept, now known as 'Poets' Corner', and bears the epigram:

The Poets Fate is here in emblem shown:
He asked for Bread and he received a
   Stone.

Poet and satirist. Born at Strensham in Worcestershire, he was educated at the King's School, Worcester. He was made famous by the publication of his satirical poem *Hudibras* which was published in three parts: part I in 1663, part II in 1664, and part III in 1678. The king, Charles II, acclaimed it and gave Butler £300, later awarding him an annual pension of £100. Despite his pension, and the patronage of many wealthy and influential persons, such as George Villiers, 2nd Duke of Buckingham, whom he satirized both in *Characters* and *Hudibras*, he died in penury and was buried in St Paul's Covent Garden because he could not afford the Abbey fees at Westminster.

Byron, George Gordon, 6th Baron Byron (1788–1824)
St Mary Magdalen Church, Hucknall Torkard, Nottinghamshire, in the family vault. A white marble memorial was placed in the floor of Westminster Abbey, London, in the South Transept, now known as 'Poets' Corner', by the Poetry Society and dedicated on 8 May 1969.
   Poet. Educated at Harrow and Cambridge, and it was while he was at the university that he published his much criticized 'Hours of Idleness' in 1807. Two years later he went abroad, travelling in Portugal, Spain, Greece and the Levant, returning to London in 1811. The following year he published the first two cantos of 'Childe Harold', which brought him much critical acclaim. This was followed by 'The Giaour', 'The Bride of Abydos' and the beautiful visionary poem in blank verse, 'The Dream', among others. In 1815 he married Anne Isabella Milbanke from whom he was separated the following year. His personal life was the subject of much controversy and after his separation he left England for good, embittered by what he described as a hypocritical society. He lived most of the time in Italy. In 1816 he published canto iii of 'Childe Harold', canto iv in 1818. He wrote the first five cantos of 'Don Juan' during 1818 to 1820, the later cantos of the unfinished poem appearing whilst he was living at Pisa. In Italy he began his connection with Teresa, Countess Guiccioli, who lived with him for a time at Venice and whom he followed to Ravenna. He also wrote several dramas including *The Two Foscari*, *Mazeppa* and *Sardanapalus*. In 1822 he joined with Leigh Hunt in the

Grave of Lord Byron, St Mary Magdalen's Church, Hucknall Torkard,
Nottinghamshire

production of the short-lived magazine, *The Liberal*. The following year, 1823, he set out to join the Greeks in their war of independence from the Turks and died of fever at Missolonghi in April 1824.

Caedmon (c.670)

St Mary's Churchyard, Whitby, Yorkshire, where there is a memorial cross. A stone in the floor of Westminster Abbey, London, in the South Transept, now known as 'Poets' Corner', commemorates Caedmon 'who first among the English made verses'.

Entered the monastery of Whitby when already an old man. Bede tells us that he was an unlearned herdsman who suddenly, in a vision, was granted the gift of song, and that he later rendered into English verse passages translated to him from the Scriptures. The only authentic fragment of his work that survives is his first Hymn, which Bede quotes.

'Carroll, Lewis' (Charles Lutwidge Dodgson) (1832–1898)

Guildford Cemetery, Guildford, Surrey.

A mathematics don at Christ Church, Oxford, who wrote several books for children, the most notable of which were *Alice's Adventures in Wonderland*, 1865, and *Through the Looking-glass*, 1872. He also published *The Hunting of the Snark*, 1876, as well as various mathematical treatises including *Euclid and his Modern Rivals*, 1879.

Chaucer, Geoffrey (c.1343–1400)

Westminster Abbey, London, in the South Transept now known as 'Poets' Corner'; it was Chaucer's tomb which originated 'Poets' Corner'.

Poet and civil servant. As the author of the *Canterbury Tales* he ranks next to Shakespeare as perhaps England's most famous poet. He entered the service of Lionel, Duke of Clarence, third son of Edward III and subsequently held various offices in the King's household. He made various diplomatic trips abroad: to Flanders in 1376 and 1377, to France and Lombardy in 1378. At home he was appointed controller of customs in the port of London, was knight of the shire for Kent in 1386, and Clerk of the King's Works in 1388, at the time when he made the pilgrimage to Canterbury. His wife Philippa was the sister of Katharine Swynford, John of Gaunt's third wife and ancestress of Henry VII and the Tudor dynasty. Chaucer's writings fall into three periods: that of French influence, 1359–1372,

Tomb of Geoffrey Chaucer, Westminster Abbey, London, in 'Poets' Corner'

which produced, amongst others, the 'Romaunt of the Rose' and 'The Boke of the Duchesse', written, it is believed, for the death of John of Gaunt's first wife, Blanche of Lancaster; the period of Italian influence, 1372–1386, which produced 'Troylus and Crysede', 'The Parlement of Foules' and 'The Legende of Good Women'; and the period of his maturity, 1386–1400, which saw the publication of the *Canterbury Tales.*

Chesterton, Gilbert Keith (1874–1936)

Roman Catholic Cemetery, Beaconsfield, Buckinghamshire (down a lane off Aylesbury End near the old town centre). Headstone sculpted by Eric Gill.

Author and essayist who, born in London, first studied art at Slade School but never painted professionally. It is said that his best work

Grave of Lewis Carroll (Charles Lutwidge Dodgson) in Guildford Cemetery, Guildford, Surrey was in the essays he wrote for various periodicals such as *The Speaker*, *The Bookman* and the one that had been his brother's (Cecil Edward: 1879–1918) *New Witness*, changed by Gilbert to *G.K.'s Weekly*. His famous detective-priest Father Brown won Chesterton popular acclaim with *The Innocence of Father Brown* (1911). Of his religion, Catholicism, to which he was a convert, he said, 'It is quite possible that everything is wrong about it, except that it is right.' He was a large man of vast girth but possessed of great zest, vigour and humour. His short novel *The Man Who Was Thursday* (1908) reveals his political humour and satire probably better than anything else he wrote.

Christie, Dame Agatha (Mary Clarissa) (1891–1976)
St Mary's Church, Cholsey, Oxfordshire, large grey stone in west part of graveyard.

An author famous for her mainly detective novels and stage plays, she was born in Torquay. Her first marriage, after a courtship of two days, was to a young subaltern, later Colonel Christie. Divorced in 1928, she married a distinguished archaeologist, Sir Max Mallowan. Her works include more than 70 mystery novels, plus some romances and children's stories, in which her most famous characters, the Belgian Hercule Poirot and the elderly village lady Miss Marple, appeared as remarkably astute detectives. She disappeared mysteriously for some time in 1926 after registering at a Harrogate hotel in the name of Miss Steele, her first husband's mistress. *The Mysterious Affair of Styles* and *The Murder of Roger Ackroyd* were among her earlier novels in the twenties, while her plays *The Mousetrap* and *Witness for the Prosecution* appeared in 1952 and 1954 respectively. The former is still running in London. She was awarded a CBE in 1956 and created a Dame in 1971 for her important contributions to literature.

Cobbett, William (1763–1835)
St Andrew's Church, Farnham, Surrey; in the tower there is a medallion bust under a simple pointed canopy.

Journalist. Self-educated son of a Farnham labourer, he served as a soldier in Florida from 1784 to 1791. Then he bought his discharge, accused some of his former officers of peculation and fled to America to avoid prosecution in 1792. There he published pro-British pamphlets under the pseudonym of Peter Porcupine. In 1800 he returned to England and edited *Cobbett's Political Register* in 1802, which established him as a Tory journalist. He published *Parliamentary Debates*, which

William Cobbett, by an unknown artist

Hansard later took over, an *English Grammar*, 1817, and a number of other works on economics. He spent some time in America during 1817 to 1819, and in 1832 became a Member of Parliament for Oldham. Perhaps the most interesting of his writings to survive are his *Rural Rides* which were collected in 1830.

Coleridge, Samuel Taylor (1772–1834)
St Michael's Church, Highgate, London, in the aisle.

Poet. Son of the Vicar of Ottery St Mary in Devon, he was educated at Christ's Hospital and Jesus College, Cambridge. Whilst only twenty-one he was contributing verses to the *Morning Chronicle* and in 1794, together with his friend and brother-in-law, Robert Southey, he published a play, *The Fall of Robespierre*. In 1796 he briefly launched a newspaper, *The Watchman*, which lasted for only ten numbers. He had met and formed a close association with Wordsworth, and they lived together for about a year at Nether Stowey and Alfoxden in Somerset. Their *Lyrical Ballads*, 1798, contained one of Coleridge's most famous and finest poems, 'The Rime of the Ancient Mariner', which together with the later poems 'Kubla Khan' and 'Christabel', is characterized by a sense of mystery. In 1809 he launched his second periodical, *The Friend*, a literary, moral and political weekly paper, which was subsequently re-written and published as a book in 1818. After his return from Malta and Italy during the years 1804 to 1806, his health broke down and he became addicted to opium. In 1825 he published his *Aids to Reflection*, which did much to introduce German philosophy to the English, and tried to influence English thinkers away from their current doctrines, advocating a more spiritual and religious interpretation of life, based on what he had learned from Kant and Schelling.

Collins, William Wilkie (1824–1889)
Kensal Green Cemetery, Kensal Green, London.

Author. Originally trained as a barrister, he forsook that profession for literature, contributing to *Household Words* from 1855. It was in this periodical that he published the work which was to establish him in the literary world, *The Woman In White*, for he was practically the first novelist to deal with the detection of crime. His contributions to the periodical brought him into collaboration with its proprietor, Charles Dickens, and they became close friends. Collins wrote numerous other novels, perhaps the best known being *The Moonstone*, 1868.

Congreve, William (1670–1729)
Westminster Abbey, London, in the south aisle of the Nave.

Dramatist. Educated at the Kilkenny School and Trinity College, Dublin, at both of which he was a fellow student of Swift, he entered London's Middle Temple, which he quickly forsook for literature. An unsuccessful attempt at a novel, *Incognita*, 1692, was followed by the success of *The Old Bachelor*, a comedy, which appeared in 1693. He subsequently published *The Double Dealer*, 1694, *Love for Love*, 1695, and *The Way of the World*, 1700, all comedies of manners, displaying the narrow world of fashion and gallantry. A friend of Swift, Pope and Steele, as well as of the enchanting actress, Anne Bracegirdle, whose rôle in his comedies contributed largely to their success. After his death, his body lay in state in the Jerusalem Chamber, and Sir Robert Walpole was one of his pall-bearers. The monument was erected by Henrietta, Duchess of Marlborough, to whom he left the bulk of his fortune, and she wrote the epitaph. She also had a statue of Congreve made in ivory, which moved by clockwork, setting it daily on her table where she talked to it as if it were alive.

Conrad, Joseph (1857–1924)
The Roman Catholic Cemetery, Canterbury, Kent.

Born of Polish parents in the Ukraine, his full names were Teodor Josef Konrad Korzeniowski. His parents were exiled to Vologda in northern Russia for revolutionary activities and his mother died there. Later he attended a school in Cracow, but in 1874 he fulfilled his ambition to go to sea, signing up as a crew member on a French ship. Four years later he joined an English merchant ship and in 1884 gained a Board of Trade certificate as a Master. He became a British citizen. In 1894 he left the sea to devote himself to writing, though his sea-faring life provided the setting for many of his subsequent novels. His best-known works are *Lord Jim*, 1900, *Nostromo*, 1904, and *The Nigger of the 'Narcissus'*, 1898, and his short stories amongst which is 'Typhoon', 1902.

Corelli, Marie, pen-name of Mary Mackay (1855–1924)
Stratford-upon-Avon Cemetery, Stratford-upon-Avon, Warwickshire.

Novelist. As a child she showed a precocious talent for the piano, in which she was encouraged by George Meredith, a near neighbour at her parents' home at Box Hill, Surrey. She pursued a musical career, being proficient as a singer as well as a player of the harp and the mandolin, before turning to writing. She first caught the public's attention with *Barabbas*, 1893, but it was her next novel, *The Sorrows of Satan*, 1895, which brought her great fame, being described as an 'hysterical triumph'. A deeply emotional woman, she often found herself at odds with those opposed to her thinking, especially at Stratford-on-Avon where she settled in 1901. During the Great War she was arrested for food-hoarding at the instigation of her local enemies, but she protested that the large sugar purchases were for jam-making, the jam to be distributed to the public; nonetheless she was convicted.

Cowper, William (1731–1800)
St Nicholas's Church, East Dereham, Norfolk.

Educated at Westminster School and thereafter, during the years 1750 to 1752, was articled to a solicitor. In 1754 he was called to the bar and nine years later was offered a Clerkship in the House of Commons. However, his fits of depression developed into insanity at the time and he tried to commit suicide. Though he recovered he lived in retirement and became a boarder in the house of Morley Unwin at Huntingdon, after whose death he removed with Unwin's widow, Mary, to Olney. There he came under the influence of John Newton, the evangelical curate, and contributed to the collection of *Olney Hymns* with such famous hymns as 'God moves in a mysterious way' and 'Hark, my soul! it is the Lord'. From 1779 onwards he wrote numerous poems, including 'John Gilpin', 1782, 'The Task', 1784, the sonnet 'To Mrs Unwin', 'To Mary', 'Yardley Oak', 1791, and 'On the loss of the Royal George'. In 1785 he undertook the translation of Homer, which was unsuccessfully published in 1791. The death of Mrs Unwin in 1796 left him bereft. His poetry is notable for its simple and more natural style than that of the classical Pope.

Crabbe, George (1754–1832)
St James's Church, Trowbridge, Wiltshire.

Poet whose family background could have provided inspiration for his didactic poems. He was born in Aldeburgh, Suffolk, and his father, a collector of salt duties, was a man with 'remarkable powers' of calculation. His father later became a drunkard and his meek wife lived in terror of his violence.

George studied medicine, but he had met a girl, Sarah Elmy, who led him to a liking for poetry, and one of the resulting poems, 'Hope', won a prize. Becoming a surgeon's assistant in Aldeburgh, he later set up on his own, but in 1780, after six years of struggling to make his practice pay, he decided to try his chances at literature. He set out for London with £3 and a box of surgical instruments. Sarah had wisely decided not to get married in poverty, and she sent him some money from time to time to help him in London. He had little success, although he wrote letters to several important men to ask for their patronage. The letters were all ignored except one to Edmund Burke, in which Crabbe said he would be in debtors' prison within a week unless he could pay a £14 debt. Burke saw promise in Crabbe's work and used his influence to get Crabbe admitted to holy orders, even though he had no degree or training. He was now able to marry Sarah. A chaplaincy to the Duke of Rutland followed, and later livings allowed him to achieve wealth and fame; the Archbishop of Canterbury even gave him an honorary L.L.B. So he could qualify for a post. In 1814 he took over the living at Trowbridge, where he remained until his death, much loved and mourned. His wife had died in 1813, and, though 'still sensitive to feminine charms', as his son said, he remained a widower. Some of Crabbe's works are: *The Library* (1781), *The Village* (1783), *The Newspaper* (1785) and *Tales* (1812).

Defoe, Daniel (c.1661–1731)
Bunhill Fields Burial Ground, City Road, Finsbury, London.

Novelist. The son of a London butcher by the name of John Foe; the change of name to Defoe occurring about 1703. In early life he became a hosiery merchant, but his business was unsuccessful. He took part in Monmouth's rebellion and, in 1688, joined the army of William of Orange, later William III. It was his poem, 'The True-born Englishman', a satire combating the prejudice against a king of foreign birth, that first brought him to the public's notice. The following year he published a pamphlet, 'The Shortest Way with the Dissenters,' portraying the absurdity of ecclesiastical intolerance for which he was fined, imprisoned from May to November 1703, and pilloried. During the ensuing years he published odes and pamphlets and was for a time employed as a secret agent in Scotland on behalf of the government, seeking support for the Union. During 1712 and 1713 he was briefly imprisoned for his ironical anti-Jacobite pamphlets; and in 1715 he escaped further punishment, when he libelled Lord Annesley, because of the favour of Lord Townshend for whom he worked as a secret agent and journalist. It was not until his late fifties that he published the first volume of his most famous work, *Robinson Crusoe*, 1719, the second volume, *Further Adventures*, following a few months later. The next five years saw the emergence of many of his most important novels: *Moll Flanders*, 1722, and *Roxana*, 1724, and *The Four Voyages of Captain George Roberts* in 1726. His guide book, *Tour Through the Whole Island of Great Britain*, in three volumes, appeared between 1724 and 1727. Despite his political manoeuvrings, he was a liberal, humane and moral writer.

Dickens, Charles (1812–1870)
Westminster Abbey, London, in the South Transept now known as 'Poets' Corner'.

Son of a government clerk who was imprisoned in the Marshalsea for debt. His early experiences as a labourer were similar to those depicted in his favourite novel, *David Copperfield*, 1849–1850. He received a scanty education but enough to enable him to obtain employment as a reporter of debates in the Commons for the *Morning Chronicle*. He contributed to various periodicals articles which were later published as *Sketches by Boz, Illustrative of Every-Day People*. His novels have had perhaps the largest circulation of any English works of fiction and include *Nicholas Nickleby*, 1838–1839, *Great Expectations*, 1860–1861, *A Christmas Carol*, 1843, *Dombey and Son*, 1848, *Bleak House*, 1852–1853, *Our Mutual Friend*, 1864–1865, *Martin Chuzzlewit*, 1843–1844, *Little Dorrit*, *A Tale of Two Cities*, 1859, *The Old Curiosity Shop*, 1840–1841, *Oliver Twist*, 1837–1838 and *The Pickwick Papers*, 1836. He also edited two journals, *Household Words* and *All the Year Round*, and took part in the movement for the abolition of the slave trade as well as carrying out other philanthropic works.

Donne, John (1572–1631)
St Paul's Cathedral, London. His monument by Nicholas Stone was one of two to survive the Great Fire of 1666 (see Bacon, Sir Nicholas).

Poet. Son of a London ironmonger, he was educated at both Oxford and Cambridge before entering Lincoln's Inn. He accompanied the Earl of Essex on two expeditions, to Cadiz and to the Islands, in 1596 and 1597, which he mentioned in his early poems 'The Storm' and 'The Calm'. Originally a Roman Catholic, he took Anglican orders in 1615 and for the last ten years of his life was Dean of St Paul's, frequently preaching before the King, Charles I. His best known

Charles Dickens, by A. Scheffer, 1855–6

poems are 'The Ecstasie', 'Hymn to God the Father', the sonnet to Death ('Death, be not proud') and 'Go and catch a falling star'.

Doyle, Sir Arthur Conan (1859–1930)

All Saints' Churchyard, Minstead, Hampshire, at the east end of the churchyard beside a large oak tree.

Educated at Stonyhurst and Edinburgh where he trained as a doctor and practised at Southsea from 1882 to 1890. He is chiefly remembered for his creation of the amateur detective, Sherlock Holmes, who appeared in a cycle of stories, *The Adventures of Sherlock Holmes*, 1891, *The Memoirs of Sherlock Holmes*, 1894, *The Hound of the Baskervilles*, 1902, and others. He also wrote a number of historical works, *Micah Clarke*, 1889, *The White Company*, 1891, *The Exploits of Brigadier Gerard*, 1896 and *Rodney Stone*, 1896. A fervent patriot, as was shown in his pamphlet 'The Great Boer War', 1900, he also wrote a one-act play, *Story of Waterloo*, which was enacted with Sir Henry Irving in the leading rôle.

Dryden, John (1631–1700)

Westminster Abbey, London, in the South Transept now known as 'Poets' Corner'.

Poet Laureate and dramatist. He was the acknowledged master of the heroic rhymed couplet. Educated at Westminster School under the famed Dr Busby, he was, in early life, an ardent admirer of Oliver Cromwell. After the Restoration he became an enthusiastic royalist and held several offices under the Crown. Soon after the accession of James II he became a Roman Catholic. His finest works, 'All for Love', 1678, and 'Absalom and Achitobel', 1681, probably the greatest English political satire, were published before his conversion, but his poem 'The Hind and the Panther', 1687, was written after. Following the Glorious Revolution Dryden refused to take the Oaths and therefore lost his laureateship as well as his office at the Customs which he had held since 1683. In consequence he died in poverty in Gerrard Street, Soho, but was buried with much ceremony near to Chaucer on 13 May 1700, and his monument was erected in 1720 by his friend, John Sheffield, Duke of Buckingham.

Grave of Sir Arthur Conan Doyle in All Saints' Churchyard, Minstead, Hampshire

Du Maurier, George Louis Palmella Busson (1834–1896)
St John's Churchyard, Church Row, Hampstead, London.
  Novelist. He was born in Paris where he studied art. His three novels, *Peter Ibbetson*, 1891, *Trilby*, 1894, and *The Martian*, published posthumously, recall his life as an art student in Paris and Antwerp. He contributed occasional drawings to *Punch* from 1860, before joining the staff as a regular illustrator in succession to John Leech in 1864.

Dunsany, Edward John Morteon Drax Plunkett, 18th Baron (1878–1957)
St Peter and St Paul's Churchyard, Shoreham, Kent.
  Best known for his plays and stories of fantasy and myth. His most famous stories include *The Gods of Pagana*, 1905, *Time and the Gods*, 1906 and *The Book of Wonder*, 1912. His first play, *The Glittering Gate*, 1909, was produced at the Abbey Theatre, and was followed by many others.

'Eliot, George' (Mary Ann Cross, née Evans) (1819–1880)
Highgate 'new' Cemetery, Highgate, London.
  Novelist. She broke away from her narrow religious upbringing when she met Charles Bray, a Coventry manufacturer. In 1850 she became a contributor to the *Westminster Review* and its assistant editor in 1851, a post she resigned two years later. In 1854 she published a translation of Feuerbach's *Essence of Christianity* and about that time went to live with George Henry Lewes the writer, and continued to live with him unmarried until his death in 1878. Under the influence of Lewes she began writing novels, *Amos Barton* appearing in *Blackwood's Magazine* in 1857. Of her novels, the most famous are *Middlemarch*, which was published in instalments during 1871 and 1872, *Daniel Deronda*, also published in instalments, from 1874 to 1876, *Adam Bede*, 1859, *The Mill on the Floss*, 1860, and *Silas Marner*, 1861. After the death of George Lewes she married J. W. Cross, but she never fully recovered from Lewes's death and died herself two years later in 1880.

Eliot, Thomas Stearns, 'T.S.' (1888–1965)
St Michael's Church, East Coker, Somerset. A stone commemorates him in Westminster Abbey, London, in the South Transept now known as 'Poets' Corner'.

Poet, dramatist and critic. Born in America he was educated at Harvard University, but later settled in London and took out British nationality. His principal poems are *The Waste Land*, dedicated to Ezra Pound, and published in the *Criterion* which he founded in 1922; and *The Four Quartets*, first published as a whole in New York in 1943. His *Sweeney Agonistes* in 1932 was an attempt to revive poetic drama and he continued with the celebrated *Murder in the Cathedral* in 1935. His other plays include *The Family Reunion*, 1939, and three 'comedies': *The Cocktail Party*, 1950, *The Confidential Clerk*, 1954, and *The Elder Statesman*, 1958. In 1948 he was awarded the Nobel Prize for Literature and received the Order of Merit.

Evelyn, John (1620–1706)
St John's Church, Wotton, Surrey.

Writer. Educated at Balliol College, Oxford, he published a number of works, chief among which was *Sylva*, 1664, on practical arboriculture, which exerted great influence, before producing his *Diary*, for which he is principally remembered. It describes his travels on the continent and contains brilliant portraits of his contemporaries. He was a founder member of the Royal Society.

Fitzgerald, Edward (1809–1883)
St Michael's Church, Boulge, Suffolk, where a rose tree, from a clipping of one that grew on Omar Khayyám's tomb grows at one end of the grave.

Writer who was educated at Bury St Edmunds and Trinity College, Cambridge. He is chiefly remembered for his translation from the Persian of the Rubáiyát of Omar Khayyám, which was published anonymously in 1859. He also translated into English the *Agamemnon* of Aeschylus and the two *Oedipus* tragedies of Sophocles. He also collected material for a dictionary of the *dramatis personae* of Madame de Sévigné's letters. He lived a retired life in Suffolk and was a friend of Carlyle, Thackeray and the Tennysons.

Fleming, Ian Lancaster (1908–1964)
St Andrew's churchyard, Sevenhampton, Wiltshire.

Novelist, the name of whose fictional secret agent James Bond has become almost as evocative as Sherlock Holmes. He joined the staff of Reuters news agency as a reporter after failing to get a job in the Foreign Office. He had been educated at Eton, where he was a top athlete, and at Sandhurst. In 1933 he reported the trial of some British engineers in Moscow who had been accused of espionage, and during World War II he was a commander in the British naval intelligence division. His James Bond novels became widely read round the world, and it has been said that President Kennedy's mention of them triggered their mass readership. Fleming's brother Peter was also a writer (see entry in this section). Ian Fleming was married in Jamaica, where he had a house and wrote during the winter months, 'with a golden pen on a golden isle'. He had one son.

Fleming, (Robert) Peter (1907–71)
Parish church churchyard, Nettlebed, Oxfordshire (distinctive blue slate headstone in family plot.

Travel author, eldest brother of Ian Fleming, q.v., he was educated at Eton and Oxford. After working in Wall Street during the financial crash he wrote his first travel book *Brazilian Adventure* (1933) which became widely popular as a Book of the Month Club edition. Other following books were *One's Company* (1934) and *News From Tartary* (1936), both being selected by the Book Society. At least five other books followed. As a Special Correspondent for *The Times*, of London, he covered activities in Manchuria, China, World War Two in Normandy, Greece and Burma. He contributed under the pen name Strix to the *Spectator*. His book *Operation Sea Lion* (1957) was an account of Hitler's projected invasion of England. He was awarded the O.B.E. and was High Sheriff of Oxfordshire. In 1935 he married the actress Celia Johnson; see Section 6 here.

Fletcher, John (1579–1625)
Southwark Cathedral, Southwark, London.

Dramatist. Son of the Bishop of London, he was educated at Benet College, Cambridge. From about 1606 to 1616 he collaborated with Francis Beaumont in the production of plays, but also worked with Massinger, Rowley and others on yet more dramas. He wrote not less than sixteen plays by himself, the principal being *The Faithful Shepherdess*, 1610, *The Island Princess*, 1621, *The Woman's Prize* or *The Tamer Tamed*, a comedy about the taming of Shakespeare's Petruchio, and *Rule a Wife and have a Wife*. He is believed to have collaborated with Shakespeare in *The Two Noble Kinsmen*, printed in 1634, and it is probable that he had a share in the composition of Shakespeare's *Henry VIII*.

Frankau, Pamela (1908–1967)
Hampstead Cemetery, Fortune Green Road, London.
Novelist. Chief among her works are *The Winged Horse, The Offshore Light* and *Pen to Paper* about her own writing. She was a notable journalist and spent ten years living in the United States of America.

Galsworthy, John (1867–1933)
Highgate 'new' Cemetery, Highgate, London, contains his memorial only, for his ashes were scattered over the Sussex Downs.
Educated at Harrow School and New College, Oxford. He is chiefly remembered for his series of novels about Soames Forsyte, a man with a passion for acquiring all things desirable, known as the *Forsyte Saga*. Of his plays the most notable are *The Silver Box*, 1909, *Strife*, 1909, about an industrial dispute, *Justice*, 1910, which criticized the existing prison system, *The Skin Game*, 1920 and *Loyalties*, 1922. Shortly before his death he won the Nobel Prize for Literature, but was too ill to go to Stockholm to receive it.

Gaskell, Elizabeth Cleghorn (1810–1865)
Brook Street Chapel, Knutsford, Cheshire.
Brought up by an aunt at Knutsford, Cheshire, which is the original of Cranford and of Hollingford in *Wives and Daughters*, she was married in 1832 to William Gaskell, the minister at the Cross Street Unitarian Chapel in Manchester. Her first novel, *Mary Barton*, based on the industrial strife during 1842 and 1843, was published in 1848. This brought her to the attention of Charles Dickens and thereafter she wrote much for his *Household Words* and *All the Year Round*. It was in *Household Words* that she first published the remarkable series of papers which were subsequently republished as *Cranford*, the work for which she is most famous. In 1857 she produced her great *Life of Charlotte Brontë*, although some of her statements therein were criticized and withdrawn. Other novels include *North and South*, 1855, *Ruth*, 1853, *Lois the Witch*, 1859, and *Wives and Daughters* which was left uncompleted at her death in 1865.

Gay, John (1685–1732)
Westminster Abbey, London. His monument in the South Transept was moved to the triforium when a fine mediaeval fresco was discovered beneath it. The epitaph was written by himself:

Life is a jest, and all things show it;
I thought so once, and now I know it.

Poet and dramatist. Born at Barnstaple in Devon, he was apprenticed to a London mercer before becoming secretary to the Duchess
of Monmouth from 1712 to 1714. He contributed to Steel's *Guardian*,
and his first notable poem, 'Shepherd's Week', appeared in 1714. He
wrote a number of plays but is principally remembered for his *Beggar's
Opera*, 1728, which was extremely successful. He also wrote the
libretto for Handel's *Acis and Galatea* which was performed in 1732.

Gibbon, Edward (1737–1794)
St Mary and St Andrew's Church, Fletching, East Sussex.

Historian. Educated at Westminster and Magdalen College,
Oxford, he converted to Catholicism at the age of sixteen and was
sent by his father to Lausanne. There he reconverted to Protestantism
and read widely. Returning to England in 1758, he published his *Essai
sur l'étude de la littérature* in 1761, the English version appearing in
1764. During a tour of Italy in 1764, while 'musing amid the ruins of
the Capitol', he formulated the idea of writing a *History of the Decline
and Fall of the Roman Empire*, the first volume of which appeared in
1776. In 1774 he entered Parliament and supported Lord North. The
second and third volumes of *Decline and Fall* appeared in 1781 and
the final three volumes, written whilst he was once again living in
Lausanne, appeared in 1788. Thereafter he once again returned to
England.

Gilbert, Sir William Schwenck (1836–1911)
St John the Evangelist Church, Great Stanmore, Greater London
(ashes only).

Formerly an officer in the militia and a clerk in the Education
Department, he became known as a writer of humorous verse through
his contributions to *Fun*, chief of which were his *Bab Ballads*, later
published in volume form. He wrote a number of dramatic comedies,
including *Pygmalion and Galatea* and *The Happy Land*, 1873, in
collaboration with Gilbert Arthur à Beckett. He is principally remembered for his work with Sir Arthur Sullivan in a long series of comic
operas for Richard D'Oyly Carte's opera company, he writing the
libretti, Sullivan composing the music. From 1882, after the produc-

tion of *Iolanthe*, they became known as the 'Savoy Operas', for from that date they were produced at the Savoy Theatre.

Godwin, William (1756–1836)
St Peter's Churchyard, Bournemouth, Dorset.

Political philosopher. Originally a dissenting minister but abandoned his ministry after becoming an atheist and philosopher of anarchical views. He believed that men acted according to reason, that it was impossible to be rationally persuaded and not act accordingly, that reason taught benevolence, and that therefore rational creatures could live in harmony without laws and institutions. In 1793 he published his *Enquiry concerning Political Justice*, followed by two novels, *Adventures of Caleb Williams*, 1794, and *St Leon*, 1797, which contains a pen portrait of his wife, Mary. He also wrote a life of Chaucer and a biography of his first wife, Mary Wollstonecraft.

Goldsmith, Oliver (c.1730–1774)
The Temple Church, Temple, Fleet Street, London. His monument was destroyed during the air-raid of 10 May 1941.

Son of an Irish clergyman who was himself rejected for ordination in 1751. He studied medicine at Edinburgh and Leyden, travelling in Europe during 1755 and 1756, thereafter returning to London where for a time he practised as a physician in Southwark and was a hack-writer on Griffith's *Monthly Review*. Failing to qualify for a medical appointment in India, he began writing and in 1758, under the name of James Willington, published his translation of *The Memoirs of a Protestant condemned to the Galleys of France for his Religion*. Subsequently he contributed to various magazines. In 1761 he met Dr Johnson and became a founder member of The Club. His novel, the *Vicar of Wakefield*, though not published until 1766, saved him from arrest for debt when Dr Johnson sold it on his behalf for £60. His first comedy, *The Good-natur'd Man*, was moderately successful despite being rejected by Garrick; his second, *She Stoops to Conquer*, produced at Covent Garden in 1773, was a huge success, and is the work for which he is chiefly remembered.

Gower, John (c.1325–1408)
Southwark Cathedral, Southwark, London, where there is a fine tomb towards the end of the north aisle.

Poet. A contemporary and friend of Chaucer who referred to him as 'moral Gower' because of the moral criticism contained in his poems. Of his chief works, the *Speculum Meditantis* or *Mirour de l'Omme* is written in French, the *Vox Clamantis* in Latin, and the *Confessio Amantis* in English. A Latin poem in leonine hexameters, *Cronica Tripertia*, relates the events of the last years of the reign of Richard II, including his deposition. Gower was a Kentish man of some wealth and is believed to have lived mostly in London and, during his later years, been well known at court. In 1400 he became blind and retired to the priory of St Mary Overies, Southwark, where he died.

Grahame, Kenneth (1859–1932)
St Cross's Churchyard, St Cross Road, Oxford.
Author of *The Wind in the Willows*, 1908, a children's book which brought its writer immense popularity and a fortune. He had previously written other works which had won him critical acclaim, notably *The Golden Age*, 1895, which was a study of childhood in the English countryside. This was followed by a sequel, *Dream Days*, in 1898.

Gray, Thomas (1716–1771)
St Giles's Churchyard, Stoke Poges, Buckinghamshire, where the Gray monument was erected in 1799 to the east of the church by John Penn to a design by James Wyatt. A monument stands in Westminster Abbey, London, in the South Transept, now known as 'Poets' Corner'.
Poet. Born in London and educated at Eton, with Horace Walpole, and at Peterhouse, Cambridge. He accompanied Walpole on a continental tour during 1739 to 1741, but they quarrelled and separated. They were reconciled in 1744 when Gray was living at Cambridge, at Peterhouse, removing to Pembroke College in 1756. He refused the Laureateship in 1757 but accepted the appointment of professor of history and modern languages at Cambridge in 1768. His first odes, 'On Spring', 'On a Distant Prospect of Eton College', and 'On Adversity' were published in 1742 together with the 'Sonnet on the Death of West', his friend Richard West. In 1750 he completed his famous poem, 'Elegy in a Country Churchyard', the setting for which is believed to be that churchyard of St Giles in Stoke Poges in which he is buried. It was the popularity of the 'Elegy' which led to the offer of the Laureateship.

Grave of Thomas Gray in St Giles's Churchyard, Stoke Poges, Buckinghamshire

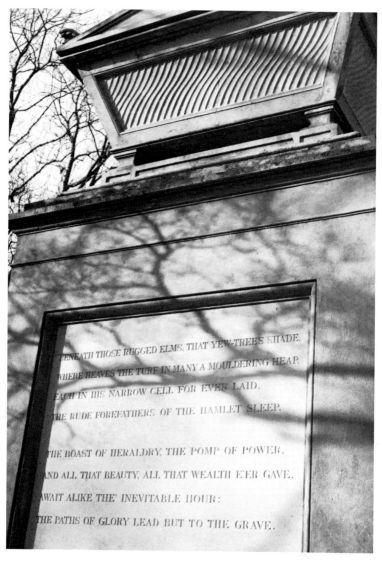

Lines from Gray's 'Elegy in a Country Churchyard' engraved on a memorial to the poet in St Giles's Church, Stoke Poges, Buckinghamshire

The grave of Thomas Hardy, St Michael's Churchyard, Stinsford, Dorset, which is inscribed 'Here lies the heart of Thomas Hardy, O.M.'

Hall, Marguerite Radclyffe (1886–1943)
Highgate 'old' Cemetery, Highgate, London.

Authoress of *The Well of Loneliness*, a novel dealing with lesbianism, a controversial theme when the book was published in the late 1920s. The novel was banned for some time. She also wrote a number of other novels but none brought her the notoriety of *The Well of Loneliness*.

Hardy, Thomas (1840–1928)
Westminster Abbey, London, ashes only in the South Transept, now known as 'Poets' Corner'; his heart is buried in the churchyard of St Michael's, Stinsford, Dorset.

Novelist and poet. His chief novels are *Far from the Madding Crowd*, 1874, *The Return of the Native*, 1878, *The Trumpet-Major*, 1880, *The Mayor of Casterbridge*, 1886, *Tess of the D'Urbervilles*, 1891, and *Jude the Obscure*, 1896. Of his poetry, the best known is that in the epic drama *The Dynasts*, 1904–1908, *Wessex Poems* and *Poems Past and Present*. He was born at Upper Bockhampton near Dorchester, the son of a builder, and started his working life as an architectural assistant in London, before returning to his native Dorset to write. The underlying theme of much of Hardy's writing, of many of the novels, is the struggle of man against the force, neutral and indifferent to his sufferings as Hardy conceives it, that rules the world; or, in another aspect, the ironies and disappointments of life and love. He was awarded the Order of Merit.

Harte, Francis Bret (1836–1902)
St Peter's Churchyard, Frimley, Surrey.

Short-story writer born at Albany in New York. At eighteen he went to California where he saw something of the mining life. Worked on various journals in San Francisco, submitting his short stories which made him famous: 'The Luck of the Roaring Camp', 1868, 'Tennessee's Partner' and 'The Outcasts of Poker Flat' which appeared in *The Luck of the Roaring Camp and Other Sketches* in 1870. From 1878–1880 he was the American consul at Crefeld in Germany, and from 1880 to 1885 at Glasgow. Thereafter he settled in England where he died.

Hazlitt, William (1778–1830)
St Anne's Churchyard, Dean Street, Soho, London.

Essayist and critic. His chief writings divide themselves into three categories: 1 – those of art and drama including the pleasant *Notes on a Journey through France and Italy*, 1826, and *A View of the English State*, 1818–1821; 2 – the essays on miscellaneous subjects which contain some of his best work, 'The Feeling of Immortality in Youth', 'Going on a Journey' and 'Going to a fight'; and 3 – the essays in literary criticism which many believe are his chief claim to fame, 'Characters of Shakespeare's Plays', 1817–1818, 'Lectures on the English Poets', 1818–1819, 'English Comic Writers', 1819, 'Dramatic Literature of the Age of Elizabeth', 1820, and 'Table Talk, or Original Essays on Men and Manners', 1821–1822. He was a quarrelsome and unamiable man.

Henty, George Alfred (1832–1902)
Brompton Cemetery, West Brompton, London.

Writer of boys' stories. After leaving Cambridge without a degree he volunteered for the Crimean War, and his letters describing the

William Hazlitt, by William Bewick, 1825

siege of Sebastopol were printed in the *Morning Advertiser*. He became a journalist for the *Standard*, volunteering as a war correspondent during the Austro-Italian war of 1866, and accompanied Garibaldi in his Tirolese Campaign. In middle life he edited the magazine for boys called the *Union Jack*, becoming its mainstay and contributing several serials in succession. They so pleased their public that they were subsequently published in book form. Altogether he wrote about eighty such works.

Hewlett, Maurice Henry (1861–1923)

All Saints' Church, Broad Chalke, Wiltshire. There is a brass to him on the south wall inside the church, but his grave is on private property; that of a local farm.

Novelist, probably of Huguenot refugee origins. His father, a civil servant, was keeper of his Majesty's revenue records, an appointment to which his son succeeded after being called to the bar by the Inner Temple. Born at Weybridge, he attended Sevenoaks grammar school and the International College at Isleworth. His first book, *The Forest Lovers* (1898), gained him great and instant fame, which he himself thought totally out of proportion with its cause, a mere romantic novel. Nevertheless he wrote two more: *The Life and Death of Richard Yea-and-Nay* (1900) and *The Queen's Quair* (1904). He followed these with both Regency and contemporary stories; one such to be noted was *Rest Harrow* (1910). He is held to have been 'in the main poet and essayist', and *Song of the Plow*, a long poem written in 1916, is called his greatest work. In 1921 *Wiltshire Essays* was published, which is held typical of his side writings. He said of himself: 'I may be a good poet or a bad one; but I am a poet of sorts.'

Hollis, Maurice Christopher (1902–1977)

St Andrew's Parish Church, Mells, Somerset, one of three low head-stones with Sassoon and Knox (whom see).

Best known as an author, he was also a Conservative MP for Devizes, Wiltshire, who went against his party's views at the time as an abolitionist of capital punishment. He was a brother of Sir Roger Hollis (d.1973) who became a controversial figure as Director General of MI5, Britain's security service.

Hollis, Thomas (1720–1774)

A field in Corscombe, Dorset. On his own instructions he was buried 10 feet deep in his field, which was then to be ploughed over, in a completely unmarked location.

Born in London, his great-uncle having been the benefactor of Harvard College in America, Thomas also supported important causes and influential libraries throughout the world, including Harvard, Berne and Zurich. He was member of Lincoln's Inn and an MP but regarded as an atheist by the church. He was a distinguished editor of Toland's *Life of Milton* (1761), Wallis's *English Grammar*, Locke's *Letters Concerning Toleration* (both in 1765) and seven other important works including not the least Algernon Sidney's works (1772), his last book. One of his eccentricities was that he named his farms and fields after famous patriots of history he felt should be honoured. A farm gate here can still be seen with 'Milton' on it.

Holtby, Winifred (1898–1935)
All Saints' Church, Rudston, East Yorkshire.
    Novelist who is principally remembered for her novel, *South Riding*, which was not published until the year of her death. A close friend of the writer Vera Brittain for whom the latter wrote the celebrated *Testament of Friendship: The Story of Winifred Holtby*.

'Hope, Anthony' (Sir Anthony Hope Hawkins) (1863–1933)
St Mary and St Nicholas's Churchyard, Leatherhead, Surrey.
    Novelist. Wrote *The Prisoner of Zenda*, 1894, and *Rupert of Hentzau*, 1898, as well as *The Dolly Dialogues*, 1894, and other novels and plays. He was knighted in 1918 for his services to the Ministry of Information during the Great War.

Housman, Alfred Edward, 'A.E.'(1859–1936)
St Lawrence's Church, Ludlow, Shropshire where his ashes lie beneath the north wall.
    Poet. A distinguished classical scholar, he is remembered for his two volumes of lyrics, remarkable for their simplicity and economy of words: *A Shropshire Lad*, 1869, and *Last Poems*, 1922.

Huxley, Aldous Leonard (1894–1963)
Compton Cemetery, Compton, Surrey.
    Novelist and essayist. He settled in California in the late 1930s where he remained until his death. His best-known novels are *Crome Yellow*, 1921, *Antic Hay*, 1923, *Point Counterpoint*, 1928, *Brave New World*, 1932, and *Eyeless in Gaza*, 1936. His essays include 'The Olive Tree', 1936, and 'Ape and Essence', 1948.

Jefferies, John Richard (1848–1887)
Broadwater Cemetery, Worthing, Sussex.

Novelist and naturalist who, born at Coate Farm near Swindon, got his beginnings at the *North Wilts Herald*. At 16 he ran away with a friend, intending to walk to Moscow, but they decided that language difficulties would debar that, so they elected to try America instead. When they ran out of money at Liverpool they returned to Swindon. Some of his first novels were *The Scarlet Shawl*, *Restless Human Hearts* and *The World's End*. His later novels of country life brought him enduring fame; *Greene Ferne Farm* and *Amaryllis at the Fair* (1888 and 1887 respectively) are full of his naturalist descriptions. One of his works, *After London* (1885), has a remarkably present-day theme: the inhabitants of London have fled, leaving a poisonous lake that is now the city, while wild beasts and a malign race of dwarfs occupy most of England.

Jerome, Jennie, Lady Randolph Churchill (d.1921)
St Martin's Church, Bladon, Oxfordshire.

Married to Lord Randolph Churchill, the High Tory politician, she was the mother of Sir Winston Churchill. An American by birth, she became a leader of London society at the turn of the century. In 1908 she published her *Reminiscences*, which was followed by two plays, *Borrowed Plumes* in 1909 and *The Bill* in 1912.

Jerome, Jerome Klapka (1859–1927)
St Mary's Churchyard, Ewelme, Oxfordshire.

Novelist and playwright. His most famous work was the celebrated *Three Men in a Boat* which appeared with *Idle Thoughts of an Idle Fellow* in 1889. His play *The Passing of the Third Floor Back* in 1908 brought him fame as a dramatist. In 1892 he founded, with others, *The Idler*, a successful monthly magazine.

Johnson, Samuel (1709–1784)
Westminster Abbey, London, in the South Transept, now known as 'Poets' Corner'.

Lexicographer and critic. Born at Lichfield and attended the local grammar school before going up to Pembroke College, Oxford. After an unsuccessful attempt at teaching, in 1737 he went to London accompanied by his pupil, David Garrick, in search of a career. His success was much slower than that of Garrick. His chief works are the

Grave of Jerome K. Jerome, St Mary's Churchyard, Ewelme, Oxfordshire

Samuel Johnson, by Barry

Gravestone of Ben Jonson in Westminster Abbey, London, in 'Poets' Corner'. His name was incorrectly spelled when the stone was renewed great *Dictionary of the English Language*, 1756, and the *Lives of the Poets*, 1779–1781. In 1750 he started the *Rambler*, a periodical written almost entirely by himself, which for two years appeared twice weekly. In 1764, together with Goldsmith, Burke and Reynolds, he founded The Club, later known as the Literary Club.

Jonson, Ben (c.1572–1637)
Westminster Abbey, London, in the north aisle of the Nave. His monument is in the South Transept, now known as 'Poets' Corner'. The tradition that he was buried upright was confirmed in the nineteenth century, in the course of digging a nearby grave. The inscription 'O rare Ben Jonson' was cut on his gravestone at the charge of Jack Young, who paid the mason eighteen pence for his work.

Dramatist and poet. He was educated at Westminster School under Camden, and was a friend of Shakespeare and Bacon. He was a tutor to the son of Sir Walter Raleigh and in 1619 became Poet Laureate. Of his many plays, the most celebrated are *Volpone, The Alchemist, Every Man in his Humour* which, when first performed at the Globe in 1598, had Shakespeare among the cast, and *Bartholomew Fair*.

Kingsley, Charles (1819–1875)
St Mary's Church, Eversley, Hampshire, where the north aisle, erected in 1876, was built as a memorial to Kingsley, who was vicar from 1844 to 1875.

Novelist. Born at Holne in Devon, he was educated at King's College, London and Magdalene College, Cambridge. He took holy orders and became the vicar of St Mary's in Eversley in 1844, holding the living there for the rest of his life. He was Professor of Modern History at Cambridge from 1860 to 1869 and thereafter held canonries at Chester and Westminster. He was an ardent social reformer, contributing, over the signature 'Parson Lot', to the *Politics of the People* in 1848 and to the *Christian Socialist* from 1850 to 1851. His principal novels were *Westward Ho!*, 1855, *The Water Babies*, 1863, and *Hereward the Wake*, 1865. He also published numerous sermons, remarkable not only for their style but for the broad spirit of humanity they display.

Kipling, Rudyard (1865–1936)
Westminster Abbey, London, in the South Transept now known as 'Poets' Corner'.

Writer and poet. Born in Bombay, his voluminous output of short stories mainly concern the British Empire and India in particular. His novels include *The Jungle Books*, 1894 and 1895, *Kim*, 1901, *Just So Stories*, 1902, *Stalky & Co.*, 1899, *Puck of Pook's Hill*, 1906, and *Rewards and Fairies*, 1910. Of his poems, the best known are *Departmental Ditties*, 1886, and *Barrack-Room Ballads*, 1892. He was awarded the Nobel Prize for Literature in 1907.

Lamb, Charles (1775–1834)
All Saints' Churchyard, Edmonton, Greater London, where his tombstone is a paved enclosure south-west of the church.

Essayist and poet. Educated at Christ's Hospital where he formed an enduring friendship with S. T. Coleridge, he found employment at the age of seventeen in the East India House, remaining there until 1825. In 1796 his sister, Mary Ann, killed their mother in a fit of insanity, and Lamb undertook to look after her to avoid her commitment to an asylum. She was subject to periodic bouts of madness and during 1795 and 1796 Lamb, himself, was briefly mentally deranged. His most famous work was the series of miscellaneous essays entitled *Essays of Elia*, which were published separately in volume form in 1823, the second appearing in 1833. Of his poems, the best known are 'Old Familiar Faces', the lyric ballad 'Hester', 1803, and the elegy 'On an Infant dying as soon as born', 1827.

Lawrence, Thomas Edward, 'Lawrence of Arabia' (1888–1935)
St Nicholas's Church, Moreton, Dorset.

He was educated at Jesus College, Oxford, became an archaeologist and travelled and excavated in Syria. During the Great War he was one of the British officers sent to help the Sheriff of Mecca in his rebellion against the Turkish Sultan. He gained great influence with the Arabs and entered Damascus with the leading Arab forces in 1918. He recalled his experiences in his celebrated *Seven Pillars of Wisdom*, which was privately printed for limited circulation in 1926, it not being commercially published until 1935. After the War he sought anonymity by joining the Royal Air Force as an aircraftman, taking the

Grave of Charles Kingsley, St Mary's Church, Eversley, Hampshire

'Lawrence of Arabia' grave, Moreton, Dorset

name of Ross, but his identity was discovered a few months later and he was forced to resign. He then joined the Tank Corps as Private T. E. Shaw, but he hated the army as much as he loved the air force and eventually was able to rejoin the Royal Air Force with the help of the Air Chief of Staff, Sir Hugh, later Lord, Trenchard. He was killed in a motor-cycle accident in Dorset.

Lemon, Mark (1809–1870)
St Margaret's Church, Ifield, near Crawley, Sussex.

A founder and first joint-editor of *Punch*, of which he was later sole editor. He also published farces, melodramas and operas, as well as contributing to *Household Words* and other periodicals. His eight-year-old daughter, Kate, was reputed to be Sir John Tenniel's model for Alice when he was illustrating Lewis Carroll's *Alice Through the Looking-glass*.

Lewis, Cecil Day (1904–1972)
St Michael's Churchyard, Stinsford, Dorset.

Poet Laureate. Born in Ireland, he was educated at Wadham College, Oxford, where he became associated with a group of young Left-wing poets, which included W. H. Auden. He became a teacher and a member of the Communist Party, his early poems reflecting his political affiliation. Later, under the infuence of Thomas Hardy, his poetry turned to more personal and pastoral themes. He also wrote several detective stories under the pseudonym of Nicholas Blake. From 1951 to 1956 he was Professor of Poetry at Oxford, and was appointed Poet Laureate in 1968.

Lewis, Clive Staples (1898–1963)
Heading Quarry churchyard, Oxford, Oxfordshire.

Writer who was much revered for his ability to bring an understanding of Christianity as he saw it to readers. He has also been described as a medievalist. His book *The Screwtape Letters* (1942) made his name familiar to a wide number of persons for its idealistic and gentle satire concerning Christian concerns. Belfast born he became Professor of Renaissance English at Cambridge. He was awarded the Hawthorne Prize for his *Allegory of Love* (1936) and one of his children's books *The Last Battle* earned him the Carnegie Prize in 1957. *The Problem of Pain* (1940),

Beyond Personality (1944), *Out of the Silent Planet* (1938), *Perelandra* (1943), the last two science fiction, were some others of his books.

Macaulay, Thomas Babington, 1st Baron (1800–1859)
Westminster Abbey, London, in the South Transept now known as 'Poets' Corner', at the foot of Addison's statue.

Historian and politician. Entered Parliament as Whig Member for Calne in 1830 and for Leeds in 1831. He held many offices including that of Secretary for War, 1839–1841, and Paymaster of the Forces, 1846–1847. His *History of England* appeared first in 1849, volumes one and two, the final two in 1855. He published a collection of his essays in 1843 and his 'Lays of Ancient Rome' in 1842, which was an attempt to reconstruct the lost ballad-poetry of Rome out of which its traditional history was thought to have grown.

Malory, Sir Thomas (d.1471)
Christ Church, Newgate Street, London. The original church was replaced by Sir Christopher Wren's between 1677 and 1691, but this was destroyed in an air-raid during 1940. Only the steeple of Wren's church now remains, the burial ground being laid out as a garden.

Identified by E. Vinaver with Sir Thomas Malory, Knight of Newbold Revel in Warwickshire and Winwick in Northamptonshire. A Member of Parliament in 1456, he is thought to have sided with Warwick the King-maker and joined the Lancastrians. Three 'prayers for deliverance' in his manuscript suggest that he wrote his celebrated *Le Morte d'Arthur* whilst in prison.

Marlowe, Christopher (1564–1593)
St Nicholas's Church, Deptford, London. The west wall records Marlowe's death in a tavern brawl nearby.

Poet and dramatist. Son of a Canterbury shoemaker, he was educated at King's School, Canterbury and Corpus Christi College, Cambridge. He joined the Earl of Nottingham's theatrical company, which produced most of his plays. His most famous dramas are *Tamburlaine*, c.1587, *Dr Faustus, The Jew of Malta*, after 1588, and *Edward II*, c.1593. He is believed to have collaborated with Shakespeare on *Titus Andronicus* and *Henry VI*. He translated Ovid's 'Amores' and paraphrased part of Musaeus's 'Hero and Leander'. He

Grave of Cecil Day-Lewis, St Michael's Churchyard, Stinsford, Dorset is thought to have been a government agent and that his death by the hand of Ingram Frisar had political complications.

Marryat, Frederick (1792–1848)

St Andrew and St Mary's Churchyard, Langham, Norfolk.

Novelist. A captain in the Royal Navy in which he served with distinction, he wrote a number of novels of sea-life of which the best-known are *Frank Mildmay*, 1829, *Peter Simple*, 1834, *Jacob Faithful*, 1834, *Mr Midshipman Easy*, 1836, *Masterman Ready*, 1841, and *The Children of the New Forest*, 1842. He spent the years 1837 to 1839 in Canada and the United States of America, publishing his *Diary in America* on his return, which contained an unflattering account of American manners.

Marvell, Andrew (1621–1678)

St Giles-in-the-Fields, St Giles High Street, London.

Poet and satirist. Educated at the Hull Grammar School and Trinity College, Cambridge. He was tutor to the daughter of Lord Fairfax and later to Cromwell's ward, William Dutton. In 1657 he became Milton's assistant in the Latin Secretaryship to the Council. He wrote several poems in Cromwell's honour, including the 'Horatian Ode upon Cromwell's Return from Ireland', and the elegy upon his death. After the Restoration he entered Parliament and became a violent politician, writing biting satires and pamphlets on Charles II's ministers and later the King. His principal verse satire is the 'Last Instructions to a Painter' on the subject of the Dutch War. Marvell vigorously defended Milton and wrote lines in praise of *Paradise Lost*, which were included in the poem's second edition. From 1660 to 1678 he wrote a series of newsletters to his constituents at Hull, which are of historical importance. Most of his poems were not published until after 1681, the satires not until 1689 after the Revolution.

Masefield, John (1878–1967)

Westminster Abbey, London, in the South Transept now known as 'Poets' Corner'.

Poet, novelist and dramatist. He ran away to sea and made his way to America where he did various menial jobs to earn his living. When he returned to England he joined the staff of the *Manchester Guardian*. During the years 1900 to 1910 he wrote continuously, publishing the *Salt-Water Ballads* in 1902 which included the famous poem, 'I must go down to the sea again'; *Ballads and Poems*, 1910; collection of short stories, *A Mainsail Haul*, 1905, and *A Tarpaulin Muster*, 1907; plays, *The Tragedy of Pompey the Great*, 1910 and *The Tragedy of Nan*, 1909; and essays. His remarkable poem 'The Everlasting Mercy', about the conversion of the ruffianly Saul Kane, was published in 1911. His novels include *Captain Margaret*, 1908, *Odtaa*, 1926, and *The Bird of Dawning*, 1933. He was appointed Poet Laureate in 1930, and was also awarded the Order of Merit.

Maugham, William Somerset (1874–1965)
Ashes scattered near the Maugham Library, King's School, Canterbury, Kent.

Novelist, short-story writer and dramatist. His principal novels were *Of Human Bondage*, 1915, *The Moon and Sixpence*, 1919, *Cakes and Ale*, 1930, *The Razor's Edge*, 1944. Of his plays, *East of Suez*, 1922, *The Circle*, 1921, *The Constant Wife*, 1927 and *For Services Rendered*, 1932, are perhaps the best known. His short stories, several of which were dramatized, include 'Ashenden', 1928, 'The Trembling of a Leaf', 1921, and 'On a Chinese Screen', 1923. For many years he lived in the South of France, where he died.

Meredith, George (1828–1909)
Dorking Cemetery, Dorking, Surrey.

Novelist and poet. After being articled to a solicitor in London he turned to journalism, contributing to *Household Words* and *Chamber's Journal*. In 1849 he married the daughter of Thomas Love Peacock but the marriage was not a success for she left him in 1858. In 1864 he married Marie Vulliamy and they lived at Flint Cottage, facing Box Hill in Surrey. His most famous novel was perhaps *Diana of the Crossways* which appeared in 1885 and brought him a popularity that his previous novels, including *The Ordeal of Richard Feverel*, 1859, and *The Adventures of Harry Richmond*, 1871, had not. He was also a considerable poet, publishing many volumes of verse.

Milton, John (1608–1674)
St Giles' Church without Cripplegate, London Wall, London.

Educated at St Paul's School, London and Christ's College, Cambridge. Whilst at Cambridge he wrote the poems 'On the Death of a Fair Infant', 1625, and 'At a Vacation Exercise', 1627. After Cambridge he lived with his father at Horton in Buckinghamshire where he

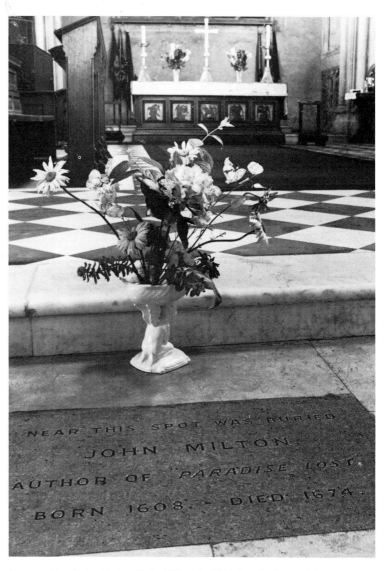

Stone marking the burial site of John Milton, St Giles' Church without Cripplegate London Wall, London composed 'L'Allegro' and 'Il Penseroso' in 1632, 'Arcades', c.1633, and 'Comus', 1634. In 1637 he produced 'Lycidas' and thereafter wrote little poetry during the next twenty years until he began the composition of 'Paradise Lost'. In 1642 he married Mary Powell, the daughter of Royalist parents, and when she did not return to him after a visit to her parents he published his notorious pamphlets on the 'doctrine and discipline of divorce'. However, his wife returned in 1645. After the execution of the King, Charles I, in January 1649 he published the 'Tenure of Kings and Magistrates' and was appointed Latin Secretary to the new Council of State. Owing to his increasing blindness he was assisted in his duties by, among others, Andrew Marvell. His first wife died in 1652 and four years later he married Catharine Woodcock, who died two years later. After the Restoration he lost both his post and his freedom, for he was briefly arrested. He was fined but released. In 1662 he married his third wife, Elizabeth Minshull, and lived with her in Bunhill Row. Aubrey believed that 'Paradise Lost' was completed in 1663 but the agreement for the copyright was not signed until 1667. 'Paradise Regained' and 'Samson Agonistes' were published together in 1671. His most famous Latin poems are 'Epitaphium Damonis', 1639, on the death of his friend, Charles Diodati, and the address to 'Mansus'. He died from gout.

Mitford, The Hon Nancy Freeman (1907–1973)
St Mary's Churchyard, Swinbrook, Oxfordshire.

Novelist and biographer. Daughter of Lord Redesdale, she achieved great popularity with her satirical novels about aristocratic life and romance, *Love in a Cold Climate*, 1949, *The Pursuit of Love*, 1945, *The Blessing* and *Don't Tell Alfred*. She was a considerable biographer, writing *The Sun King* about Louis XIV of France, *Madame de Pompadour*, *Voltaire in Love*, *The Stanleys of Alderley* and *Frederick the Great*. She also wrote a most witty enquiry into the identifiable characteristics of the English aristocracy entitled *Noblesse Oblige*. For many years she lived just outside Paris at St Cloud.

Mitford, William (1744–1827)
St Catherine's Churchyard, Exbury, Hampshire; remains translated from the Mitford vault in the eastern wall to the churchyard when church was lengthened c.1907.

A historian who knew the Utilitarian philosopher Jeremy Bentham at Oxford, and Edward Gibbon, who had been a brother officer in the South

Hampshire Militia. It is said of Mitford that at Queen's College, Oxford he was distinguished by his good looks and physical strength. He did not study much, either at university or at the Middle Temple as a law student, never practising law, and when he was 17 years old he succeeded to the property at Exbury. Here it was that Gibbon, the historian of Rome, suggested that Mitford write a history of Greece. He could read Greek well and had made a hobby of studying that country's history. The Greek history he wrote became extremely popular, especially among those who favoured his attempts to show that the French Revolutionary visionary ideas of the time, based on Greek democracy, were impracticable. Other works included an *Essay on the Harmony of Language* (1774), an essay on the Corn Laws (1791), contending that England could be self-sufficient in wheat, and a *Review of the Early History of the Arabs* (1816). He is commemorated by a tablet in the church on the north wall of the nave. Nancy Mitford (1904–1973), the authoress, was descended from his younger brother, Lord Redesdale.

Moore, Thomas (1779–1852)

St Nicholas' Churchyard, Bromham, Wiltshire; under a large Celtic cross.

Irish poet, born in Dublin of a wine merchant, he became noted for his wit and literary abilities as a Trinity College, Dublin, student. In London his singing and playing ability brought him great popularity. He achieved fame and money with his *Irish Melodies*, for which over nearly thirty years he received more than £12,000. The story is told of him sitting with Byron on the banks of the Thames discussing fame. From the river came the voices of boaters singing Moore's popular songs, such as 'The Harp that once Through Tara's Halls' and 'She Wore a Wreath of Roses'; Byron said to Moore: 'That, is fame.' Moore now lived with his actress wife near Lord Lansdowne, his friend, whose Bowood House was near Bromham. Earlier, his success had induced Longman's to pay him £3,000 for a poem he had not even written at the time. It turned out to be *Lalla Rookh*, which was about the East, a subject made fashionable by Byron. Around 1815 Moore's *National Airs and Sacred Songs* were adapted to music and became as popular as his *Irish Melodies*. They included 'Oft in the Stilly Night' and 'Sound the Loud Timbrel'. After Byron died, Moore was asked to write his biography from the memoirs that Byron had given him, but Moore had burnt them. To get out of debt later, however, he wrote a life of Byron. Moore's last work, *The History of Ireland*, turned out to be such an exhausting and arduous task, needing four volumes to complete, that he could not even write a word of the preface and at times seemed to be reduced to a condition of 'little better than imbecility', aggravated no doubt by the deaths of five of his children. Moore was an 'amiable, generous, and affectionate' man who, rather than see his wife spurned by London society, for which she had neither the wit nor desire, had moved to Bromham to live in Sloperton Cottage. She died in 1865 and was buried in his grave.

Morris, William (1834–1896)
St George's churchyard, Cotswold-style gravestone, Kelmscott, Oxfordshire.

As a poet, author of prose romances, founder of both a publishing house and a firm of house decorators, his first intentions were to take holy orders. He was educated at Marlborough and Exeter College, Oxford. Through the poet Rossetti Morris turned to painting and handicrafts, which in turn gave him eventually an aversion to the growing technology, mass production and capitalism of the Victorian era. He became attracted to socialism. He was a typical Utopian, organising the Socialist League and also the Arts and Crafts Societies through which he was able to promote his socialism to the mostly manual workers of the Societies. *The Dream of John Ball* in 1888 was one of two romances he wrote as socialist propaganda. Other works of a more realistic nature followed, including *The House of Wolfings*, *The Roots of Mountains*, *The Story of the Glittering Plain*, all written between 1889 and 1891. His first volume of poetry *The Defence of Guinevere* had appeared in 1858. He established the Kelmscott Press at Hammersmith in 1890 where he published his own works and assorted reprints of classical works, including his own earlier translations of the Aeneid and the Odyssey. Margaret Grennan epitomized him as a 'Mediaevalist and Revolutionary' in her 1945 book.

Mulock, Dinah Maria, Mrs Craik (1826–1887)
Keston Churchyard, Keston, Kent, near hedge border and tall Celtic cross.

Novelist whose best-known work was *John Halifax, Gentleman*, 1857, which placed her in the front rank of the day's women novelists. Her other novels never commanded the great respect of the former but *A Life for a Life* brought her some financial success. She wrote many children's tales and some short stories as well as poems. In 1864 she married G. L. Craik, a partner in the firm of Macmillan & Co.

'Orwell, George', Eric Blair (1903–1950)
All Saints' Churchyard, Sutton Courtenay, Oxfordshire.

Satirical novelist. Born in Bengal, he was educated at Eton College. From 1922 to 1927 he served with the Indian Imperial Police in Burma, and his experiences are the basis for his first novel, *Burmese Days*, 1934. Later he returned to Europe, undertaking a series of ill-paid jobs in Paris and London which inspired *Down and Out in Paris and London*, 1933. He fought for the Republicans in the Spanish Civil War and his *Homage to Catalonia*, 1938, is a biographical record of that war. A democratic Socialist with a dislike for totalitarianism which brought a disillusion with the aims and methods of Communism, he wrote two satirical political novels, *Animal Farm*, 1945, and *Nineteen Eighty Four*, 1949, reflecting his views, which brought him great popularity. He wrote a number of essays and studies, such as *The Road to Wigan Pier*, 1937, about unemployment.

Palgrave, Francis Turner (1824–1897)
Barnes Cemetery, Barnes, Greater London.

Educated at Charterhouse and Balliol College, Oxford. A close friend of Tennyson, he is chiefly remembered for his anthology, *The Golden Treasury of Songs and Lyrics*, 1861. He was himself a poet, publishing *The Visions of England* which was perhaps his best sole work. From 1885 to 1895 he was Professor of Poetry at Oxford.

Parnell, Thomas (1679–1718)
Holy Trinity Church, Chester, Cheshire.

Irish poet who coined the phrase 'Pretty Fanny's Way' which denotes a perverse or annoying habit regarded with tolerance by the friends of the person guilty of it. It appears in his 'Elegy to an Old Beauty':

And all that's madly wild, or oddly gay
We call it only pretty Fanny's way.

His works were published posthumously by Pope and include 'The Night Piece on Death', 'The Hymn to Contentment' and 'The Hermit'. He died at Chester on his way home to Ireland.

Pepys, Samuel (1633–1703)
St Olave's Church, Hart Street, City of London, beside the communion table alongside his wife Elizabeth. The bust he erected to his wife after her death in 1669 records that she bore no children because she could bear none worthy of herself.

Diarist. Educated at St Paul's School, London and at Trinity Hall and Magdalene College, Cambridge, he entered the household of his father's cousin, Sir Edward Montagu, later the Earl of Sandwich, under whose patronage he rose. He held many government appointments, though lost them briefly when he was committed to the Tower of London on suspicion of complicity in the 'Popish Plot' of 1679. He was soon released and regained his post of Secretary to the Admiralty in 1684. His famous *Diary* opens on 1 January 1660 and for nine years, until failing eyesight forced its closure on 31 May 1669, he kept a detailed record of his own life and times, not only revealing the author's own lovable nature but portraying a vivid picture of contemporary everyday life, of the administration of the navy, and of the ways of the court.

Plath, Sylvia (1932–1963)
St Thomas's Churchyard, Heptonstall, Hebden Bridge, West Yorkshire.

American-born poet, born in Boston, Massachusetts, who married Poet Laureate Ted Hughes in 1956 after graduating from college in America. Her poems and writings have been considered as reflecting a disturbed mind, for she seemed obsessed with disgust for the natural functions of the human body, including childbirth. She wrote an autobiographical novel *The Bell Jar* (1963), and her collected poems, *The Colossus* (1960) and others which attracted a Pulitzer Prize in 1982, were more successful after her death. Her poems were popular with the feminist movement. Her poem *Daddy*, about her love–hate relationship with her father, was written just before her suicide.

Pope, Alexander (1688–1744)
St Mary's Church, Twickenham, Greater London, where a monument was erected in 1761 bearing the inscription, 'To one who would not be buried in Westminster Abbey'. Pope is reputed to haunt the church following the exhumation of his skull which had been purchased for phrenological examination.

Poet and essayist. Largely self-taught, he showed precocious met-

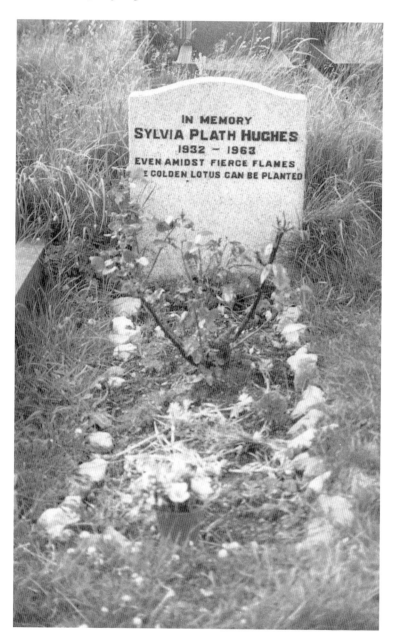

Sylvia Plath's grave, Hebden Bridge

rical skill in his 'Pastorals' written, he claimed, when he was sixteen. His 'Essay on Criticism', written when he was only twenty-three, was published in 1711, and contains the famous and oft-quoted lines, 'To err is human, to forgive, divine' (l.525) and 'A little learning is a dang'rous thing' (l.215). Its publication brought him into association with Addison's circle which led to the publication of his 'Messiah' in the *Spectator* in 1712. He became a member of the Scriblerus Club which included Swift, Gay and Arbuthnot among its members, and in 1715 issued the first volume of his translation in heroic couplets of Homer's *Iliad*. It was regarded as one of the great poems of the age and was completed in 1720. In 1719 he bought a lease of a house in Twickenham in Middlesex where he spent the remainder of his life. In 1733 he published the first of his miscellaneous satires, 'Imitations of Horace', entitled 'Satire 1', a paraphrase of the first satire of the second book of Horace, in the form of a dialogue between the poet and William Fortescue, the lawyer. This was followed by others.

Potter, Beatrix (1866–1943)
Ashes scattered on one of her fields at Near Sawrey, Cumbria, by her shepherd Tom Storey, who promised not to reveal the spot. He died in 1988 at 90, having passed the secret on to his son, who suddenly dropped dead in 1989. No one knows now the exact spot, which is what she wanted (I am indebted to Mrs Irene Whalley of the Beatrix Potter Society for this information.-DG.)

An authoress, born in London, whose books became children's classics. She published her first two animal-story books *The Tale of Peter Rabbit* (1902) and *The Tailor of Gloucester* (1903), at her own expense. Later 23 of her animal stories were published. They were translated into many languages. She also illustrated her books with drawings and watercolours. Later she became a successful cattle breeder and landowner. Her first farmhouse, Hill Top, is owned by the National Trust, to whom she left her extensive farm properties. The small pub next to Hill Top is also a National Trust property.

Powys, John Cowper (1872–1964), Llewelyn (1884–1939),
Theodore Francis ('T.F.') (1875–1953)
Abbotsbury, Chesil Beach, ashes scattered (John Cowper); Swyre Head, near Chaldon Herring, ashes under stone monument to him by Elizabeth Muntz (Llewelyn); St Peter and Paul Church, Mappowder (Theodore Francis), all in Dorset.

Three brother novelists who had virtually a cult following in the USA. Between them they wrote scores of fiction and non-fiction books. Their reputation probably rests largely on *Wolf Solent* (1929), set in Bradford Abbas, Dorset, and *A Glastonbury Romance* (1932) by John Cowper; *Dorset and Somerset Essays*, and *Skin for Skin* (1925) by Llewelyn; *Unclay* (1931) and *Mr Weston's Good Wine* (1927), set in Chaldon Herring, Dorset, by Theodore Francis.

Priestley, John Boynton, 'J.B.' (1894–1983)
St Michael and All Angels Church, Hubberholme, Upper Wharfedale, North Yorkshire.

Novelist and playwright who was born in Bradford, Yorkshire, from which town and county he drew his characters in *The Good Companions*, which became an immediate best-selling novel in 1929. Previously, after being educated at Trinity College, Cambridge, he had produced several critical books such as *The English Comic Character* (1925) and *English Humour* (1928). His stage comedy *Laburnum Grove* (1933) was a West End success, as were his more serious plays *Dangerous Corner* (1932) and *Time and the Conways* (1937) with its theme of being able to foresee the future by dreams. With his wife Jacquetta Hawkes (1910–1989), an archaeologist, he wrote *Journey Down the Rainbow* (1955), a good-natured critique of American life. Four of his plays *Eden End* (1934), *Cornelius* (1935), *Johnson Over Jordan* (1939) and *An Inspector Calls* (1945) were graced by Sir Ralph Richardson (whom see) in their leading roles.

Prior, Matthew (1664–1721)
Westminster Abbey, London, in the South Transept known as 'Poets' Corner'.

Poet about whose Wimborne, Dorset, birthplace controversy once raged. Opinion now generally accepts that town. Traditionally he was a student at the free grammar school there but he came under the sponsorship of Lord Dorset in London and attended Westminster School and St John's College, Cambridge. He had been noticed reading *Horace* behind a public-house bar by Dorset, who discovered the boy's talent as a translator. He became not only a poet but also a diplomatist and courtier. His lyrics and epigrams brought him fame, his more serious works tending to pall.

That he repaired a hole he had burnt in Sir Walter Raleigh's *History of the World* in Wimborne Minster's chained library is proven to be a myth because the books were not placed in the library (by the Rev. William Stone) until Prior was away from Wimborne at Cambridge. He wrote his own epitaph: 'Nobles and Heralds, by your leave, Here lies what was once Matthew Prior, The son of Adam and of Eve: Can Bourbon or Nassau claim higher?' It is not, however, the one over his grave.

'Q', Sir Arthur Thomas Quiller-Couch (1863–1944)
St Nicholas's Church, Fowey, Cornwall.

Poet, novelist and critic. He became Professor of English Literature at Cambridge in 1912 and wrote many novels including *Dead Man's Rock*, 1887, *Troy Town*, 1888, and *The Splendid Spur*, 1889. He compiled *The Oxford Book of English Verse*, 1900 and 1939, *The Oxford Book of Ballads*, 1910, *The Oxford Book of Victorian Verse*, 1912 and *The Oxford Book of English Prose*, 1925. His books of criticism included *On the Art of Writing*, 1916, and *On the Art of Reading*, 1920. He died after being hit by a jeep whilst walking near his home in Cornwall.

Roget, Peter Mark (1779–1869)
St James's Churchyard, West Malvern, Hereford and Worcester.

English physician and savant. He was for twenty-two years, from 1827 to 1849, the Secretary of the Royal Society. He played a rôle in the founding of London University but is principally remembered for his *Thesaurus of English Words and Phrases*, which was published in 1852 and has run into many editions.

Ruskin, John (1819–1900)
St Andrew's Churchyard, Coniston, Cumbria. A bronze medallion portrait head commemorates Ruskin in Westminster Abbey, London, in the South Transept now known as 'Poets' Corner'.

Art critic and social theorist. As an art critic he was the greatest influence of his generation and was instrumental in promoting the Pre-Raphaelite school of painting. His *Stones of Venice*, 1851–1853, and *Modern Painters* which was begun as a defence of Turner, are masterpieces. During the 1860s his mind was concerned with economics and he began publishing essays on the subject which aroused strong opposition by their heterodoxy. He advocated a system of national education, the organization of labour, and other social reforms in these and other pamphlets. He attacked a politico-economic system based on the idea of 'economic man', actuated by no other motive than profit. Wealth, he insisted, is not the only thing worth having. His interest in social reform is reflected in his most popular work, *Sesame and Lilies*, 1865, and *The Crown of Wild Olive*, 1866. He inherited a large fortune which he distributed chiefly on philanthropic ventures and in 1871 he founded the Guild of St George on the principles that 'food can only be got out of the ground and happiness out of honesty', and that 'the highest wisdom and the highest treasure need not be costly or exclusive'. The members of the guild were to give a tithe of their fortunes to philanthropic purposes, and to these he contributed generously.

Saintsbury, George Edward Bateman (1845–1933)
Old Cemetery, Southampton, Hampshire.

Historian and literary critic. He was the author of a large number of works on English and European literature, including a *Short History of English Literature*, 1898, *Elizabethan Literature*, 1887, and *A History of Criticism*, 1900–1904. He also wrote interesting and entertaining *Notes on a Cellar Book*, 1920, *A Letter Book*, and *A Scrap Book*, 1922. He wrote several lives of, among others, Dryden, Sir Walter Scott and Matthew Arnold.

Sassoon, Siegfried (1886–1967)
St Andrew's Parish Church, Mells, Somerset, one of three low head-stones with Knox and Hollis (whom see).

Poet, novelist and biographer. Educated at Marlborough and Clare College, Cambridge, he enlisted in the first world war and won the Military Cross. His bitter war poetry attacks the hypocrisy and romanticism of the war mood. His published poems include *The Old Huntsman*, 1917, *Counterattack*, 1918, *Satirical Poems*, 1926, *The Heart's Journey*, 1928, *Vigils*, 1935, and *Collected Poems*, 1947. He wrote a number of works of semi-autobiographical fiction including *Memoirs of a Fox-Hunting Man*, 1928, *Memoirs of an Infantry Officer*, 1930, and *Sherston's Progress*, 1936, as well as a biography of George Meredith in 1948.

Sayers, Dorothy Leigh (1893–1957)
St Anne's Church, Soho, London; ashes and memorial.

Novelist and playwright who appeared first in *Clouds of Witness* (1926). Born at Oxford, she was credited with being the 'most celebrated detective-story writer since Conan Doyle' in her earlier days. She set her scenes accurately and paraded her characters with taste and style. Among other titles of her mystery stories were *Murder Must Advertise* (1933), *The Nine Tailors* (1934) and *Busman's Honeymoon* (1937), the last of that genre. Later she used Christianity as a theme for two successful plays, *The Zeal of Thy House* (1937) and *The Devil to Pay* (1939) along with a broadcast series *The Man Born to be King* (1943). She was also an essayist on the same subject, for which she was no apologist but a sincere believer. A translater of Dante's *Inferno* (1949) and *Purgatorio* (1955), her *Paradiso* was unfinished at her death.

Sewell, Anna (1820–1878)
Old Quaker Meeting House Garden, Lamas, Norfolk.

Remembered solely for her great children's classic, *Black Beauty*, the 'autobiography' of a horse, which was published a year before she died.

Shakespeare, William (1564–1616)
Holy Trinity Church, Stratford-on-Avon, Warwickshire, by the north wall of the chancel. On his gravestone are the lines:

Good friend, for Jesus' sake forebeare
To digg the dust enclosed heare;
Bleste be the man that spares thes stones,
And curst be he that moves my bones.

Whilst his bust on the wall above bears the inscription:

IVDICIO PYLIVM GENIO SOCRATEM ARTE MARONEM
TERRA TEGIT POPVLVS MAERET OLYMPVS HABET
Stay Passenger, why goest thou by so fast,
Read if thou canst, whom envious death has plast,
Within this monument Shakespeare: with whome,
Quick nature dide: whose name does deck Y_s tombe,
Far more, then cost: Seih all, Y_t he hath Writt
Leaves living art, but page, to serve his Witt.

He was educated at the free grammar school in Stratford, and it is believed that before he went to London he may have been a schoolmaster. In 1582 he married Anne Hathaway and his first child, Susannah, was baptized in 1583. In 1585 he moved to London and secured Lord Southampton as his principal patron. It is established that by September 1592 Shakespeare was both an actor and playwright. He took part in the original performance of Ben Jonson's *Every Man in his Humour* in 1598 and *Sejanus*, 1603, after which he seems to have given up acting. He had a share in the establishment of the new Globe Theatre on the Bankside in 1599. His earliest work as a dramatist, the three parts of *Henry VI*, date from 1590 to 1591. Thereafter he wrote over thirty plays, all of which have been performed throughout the world. *Henry VIII* was written during 1612 and 1613 and is believed to have been with the collaboration of John Fletcher.

Shaw, George Bernard (1856–1950)

Shaw's Corner, Ayot St Lawrence, Hertfordshire, his ashes being scattered in the garden of his home.

Irish playwright and critic. He began as a journalist, then turning to writing for the stage where his unorthodox turn of mind and distrust of conventions and accepted institutions soon revealed itself. *Man and Superman*, 1903, introduced Shaw's conception of the 'Life Force', a power that seeks to raise mankind, with their co-operation, to a higher and better existence, and he continued this doctrine in *Heartbreak House*, 1917, and *Back to Methuselah*, 1925, in which the causes of the failure of our civilisation, as demonstrated by the Great War, are examined. He became a founder member of the Fabian Society. He wrote numerous other plays including *St Joan*, 1924, *Candida*, *Mrs Warren's Profession* and the immensely popular *Pygmalion*.

Shelley, Mary Wollstonecraft (1797–1851)

St Peter's Churchyard, Bournemouth, Dorset.

Daughter of Mary Wollstonecraft and William Godwin, she became the second wife of Percy Bysshe Shelley. She was the author of *Frankenstein, or the Modern Prometheus*, 1818, *The Last Man*, 1926, about the destruction of the human race by an epidemic, *Valperga*, 1823, a mediaeval Italian romance, and the autobiographical *Lodore*, 1835.

Shelley, Percy Bysshe (1792–1822)

St Peter's Churchyard, Bournemouth, Dorset, where his heart was reinterred from its original resting place at the English Protestant Cemetery in Rome.

George Bernard Shaw (International News Photos)

Poet. Educated at Eton College and University College, Oxford. He published his first poems whilst still at Eton, namely *Zastrozzi*, and in 1810, aged eighteen, published *St Irvyne*, romances in the style of 'Monk' Lewis. He was sent down from Oxford in 1811 for circulating a pamphlet on 'The Necessity of Atheism'. That year he married Harriet Westbrook, but his wandering life brought the marriage to an end and they separated three years later. During that time he wrote *Queen Mab*. In 1814 he left England with Mary Godwin, whom he later married when the unfortunate Harriet Westbrook drowned herself in the Serpentine in London in 1816. That year he formed his friendship with Byron and Shelley and Mary spent the summer with him in Switzerland. The next few years saw a large output of his work including the composition of his great lyrical drama *Prometheus Unbound*, 1820, *The Cenci*, 1819, and a translation of Plato's *Symposium*, *Adonais*, 1821 and *Epipsychidion*, also 1821. He was drowned while sailing near Spezia, and his body was burned on the beach. Trelawny at the last moment snatched his heart, which would not burn, from the flames and gave it to Mary Shelley.

Sheridan, Richard Brinsley (1751–1816)
Westminster Abbey, London, in the South Transept now known as 'Poets' Corner'.

Parliamentary orator and dramatist. Educated at Harrow School, and, when only twenty-three, wrote his great play, *The Rivals*, which was performed at Covent Garden in 1775. He acquired David Garrick's share in the Drury Lane Theatre in 1776 and the following year produced there *A Trip to Scarborough* and *The School for Scandal*. His famous farce, *The Critic*, was performed in 1779, but his play *Pizarro*, an adaptation of Kotzebue's *The Spaniards in Peru*, was performed in 1799 and showed a decline in style. In 1780 he entered Parliament as a supporter of Charles James Fox and became famous for the eloquence of his oratory, his speech of impeachment against Warren Hastings in 1788 being particularly memorable. His new theatre in Drury Lane was destroyed by fire in 1809 and he was ruined financially, being arrested for debt in 1813. He suffered from brain disease during the last years of his life. He received a great public funeral.

Sitwell, Dame Edith (1887–1964)
St Mary's Churchyard extension, Weedon Lois, Northamptonshire. The monument is by Henry Moore and is a large tapering, upright slab, and attached to it is a square bronze plaque with two delicate hands in high relief, signifying Youth and Age.

Poet, novelist, biographer and essayist. She published a number of poems during the 1920s which exploited the musical qualities of the language. Some of them were set to music by William Walton and entitled *Façade*. Her biographical studies included that of *Alexander Pope*, 1930 and *The English Eccentrics*, 1933, and her historical novels included one on Elizabeth I and Mary, Queen of Scots entitled *The Queens and the Hive*. Her later poems developed a graver tone, in *Street Songs*, 1943, *Green Song*, 1944 and *Song of the Cold*, 1945. She was made a Dame of the British Empire in 1954.

Southey, Robert (1774–1843)
St Kentigern's Churchyard, Crosthwaite, Keswick, Cumbria, where his monument shows a recumbent white marble figure, asleep, one hand on his heart, the other holding a book.

Poet. Son of a Bristol linen-draper. He was expelled from Westminster School for a precocious essay on flogging, and went on to Balliol College, Oxford. He became friends with S. T. Coleridge and joined in his scheme for a 'pantisocratic' settlement. He married Edith Ficker, whose sister married Coleridge. He wrote an immense amount both of verse and prose, and is best known for his shorter poems, such as 'My days among the dead are past', 'The Battle of Blenheim', 'The Holy Tree', and 'The Inchcape Rock'. Of his prose works the most celebrated are his valuable *History of Brazil*, 1810–1819, *History of the Peninsular War*, 1823–1832; and he revised the old translations of Amadis of Gaul, 1803, and *Palmerin of England*, 1807, and edited Malory, 1817. He died of 'softening of the brain'.

Spenser, Edmund (c.1552–1599)
Westminster Abbey, London, in the South Transept now known as 'Poets' Corner'. The monument was erected by Ann Clifford, Countess of Dorset, Pembroke, and Montgomery, but, having fallen into decay it was replaced by an exact copy in 1778. The epitaph reads:

Heare lyes (expecting the Second comminge of our Saviour Christ Jesus) the body of Edmond Spencer the Prince of Poets in his tyme whose Divine Spirrit needs noe othir witnesse then the works which He left behinde him.

Poet. Educated at Merchant Taylors' School and Pembroke Hall, Cambridge. In his youth he wrote the 'Hymnes in honour of Love and Beautie', which reflect the Platonic influence. In 1578 he obtained a place in the household of the Earl of Leicester, Elizabeth's favourite, and there made the acquaintance of Sir Philip Sidney, with whom, and with Dyer and others, he formed a literary club called the Areopagus. He began his most famous poem, which he dedicated to Queen Elizabeth, 'The Faerie Queen'. In 1580 he was appointed secretary to Lord Grey de Wilton, Lord Deputy for Ireland. In 1586 he became one of the 'undertakers' for the settlement of Munster, and acquired Kilcolman Castle in County Cork where he reluctantly settled and occupied himself with literary work. In 1594 he married Elizabeth Boyle, celebrating the marriage in his 'Epithalamion'. In October 1598 his castle was burnt in an insurrection and he and his family – by then he had four children – fled to Cork. He died in London in financial distress at a lodging in King Street, Westminster, and the expenses of his funeral were borne by the Earl of Essex.

Stacpoole, Henry de Vere (1863–1951)
St Boniface's Church, Bonchurch, Isle of Wight.
Novelist. After qualifying as a doctor he sailed the world as a ship's physician. He was a prolific novelist, some fifty in all, but he achieved little financial success with them until his *Blue Lagoon* (1908) which, with his novel of the previous year, *The Crimson Azaleas*, proved immediately popular because of their exotic and tropical setting. The *Blue Lagoon*, reprinted twenty-three times in the next twelve years, was made into a episodic play which was put on at the Prince of Wales Theatre in London in 1920, and also filmed. He was acquainted with many of the authors of the *Yellow Book* period, including Aubrey Beardsley.

Sterne, Laurence (1713–1768)
Originally buried in the St George's burial ground in the Bayswater Road, London, but a seemingly authentic rumour says his body was disinterred and sold for dissection. A monumental stone was later erected near the site. When the burial ground was built over his

remains were removed to the churchyard of St Michael's, Coxwold, North Yorkshire, where he was vicar from 1760 to 1768.

Novelist. After leaving Jesus College, Cambridge, he was ordained and became Vicar of Sutton-in-the-Forest in 1738, remaining there until 1759. He married Elizabeth Lumley in 1741 but his philanderings caused her much distress and she became insane in 1758. He began his famous novel, *Tristram Shandy*, in 1759, volumes i and ii being published the following year. He then came to London and published the first volumes of his *Sermons of Mr Yorick*. After the publication of four more volumes of *Tristram Shandy*, it was denounced by Dr Johnson, Richardson, Horace Walpole, Goldsmith and others on moral and literary grounds. In 1760 he was granted the perpetual curacy of Coxwold in North Yorkshire in the patronage of his friend Lord Fauconberg. He travelled abroad in France and Italy during 1765 and 1766, part of which journey is described in *A Sentimental Journey*, 1768. He died of pleurisy in lodgings in Old Bond Street.

Stow, John (c.1525–1605)
St Andrew Undershaft, corner of St Mary Axe and Leadenhall Street, City of London. The monument of Derbyshire marble and alabaster in the north-east corner shows him bald-headed writing in a book at a table, flanked by square pillars richly decorated with ribbon-work, lions' heads, books and crosses. Each year, near the anniversary of his death on 5 April, the Lord Mayor of London, attended by Sheriffs, renews his quill pen and presents a copy of Stow's book to the writer of the best essay on London received that year.

Chronicler and antiquary. Formerly a tailor and a freeman of the Merchant Taylors' Company from 1547. He is chiefly remembered for *A Survey of London*, 1598 and 1603, a work invaluable for the detailed information it gives about the ancient city and its customs. He also wrote *The Woorkes of Geffrey Chaucer*, 1561, *Summarie of Englyshe Chronicles*, 1565, and *The Chronicles of England*, 1580. He occupied himself from 1560 onwards in transcribing and collecting manuscripts, spending all his money in their pursuit. He was suspected of favouring the Roman religion and was charged in 1568, 1569 and 1570 with being in possession of popish and dangerous writings, but, after examination before the ecclesiastical commission, escaped without punishment.

Swinburne, Algernon Charles (1837–1909)
St Boniface's Church, Bonchurch, Isle of Wight.

Poet. Educated at Eton and Balliol College, Oxford, he became friendly with Rossetti and his circle. His first publication, *The Queen Mother. Rosamond. Two Plays*, 1861, attracted no attention but *Atalanta in Calydon*, 1865, a drama in the classical Greek form, did. Many regard his most perfect work as *Tristram of Lyonesse*, a romantic poem in rhymed couplets, which appeared in 1882. He suffered from illness but was supported by his friend and fellow critic, Theodore Watts-Dunton, who took him to live in his house in Putney from 1879 to his death, during those thirty years exercising a devoted and tactful control over the poet.

Tennyson, Alfred, 1st Baron Tennyson (1809–1892)
Westminster Abbey, London, in the South Transept now known as 'Poets' Corner'.

Poet. Educated at home by his father, who was Rector of Somersby, and at Trinity College, Cambridge, where he became the friend of Arthur Hallam, and where he also won the Chancellor's medal for English verse in 1829, with a poem 'Timbuctoo'. He is chiefly remembered for his 'In Memoriam', commemorating the death of his friend Arthur Hallam, and for the 'Ode on the Death of the Duke of Wellington', 1854, and the 'Idylls of the King'. He became Poet Laureate in 1850 in succession to William Wordsworth. In later life he published several historical plays, some of which were produced by Sir Henry Irving. His poem, 'Crossing the Bar', was set to music by Sir Frederick Bridge and was first sung at his own funeral in the Abbey. He was made a baron by Queen Victoria in 1884.

Thackeray, William Makepeace (1811–1863)
Kensal Green Cemetery, Kensal Green, London. A monument bust by Marochetti was erected in Westminster Abbey, London, in the South Transept now known as 'Poets' Corner'.

Novelist and essayist. He was born in Calcutta but was educated in England at Charterhouse and Trinity College, Cambridge, which he left without taking a degree. He attempted the law but also gave that up and in 1833 became the proprietor of *The National Standard*, for which he wrote and drew. It had a short existence and he then went to Paris to study drawing, where he married Isabella Shawe, whilst correspondent for *The Constitutional*, which, too, failed. He returned to London in 1837 and began writing for various journals. His wife's insanity brought about a breakdown in their marriage in 1840. In 1842 he began his contributions to *Punch* where the celebrated *Snobs of England* first appeared. His most memorable novels are *Vanity Fair*, portraying the appealing Becky Sharp, 1848, *Pendennis*, 1848, *Esmond*, 1852, and *The Virginians*, 1857–1858. He retired from *Punch* in 1854 and took up the editorship of the *Cornhill* in 1860.

Thomas, Brandon (1850–1914)
Brompton Cemetery, West Brompton, London.

Actor-playwright who wrote one of the most famous comedies ever written for the English stage, *Charley's Aunt*, which was first produced in 1892. As an actor Thomas often appeared with the actress Marie Tempest.

Tolkien, John Ronald Reuel (1892–1973)
Wolvercote Cemetery, north Oxford, Oxfordshire, with his wife Edith.

Author whose books *The Hobbit* (1937) and *The Lord of the Rings* (3 vols. 1945–55) enjoyed virtually a cult following that still exists to a somewhat lesser degree. Their allegorical connection to the present world, however, persists. Born in Bloemfontein, South Africa, he was educated at King Edward VI School, Birmingham and Oxford University. From 1925 to 1959 he taught Anglo-Saxon there as a professor of English language and literature. His great interest in philology led to the publication of several studies in that field. An edition of *Gawain and the Green Knight* (1925) was followed by studies of Chaucer and *Beowulf*. For *The Hobbit* he constructed an entire language and mythology. Its plot involved a perilous journey for his character Bilbo Baggins and other dwarfs. They had to recover treasure from a dragon, Smaug. Sequels had Bilbo's nephew Frodo on a mission in Mordor, the land of darkness and evil, out to destroy a powerfully dangerous ring of treacherous conspirators. It has been considered by some that there are indeed Biblical echoes in the allegory. Tolkien died as a widower while on holiday in Bournemouth. There is a picture of his grave on the Internet along with widely linked information about him. Its U.R.L. is http://users.ox.ac.uk/~talksoc/tolkiensOxford/grave.html

Trollope, Anthony (1815–1882)
Kensal Green Cemetery, Kensal Green, London.

Novelist. His early life was made miserable by his father's debts, necessitating frequent changes of school and finally a refuge in Belgium where his mother supported the family by his writings. Trollope entered the Post Office as a clerk in 1834, and proved a valuable civil servant. His literary output was prolific and he is chiefly remembered for his Barsetshire novels, of which the first was *The Warden*, and the Palliser novels, sometimes called his political novels. Trollope regarded his presentation of Plantaganet Palliser, who became Prime Minister, and his wife Lady Glencora, as the best work of his life.

Wallace, Edgar (1875–1932)
Town Cemetery, Ferne Lane, Little Marlow, Buckinghamshire.

Mystery-story writer, journalist and playwright, he was called by his biographer Margaret Lane a 'phenomenon'. His life, from being found abandoned at nine days old and brought up by a Billingsgate, London, fish-porter to become one of England's best-known story writers, deserves such an appellation. After being a war correspondent for the *Daily Mail* during the Boer War in South Africa, in the twenties his output of, mostly, 'thrillers' involving Scotland Yard and various types of detectives was so great that 'this week's Edgar Wallace' novel became virtually an accurate description of his prolific production. His first success was *The Four Just Men* (1905); still in print. Two of his more serious works were *Sanders of the River* (1911) and *Bones* (1915), while his plays include *The Ringer* and *The Squeaker*. He died in Hollywood while working on *King Kong* of pneumonia aggravated by a long-standing diabetic condition.

Walpole, Sir Hugh Seymour (1884–1941)
St John's Churchyard, Keswick, Cumbria.

Novelist. His chief works are *Rogue Herries*, 1930, which was part of an historical sequence known as the Herries novels, *Judith Paris*, 1931, *The Fortress*, 1933, and *The Cathedral*, 1922.

Walton, Izaak (1593–1683)
Winchester Cathedral, Winchester, Hampshire.

Writer. His early years were spent as an apprentice to an ironmonger, and he carried on the trade on his own behalf in London. A friend of Donne and Sir Henry Wotton, he wrote their biographies, publishing the Donne in 1640, and the Wotton in 1651. He is chiefly known for *The Compleat Angler, or, The Contemplative Man's Recreation*, 1653, which he largely rewrote for its second edition in 1655.

Waugh, Evelyn Arthur St John (1903–1966)
St Peter and St Paul's Churchyard, Combe Florey, Somerset.
   Novelist. Famous for his satirical, sophisticated and witty novels which include *Decline and Fall*, 1928, *Vile Bodies*, 1930, *Brideshead Revisited*, 1945, *Men at Arms*, 1952, *Officers and Gentlemen*, 1955, and *The Ordeal of Gilbert Pinfold*, 1957. He also wrote a life of Edmund Campion, 1935.

West, Dame Rebecca (Mrs H. M. Andrews) (1892–1983)
Brookwood Cemetery, Brookwood, Surrey.
   Novelist and social critic, she was educated at Edinburgh and first attempted an acting career but soon turned to writing. She had a forthright style and soon became accepted as a notable novelist. Some of her books include *The Judge* (1922), *The Thinking Reed* (1936) and an outspoken work, *The Meaning of Treason* (1947), based on the Nuremberg Trials after the last war. She became a Dame of the British Empire in 1959 and in 1968 a Companion of Literature.

Wheatley, Dennis Yates (1897–1977)
Brookwood Cemetery, Brookwood, Surrey.
   Novelist whose 75 books were remarkable for their wide-ranging subjects from modern and historical adventures to satanism. The son of a wine merchant, he carried on in his father's business until failing in the financial crash of 1930, after which he turned to writing. Among his early novels were *They Found Atlantis* and *The Forbidden Territory*, which was still selling forty years later and sold a million and a half copies. It had introduced his character the Duc de Richelieu, who appeared in ten later stories. Another of his characters, Gregory Sallust, was the hero in eleven other novels. His 'black magic' book, *The Devil Rides Out* (1935), gave him a reputation, with eight of the same genre, of being an expert on the subject but was merely a measure of his literary research into such lore. During the second world war he worked with an RAF commission to deceive the enemy. In his youth he had also been a naval cadet and a Royal Artillery

Corps officer, being gassed in the trenches. His short biography of Charles II, *Old Rowley* (1933), is now virtually a classic.

Wollstonecraft, Mary (Mrs Godwin) (1759–1797)
St Peter's Churchyard, Bournemouth, Dorset.

Educational writer famous for her *Vindications of the Rights of Women*, 1792, which was a courageous attack on the conventions of the day. She had originally founded a school in Newington Green with her sister, Eliza, and then went as governess to the children of Lord Kingsborough. During her sojourn in Paris from 1793 to 1795, she became the mistress of an American, Gilbert Imlay, by whom she had a daughter, Fanny, who, years later after the death of her mother, poisoned herself for no apparent reason. Subsequently, Mary Wollstonecraft married William Godwin, the political and philosophical writer, but died bearing him a daughter, Mary, who was to become Percy Bysshe Shelley's second wife.

Woolf, Virginia (1882–1941)
Monks House, Rodmell, Sussex, where her ashes were buried in the garden.

Novelist. The daughter of Sir Leslie Stephen, she made a positive contribution to the development of fiction in this century. She experimented with the form of the novel, minimizing the importance of fact, events, and character analysis in order to concentrate on the moment-by-moment experience of living. She eliminated the author as narrator or commentator. Her principal novels were *Mrs Dalloway*, 1922, *To the Lighthouse*, 1927, *Orlando: A Biography*, 1928, *The Waves*, 1931, and *Between the Acts*, 1941. She also wrote a number of essays and other works which included *A Room of One's Own*, 1929, and *A Haunted House*, 1943. She suffered from mental illness and committed suicide by drowning. She was married to Leonard Woolf.

Wordsworth, William (1770–1850)
St Oswald's Churchyard, Grasmere, Cumbria. His monument is in Westminster Abbey, London, in the South Transept now known as 'Poets' Corner'.

Poet. Educated at the grammar school in Hawkshead and at St John's College, Cambridge. In 1790 he went on a walking tour in France, Italy and the Alps, during the height of the French Revolution which exercised a powerful influence on him. He met and fell in love with Annette Vallon, the daughter of a surgeon at Blois, and she bore him a daughter. The episode is reflected in 'Vaudracour and Julia', written in 1805. His enthusiasm for the Revolution gave way to pessimism which is also reflected in 'The Borderers' written during 1795 and 1796. In 1795 he received a legacy of £900 from his friend Raisley Calvert, and that same year saw his acquaintanceship with S. T. Coleridge which brought an enduring friendship. He married Mary Hutchinson of Penrith in 1802. He is chiefly remembered for 'The Prelude', completed in 1805 but not published until after his death, 'The White Doe of Rylstone', 1805, 'Lines written above Tintern Abbey', 1798, 'Ruth', 'Lucy Gray', 'Nutting' and 'Lucy', all written whilst at Goslar in Germany during the winter of 1798, and 'Michael', surely one of his most harmonious poems, which was written in 1800. He succeeded Southey as Poet Laureate in 1843. His prose works include the essay 'Concerning the Relations of Great Britain, Spain, and Portugal . . . as affected by the Convention of Cintra', published in 1809 as an attack on the lack of vigour shown in English policy, and 'A Description of the Scenery of the Lakes in the North of England', written as an introduction to T. Wilkinson's *Select Views in Cumberland*.

Yonge, Charlotte Mary (1823–1901)
St Matthew's Churchyard, Otterbourne, Hampshire; beside Keble memorial cross.

Novelist whose story *Le Chateau de Melville* was sold when she was only 15 years old. Her father, who had fought at the Battle of Waterloo, taught her classical languages and mathematics while tutors her French and Spanish. She was friendly with John Keble (*see* Hursley), whose parish included Otterbourne and who discovered her writing gifts and encouraged her. He also made her change some of her expressions that he and his wife thought 'coarse', such as when, in *Heartsease* (1854), she referred to the heart as a 'machine for pumping blood'. In Charlotte's first novel, *The Heir of Redclyffe* (1853), she had to substitute such words as 'jackanapes' for 'coxcomb', and no allusions to drukenness or insanity were allowed. Before its publication her family had also decided that it was not right for a woman to write commercially unless she devoted her earnings to some good cause. From her novel *The Daisy Chain* (1856) she gave £200 to a New Zealand missionary college. Her first works, which included *Abbey Church, or Self-control and Self-conceit* (1844); *Henrietta's Wish, or Domineering*: and *Kenneth, or the Rearguard of the Grand Army* (both in

1850) were brought out anonymousy under the stricture of her family's sensibilities about her writing. Other, later novels under her own name brought her wide fame. Such titles as *The Clever Woman of the Family* (1865) and *The Pillars of the House* (1873), and historical novels such as *The Pigeon Pie: a Tale of Roundhead Times* (1860) and *The Prince and the Page: a story of the Last Crusade* (1865) all appealed to the wide variety of her readers. Altogether she published 160 books, besides being the editor of *The Monthly Packet*, started in 1851 to imbue young women with the principles of the Oxford Movement, which she strongly supported along with its 'founder' John Keble. *The Heir of Redclyffe*, which appeared in 22 editions in about as many years, was eagerly read by officers in the Crimean War, and Charles Kingsley is said to have wept over *Heartsease*. She travelled only once out of her small village, when she visited Normandy, and, except for her writing, she devoted herself to the church and to teaching scripture at the village school. A year before she died she bought a new lychgate for St Matthew's Church with a present of £200 from subscribers to her magazine. In her last book, *Modern Broods* (1900), she contrasted the modern generation with the past one, with which she felt more in sympathy.

[7] Actors, Artists and Musicians

Arne, Thomas Augustine (1710–1778)
St Paul's Church, Covent Garden, London.

Composer of 'Rule, Britannia!', which he wrote for the masque *Alfred* by Mallet and Thompson, performed in the gardens of the house of Frederick, Prince of Wales at Cliveden in August 1740. A prolific composer, he set to music such Shakespearean songs as 'Where the Bee sucks', as well as composing operas, *Artaserse*, oratorios, *Judith* and *Abel*, and a wealth of instrumental music.

Bach, Johann Christian (1735–1782)
St Pancras Old Churchyard, St Pancras Road, London.

Composer. The eleventh son of Johann Sebastian Bach, he studied music under his brother Emmanuel in Berlin after the death of his father in 1750. In 1754 he went to Italy to study under Padre Martini, and from 1760 to 1762 held the post of organist at Milan Cathedral, for which he wrote two Masses, a *Requiem*, a *Te Deum*, and other works. In 1762, having gained a reputation as the composer of opera, he was invited to England and became the most popular musician in England, his dramatic works being staged at the King's theatre, and his concerts, given in partnership with Abel at the Hanover Square rooms, being the most fashionable of London entertainments at the time. He was appointed music-master to Queen Charlotte and he has gone on record as the first composer to prefer the pianoforte to the older keyboard instruments.

Banks, Leslie James (1890–1952)
St Nicholas's Churchyard, Worth Matravers, Dorset; at the north-east side.

An actor, born at Derby, who, after winning a scholarship to Keble College, Oxford, and studying classics there, was attracted to the theatre. He played his first professional role in 1911 as old Gobbo in *The Merchant of Venice* at the Town Hall, Brechin, in Sir Frank Benson's company, later touring the United States and Canada. During the first world war he was wounded in the face but found that the resulting disfigurement did not handicap him in his acting.

He became a sought-after player whose name guaranteed success in any play he was in. He appeared in such plays as *The Circle*, *Goodbye, Mr Chips*, and *Life With Father* after the second world war, before which he had made his name in provincial repertory and in London. His many film appearances included Alfred Hitchcock's *The Man Who Knew Too Much* and *Jamaica Inn*. In private life his unassuming nature was praised by A. A. Milne as 'the man next door, a good neighbour and a good friend'. He was said, however, to have been brought to ruin by a 'streak of wild recklessness'. He was awarded the CBE in 1950. He lived in Worth Matravers during the summer but died in London.

Barbirolli, Sir John (1899–1970)
St Mary's Roman Catholic Cemetery, Kensal Green, London.

Conductor and cellist. He conducted many famous orchestras including that of the New York Philharmonic, which he took over from Toscanini, from 1937 to 1942, and that for which he is principally remembered, the Hallé Orchestra which he conducted from 1943 to 1970.

Baring-Gould, Sabine (1834–1924)
St Peter's Churchyard, Lew Trenchard, Devon.

Chiefly remembered for his famous hymn 'Onward Christian Soldiers', which was but one of the hymns that he wrote. He was also a notable divine and author, publishing several theological works, including *The Origin and Development of Religious Belief*, 1869–1870, as well as folk-lore books and novels, the best known of which are *Mehalah*, 1880, which Swinburne likened to *Wuthering Heights*, and *The Brown Squire*, 1896. In all, from 1857 to 1920, he published 159 books. He was rector of the church in which he was buried, being a high churchman with a belief in the Catholicity of the Church of England.

Beecham, Sir Thomas (1879–1961)
Brookwood Cemetery, Brookwood, Surrey.

Conductor and impresario. He founded the London Philharmonic Orchestra in 1931, championed the music of Delius and introduced the operas of Richard Strauss and the Russian Ballet of Diaghilev to England.

Britten, (Edward) Benjamin, 1st Baron Britten of Aldeburgh
(1913–1976)
St Peter and St Paul's Church, Aldeburgh, Suffolk. Blue slate stone
in churchyard.

Composer born at Lowestoft who founded the Aldeburgh Festival
in 1948. He was an accomplished pianist and conductor whose more
important compositions besides his numerous operas were the *Seven
Sonnets of Michelangelo* (1940) and *War Requiem* (1962). *Variations on a
Theme of Frank Bridge* won him his first world acclaim in 1937. Given
the Aspen Award in 1964, in 1976 he became the first musician to
become a life peer.

Butt, Dame Clara (1872–1936)
St Mary the Virgin Churchyard, North Stoke, Oxfordshire; near the
fence stile behind the church.

Contralto concert singer, she was born at Southwick near Brighton,
her father being a sea captain. Both he and her mother sang and
played the piano. She was educated at Bristol, where her parents had
gone, and she first sang in the Bristol Choir and achieved a scholarship
to the Royal College of Music in 1890. Her debut at the Royal Albert
Hall was in the part of Ursula in Sir Arthur Sullivan's *The Golden
Legend*, after which she went on to achieve both popular and critical
acclaim on the concert stage. Her six-foot-tall figure created an
impressive presence. *Abide With Me* was set to music for her, while
Sir Edward Elgar composed *Sea Pictures* and *The Dream of Gerontius*
for her also. 'With her whole heart she sang songs, and loved him that
made her' is inscribed on her gravestone.

Coates, Eric (1886–1957)
Golders Green Crematorium, Golders Green, London; ashes dispersed in the Garden of Rest, section 1J.

As a conductor and composer Coates gained much of his experience
as a leading viola player in London orchestras. He holds a special
place among most English composers for his delightfully light, yet
strangely stirring music such as *Knightsbridge March* (first chosen by
the BBC for its In Town Tonight program in the early thirties, making
Coates's composition famous), *London Calling March*, *The Three Bears
Suite* and many others. He was born in Hucknall, Nottinghamshire,
the younger son of a well-known surgeon. A musical prodigy, Coates
received a scholarship to the Royal Academy of Music when he was

20 years old, studying composition and the viola. He composed a world-wide 'hit' called *By the Sleepy Lagoon* in 1930. Several of Coates's works were featured by Sir Henry Wood in his early Promenade Concerts, in which the composer had been lead viola.

Constable, John (1776–1837)
St John's Churchyard, Church Row, Hampstead, London.

Landscape painter. Born at East Bergholt, Suffolk, he was the son of a mill owner and, after schooling at Dedham Grammar School, he entered one of his father's mills. After initial attempts at painting he was allowed by his father to enter the Royal Academy as a student in 1799. He was strongly influenced by Benjamin West, the president of the Academy, as can be seen from the altarpiece painted by Constable for Brantham Church in 1804. However, Gainsborough, the Dutch masters and Girtin are the predominant influences in his landscapes. He took to portrait-painting around 1811, when trying to earn himself the money to marry Maria Bicknell, but this he was unable to do until after his father's death in 1816. He then settled in London, in Keppel Street, Russell Square, where a succession of his well-known paintings were completed: 'Flatford Mill', 1817, 'A Cottage in a Cornfield', and 'The White Horse', 1819. His famous 'Haywain', 1821, which was sold to a Frenchman, was exhibited at the Louvre and won him a gold medal. Other famous paintings include 'Salisbury Cathedral from the Bishop's Garden', 1823, 'Salisbury Cathedral from the Meadows', 1831, 'The Valley Farm', 1835, and 'Arundel Mill and Castle', 1837.

Cooper, Dame Gladys (1888–1971)
Hampstead Cemetery, Fortune Green Road, London.

Actress. She began her career as Bluebell in *Bluebell in Fairyland* at the Theatre Royal, Colchester, when just seventeen. Thereafter she appeared in numerous rôles both on the stage, in films and on television. She was made a Dame of the British Empire.

Cotman, John Sell (1782–1842)
St John's Wood Chapel, Wellington Road, St John's Wood, London.

Landscape painter and architectural draughtsman. He was born in Norwich, and after showing a talent for art was sent to London to study where he became friends with Turner, T. Girtin and other artists. He first exhibited at the Royal Academy in 1800. He returned to Norwich in 1807, joined the Norwich Society of Artists, and became its president in 1811. In 1825 he became an associate of the Society of Painters in Water-colours; in 1834 was made drawing-master at King's College, London, and in 1836 was elected a member of the Institute of British Architects. His work was not considered important in his lifetime but he now ranks as one of the great figures of the Norwich School, a fine draughtsman and a remarkable painter both in oil and water-colour. His architectural etchings, published in a series of volumes, the result of tours in Norfolk and Normandy, are valuable records of his interest in archaeology.

Crome, John 'Old Crome' (1769–1821)
St George's Church, Colegate, Norwich, Norfolk.
   Landscape painter and chief representative of the Norwich School of painting. He was first apprenticed as a housepainter but through the influence of an art-loving patron he was able to exchange that trade for the position of drawing-master, remaining one for the remainder of his life. About 1790 he was introduced to Sir William Beechey, who encouraged and helped Crome in his art. In 1805 the Norwich Society of Artists was formed, with Crome as its president and the largest contributor to its exhibitions. He first exhibited at the Royal Academy in 1806, but throughout the next twelve years contributed only fourteen paintings. His important works include 'Mousehold Heath, near Norwich', 'Oak at Poringland', the 'Willow' and 'Slate Quarries'. He enjoyed only a limited reputation during his lifetime.

Delius, Frederick (1862–1934)
St Peter's Churchyard, Limpsfield, Surrey, under an ancient elm tree.
   Composer. Of German parentage, the idiosyncratic idiom of his music was more appreciated in Germany than in England, and it was not until Sir Thomas Beecham championed it that it became widely known in England. His most famous works are the atmospheric tone-poems for orchestra, such as *Brigg Fair*, the vocal and orchestral *A Mass of Life*, *Sea Drift* and *Appalachia*, and the opera *A Village Romeo and Juliet*. After temporary burial in the churchyard at Grez-sur-Loing, France, where he had lived since the 1880s, his body was brought to England and buried at Limpsfield, with Sir Thomas Beecham reading the funeral oration and conducting a picked orchestra in playing a selection of Delius pieces fitting for the occasion.

Dors, Diana (1931–1984)
Sunningdale Roman Catholic church, Sunningdale, Berkshire.

Actress who has been called 'the English Marilyn Monroe', perhaps mainly because of her blond hair and striking figure. She was also called 'The only sex symbol Britain has produced since Lady Godiva'. But, as in the case of Miss Monroe, her screen personality and ability gave her a universal appeal both on film and off. Not only that, after training at the Royal Academy of Dramatic Art she starred in over thirty-six films after appearing as young as fifteen in background 'sexy girl' bits. Some of her major films were *There's a Girl in My Soup* (1970) as an ex-wife of Peter Sellers, *Steptoe and Son Ride Again* (1973), in BBC Television Shakespeare *Timon of Athens* as Timandra (1981), *All Our Saturdays* (1973), a TV series; a hard-working actress in many substantial roles. Two of her three marriages ended in divorce; she had three sons. Born in Swindon she died at Windsor of meningitis. Before she died she devoted much of her time to religious and charity groups.

Elgar, Sir Edward William (1857–1934)
St Wulstan's Churchyard, Wells Road, Little Malvern, Hereford and Worcester. A memorial stone lies in Westminster Abbey, London, in the floor of the north choir aisle of the Nave.

Composer. Generally considered the principal composer in the trio, comprising himself, Hubert Parry and Charles Stanford, that led to the revival of English music in the nineteenth century. Although influenced by Brahms they nonetheless established a new English tradition that has been carried on in the present time. His principal works include *The Dream of Gerontius*, an oratorio, over the score of which Elgar wrote 'This is the best of me', his symphonic study, *Falstaff*, his overtures, *Cockaigne*, a happy evocation of London, and *In the South*, written after a visit to Italy, his *Enigma* variations, a series of sound portraits of his friends, and his *Pomp and Circumstance* marches which include the famous 'Land of Hope and Glory'. He was made Master of the King's Musick in 1924 and granted the Order of Merit in 1911, the first musician to receive the order, was knighted in 1904, and made a baronet in 1931.

Formby, George O.B.E. (1904–1961)
Manchester Road Catholic Cemetery, Warrington, Cheshire.

Variety artist and film actor who was best known for his ukulele playing and comic singing. Born in Wigan, the son of a music-hall performer, George was warned by his father not to go on stage; its life, especially in those Edwardian days, was too hard, he believed. Formby senior died in 1921 and George did start to 'tread the boards' imitating his father's act, but poorly. Of his first appearance at the Hippodrome, Earlstown he said 'I died the death of a dog!' In 1923 he married Beryl Ingham, of a clog-dancing team, who improved his act. After being signed up to make films at Ealing Studios by Basil Dean, their head, many successful films followed. The first film he made was *Off the Dole* in 1935. During the war he toured battlefronts in virtually every theatre of the war, including Normandy less than a week after D-day, where he was awarded the OBE. In 1951 he starred in his first West End musical, a new version of *Brewster's Millions*, which became a smash hit. While still in the show he suffered a major heart attack in 1952 while driving home after a performance. His wife nursed him back to health, however, and he eventually was able to appear about eighteen months later in Palladium and Palace Theatre shows such as *Fun and the Fair*, with Terry-Thomas and *Dick Whittington*. Shortly after his wife died in 1961, however, and an engagement to a younger woman he suffered another heart attack, which proved fatal. On his own request he was buried beside his father.

Gainsborough, Thomas (1727–1788)
St Anne's Church, Kew Green, Kew, Surrey.

Portrait and landscape painter. Born at Sudbury in Suffolk where his father owned a woollen-carpet-making business. His mother excelled in flower painting and encouraged her son in the use of the pencil. He was sent to study in London at the academy in St Martin's Lane, where he spent three years before returning to the country. He fell in love with Margaret Burr, who was reputedly the daughter of either the Duke of Bedford or one of the exiled Stuarts. They married after he had painted her portrait and settled in Ipswich. He painted portraits to earn his living and used the surrounding countryside for his landscapes. In 1759, anxious to improve his reputation, he moved with his family to the more fashionable Bath where his skill as a portrait painter was much sought after. During this period he painted Sterne and Richardson, the authors, as well as Quinn, Henderson and Garrick, all actors. In 1774, his reputation fully established and his financial position assured, he moved to London and settled at Schomberg House in Pall Mall. Within a few months he was summoned to the palace and he shared with West the favour of the court, and with the Reynolds the favour of fashionable society. His most famous portraits are 'Lady Ligonier', 'Georgiana, Duchess of Devonshire', 'Master Buttall', known as 'The Blue Boy', 'Mrs Siddons', and 'The Hon Mrs Graham'. Of his other works the principals include 'the Cottage Door', 'the Return from the Harvest', 'Waggon and Horses passing a Brook' and 'the Market Cart'. His total output exceeded 300 paintings, of which 220 were portraits.

Garrick, David (1716–1779)
Westminster Abbey, London, in the South Transept, now known as 'Poets' Corner'.

Actor-manager. Son of an army officer, he was born in Lichfield. He was Dr Johnson's solitary scholar when Samuel Johnson set up a school near Lichfield, and he accompanied Johnson to London when the two set out to seek their fortunes, as Dr Johnson said, 'with twopence halfpenny in his pocket,' and Garrick 'with three halfpence in his'. Both Garrick's father and uncle shortly afterwards died and he was left £1,000. He and his brother decided to set up a wine business in Lichfield and London, David looking after the London office. It was not successful and he had soon spent half his capital. He was engrossed in the theatre and made an incognito appearance on the stage in *Harlequin Student, or The Fall of Pantomime with the Restoration of Drama*, March 1741. By October of that year he had gained popular applause for his rôle of Richard III at Goodman's Fields. He immediately gave up his wine business and took to the stage full-time. Within six months he had acted in eighteen rôles and was immediately successful. His own farce, *The Lying Valet*, in which he played the part of Sharp, was so successful that his fortune was made. For the season of 1742 he was employed by Fleetwood for the Drury Lane Theatre, and he remained there until 1745 when he went to Dublin. He remained there as joint manager with Sheridan of the Theatre Royal in Smock Alley. In 1747 he took over the managership of the Drury Lane Theatre, opening in September of that year with a strong company of actors. He ceased to act in 1766 but continued with the managership of Drury Lane. He sold his share in the theatre in 1776 for £35,000 and took his leave by playing a round of his favourite characters: Hamlet, Lear and Richard III.

Greenaway, Kate (1846–1901)
Hampstead Cemetery, Fortune Green Road, London.

Artist and book illustrator. She was the daughter of John Greenaway, a well-known draughtsman and engraver on wood, and was born in London. She studied at South Kensington and at the Slade School, and began exhibiting her water-colours at the Dudley Gallery, London in 1868. Her illustrations for children, particularly *Little Folks*, 1873, attracted a great deal of attention. In 1879 she produced the work for which she is chiefly remembered, *Under the Window*, which is reputed to have sold 150,000 copies. She was elected a member of the Royal Institute of Painters in Water-Colours in 1890.

Grimaldi, Joseph (1779–1837)
St James's Church (site of), Pentonville, London. Newly restored grave in iron-railed surround.

Clown, famous throughout the world in his time, who died penniless as a lifelong resident of Islington, London. A successful campaign by the Joseph Grimaldi Society, spearheaded by Lord Miles (actor Bernard Miles), saw the grave renovated and landscaped in 1987 on the 150th anniversary of the clown's death. A group of fourteen clowns attended the celebration, one of them wearing Grimaldi's original costume and wig. Grimaldi's career began as an infant dancer at Sadler's Wells. He later acted there and at Drury Lane for many years, as well as in the provinces and at Dublin. Covent Garden saw him in his most famous rôle as Squire Bugle in *Mother Goose*.

Gwyn, Eleanor, 'Nell' (1650–1687)
St Martin-in-the-Fields, St Martin's Place, London.

Actress. Born in London, probably in an alley off Drury Lane. Her father was described as a broken-down soldier. She first sold oranges in the precincts of the Drury Lane Theatre and graduated to the stage around the age of fifteen, through the influence of the actor Charles Hart and a guards officer, Robert Duncan or Dùngan, who had some influence with the management. Her first recorded appearance was in 1665 as Cydaria, Montezuma's daughter, in Dryden's *Indian Emperor*. Pepys in his diary entry for 25 March 1667 recorded that he was delighted with the acting of 'pretty, witty Nell,' and when he saw her playing Florimel in Dryden's *Secret Love, or the Maiden Queen*, he wrote 'so great a performance of a comical part was never, I believe, in the world before' and 'so done by Nell her merry part as cannot be

Nell Gwyn, from the studio of Lely

better done by nature'. Her success brought her many leading rôles and she stayed with the Drury Lane company until 1669. But it is as the mistress of Charles II that she is principally remembered. As his mistress she was popular with the public, probably to counter the public's distrust of Louise de Kéroualle, Duchess of Portsmouth, Charles's other mistress who was both Catholic and French, both characteristics likely to offend the English public. She bore Charles two sons, the future Duke of St Albans, and the young Lord Beauclerk who died in 1680. When Charles died he implored his brother, James II, 'Let not poor Nell starve', and the new King honoured his brother's dying wish. He settled an estate on the former mistress with reversion to her surviving son, the young Duke. Nell Gwyn did not long survive Charles II, dying in November 1687, her funeral sermon being preached by Thomas Tenison, Vicar of St Martin-in-the-Fields and afterwards Archbishop of Canterbury.

Handel, George Frederick (1685–1759)
Westminster Abbey, London, in the South Transept, now known as 'Poets' Corner'. The statue is said to be an exact likeness, for the face was modelled from a death mask.

Composer. Born at Halle in Lower Saxony, the son of a surgeon-barber who disapproved of music. As an eight-year-old Handel contrived to be overheard by the Duke of Saxe-Weissenfels, to whom his half-brother was valet-de-chambre, when he was practising on the ducal organ. The Duke persuaded his father to exploit his son's talent and he was sent to become a pupil of Zachau, the cathedral organist at Halle. At twelve Zachau sent him to Berlin where he made an immediate and great impression and the Elector of Brandenburg, later Frederick I of Prussia, offered to send him to Italy for training. However, George's father declined and he returned to Halle to continue his education there. After his father's death he trained as a lawyer but in 1702 accepted the post of organist at Halle Cathedral. A year later, having completed his probation period at the cathedral, he suddenly left for Hamburg where the only German opera worthy of the name was flourishing, and there met Matheson, a prolific composer and writer on music. His first opera, *Almira*, was performed in Hamburg on 8 January 1705 and was followed a few weeks later by another work, now lost, *Nero*. The following year he travelled to Italy where he met many of the famous composers of the day including Domenico and Alessandro Scarlatti, and Domenico is reputed to have said on first hearing him play incognito that 'It is either the devil or the Saxon'; Handel being referred to in Italy as *Il Sassone*, the Saxon. In 1709 his fame led to an offer from the Elector of Hanover to become his Kapellmeister and Handel accepted on condition he should be allowed to travel to England for a visit. He arrived in London at the end of 1710 and earned his first success with his opera *Rinaldo* performed at the Haymarket Theatre on 24 February 1711. He returned to Hanover briefly then once more journeyed to England where he stayed, being in an awkward position when his deserted master arrived in London as George I. However, at the intercession of Baron Kielmansegge he was restored to favour when he composed his *Water Music*, and given a pension of £400 per annum. He composed over forty operas, chief of which are *Atlanta*, *Berenice*, and *Serse*; thirty-two oratorios, including *Saul*, *Samson*, *Messiah*, *Judas Maccabaeus* and *Jephtha*; and numerous other works. Eight years before his death he became blind and relied on the services of his friend, John Christopher Smith, to commit his music to paper.

Hogarth, William (1697–1764)
St Nicholas's Churchyard, Chiswick Mall, Chiswick, London.

Painter and engraver. He satirized the life of his day in numerous works chief of which were *Harlot's Progress*, 1732, followed by *Rake's Progress* in 1735, *Marriage à la Mode*, *Industry and Idleness*, and *The March to Finchley*.

Holbein, Hans 'The Younger' (1497–1543)
St Katherine Cree Church, Leadenhall Street, City of London. There is a brass tablet on the south wall of the church of St Andrew Undershaft, Leadenhall Street, commemorating the fact that Holbein lived within the parish. However, it is generally accepted that he was buried at St Katharine Cree nearby.

Painter. The favourite son of the painter, Hans Holbein the Elder, he was probably born at Augsburg. With his brother Ambrose, he sought employment as a book illustrator in Basel in the year 1515, and his first patron was believed to be Erasmus, for whom he illustrated, with a series of pen-and-ink sketches, an edition of the *Encomium Moriae*. He settled in London in 1532, residing in the parish of St Andrew Undershaft in the City, where he was rated as a 'stranger'. He enjoyed the patronage of the King, Henry VIII, for whom he

Grave of William Hogarth, St Nicholas's Churchyard, Chiswick Mall, Chiswick, London executed a number of portraits, including those of members of the royal family: Jane Seymour, Prince Edward, later Edward VI, and Anne of Cleves whom Henry later married and divorced. He also painted many of the members of Henry's court, including the famous 'Duke of Norfolk'. He died of the plague in November 1543.

Hunt, William Holman (1827–1910)
St Paul's Cathedral, London.

Pre-Raphaelite painter. Born in London, he started work as a clerk in a city office but during his seventeenth year he entered the Royal Academy schools, where he met his lifelong friend, John Everett Millais. His first painting to be exhibited at the Royal Academy was 'Hark!' which appeared in 1846. In 1848, he, Millais, Dante Gabriel Rossetti and others formed the movement known as the Pre-Raphaelite Brotherhood, which was championed by Ruskin. His most famous painting, 'The Light of the World', was purchased and given to Keble College. Because he was dissatisfied with the way in which it was hung he executed a new painting, slightly altered from the original 'Light of the World'. This now hangs in St Paul's Cathedral. He spent two years in the Holy Land in order to revivify on canvas the facts of the Scriptures 'surrounded by the very people and circumstances of the life in Judaea of old days'. From his experiences there he produced 'The Scapegoat', exhibited at the Royal Academy in 1856, and this was followed by 'The Finding of our Saviour in the Temple', 1860. His other major work is 'The Triumph of the Innocents'.

Irving, Sir Henry (1838–1905)
Westminster Abbey, London, in the South Transept, now known as 'Poets' Corner'.

Actor-manager. He revolutionized the dramatic art of the nineteenth century by his revivals of Shakespeare, and other plays, at the old Lyceum Theatre from 1878 to 1899. His performances of Shylock and Malvolio were renowned. For many years he acted with Ellen Terry.

John, Augustus Edwin (1878–1961)
Town Cemetery, Fordingbridge, Hampshire, beside the path from the second entrance. There is a statue of him by Ivor Robert-Jones in Fordingbridge Park.

Portrait painter whose Bohemian lifestyle made him unpopular with the art establishment. He was born, a solicitor's son, at Tenby, Dyfed, Wales, and entered the Slade School of Art in 1894 as a shy student. Swimming one day he dived into shallow water and cut his head on a rock. 'He hit his head whilst diving', wrote Virginia Shankland, 'and emerged from the water a genius!' He won a Royal Academy prize and produced a succession of masterly portraits until the later 1920s. His biographer Michael Holroyd said that his life was that of 'the great artist, the great lover, and great Bohemian.' He had eight children by his two wives, Ida Nettleship and Dorothy McNeill, and three illegitimate children. His second son Casper became First Sea Lord from 1960 to 1963.

Johnson, Celia (Mrs Peter Fleming) (1908–1982)
Parish Church churchyard, Nettlebed, Oxfordshire.

Actress who appeared in many popular films. Perhaps two of the best remembered are *Brief Encounter* (1945) by Noel Coward with Trevor Howard co-starring, and *The Captain's Paradise* (1953), with Alec Guinness. Two of her major films were *In Which We Serve* (1942), co-directed and produced by Noel Coward, who played Captain Kinross (she played his wife) and *This Happy Breed* (1944) based on the play by Noel Coward in which she played opposite Robert Newton. In 1969 the British Film Academy named her Best Supporting Actress in *The Prime of Miss Jean Brodie*. She was married to Peter Fleming, see in Section 6 here.

Karloff, Boris; born William Pratt (1887–1969)
Mount Cemetery, in Garden of Remembrance, Guildford, Surrey.

Actor who is generally best known for his portrayal of Frankenstein's monster in the film of that name. He was, however, an accomplished stage actor and his return to the stage in *Arsenic and Old Lace* (1941) and as Captain Hook in 1951 brought him critical acclaim. Earlier, as the youngest child of a civil servant, he had been educated at Uppingham and the Merchant Taylor's School and had hoped for a diplomatic career after London University. After going to Canada and the United States at the age of twenty-one, though, he was for ten years in a repertory company, which culminated in his making several films in Hollywood before the one that brought him fame. As Frankenstein's monster and in other parts involving ghosts and resurrected mummies, to all of which he managed to bring a characterisation well above the otherwise crude pathos involved, he became a traditional role model. But a strong performance in a 1934 World War I film, *The Lost Patrol*, notably revealed his versatility. He also worked in television and remained active in his craft until his death.

Kean, Charles John (1811–1868)
All Saints' Church, Catherington, Hampshire.

Actor. Son of the actor Edmund Kean who, despite his father's wishes to the contrary, went on the stage. He played opposite his father during the latter's last appearance on the stage in *Othello*, his father playing the title rôle and he Iago. With his wife, Ellen Tree, he played in spectacular revivals at the Princess's Theatre, London, during the 1850s.

Kean, Edmund (1787–1833)
St Matthias's Churchyard, Friars' Stile Road, Richmond, Surrey.

Actor. He made his first appearance on the stage as Cupid in Noverre's ballet of *Cymon* when only four years old. As a child he became a cabin boy but so disliked it that he feigned deafness and lameness with such skill that he deceived the physicians. At fourteen he joined the York Theatre playing Shakespeare for twenty nights and thereafter joined a troupe of strolling players. He recited before George III at Windsor, and in 1807 was playing opposite Mrs Siddons in Dublin. In 1814 he opened at the Drury Lane Theatre as Shylock and the triumph was so great that he remarked 'I could not feel the stage under me'. He played twice in the United States, in 1820 and 1825, and last appeared on the English stage at Covent Garden on 25 March 1833 playing Othello to his son, Charles's Iago and his daughter-in-law, Ellen Tree's Desdemona. During the third act he became ill and, crying in a faltering voice, 'O God, I am dying. Speak to them, Charles,' he fell unconscious into his son's arms. He died a few weeks later at Richmond.

Kendall, Kay (1927–1959)
St John's Churchyard extension, Church Row, Hampstead, London.

Actress. A talented comedienne, she starred in many films, perhaps the most popular being *Genevieve*. She appeared also in Cole Porter's *Les Girls*. She was married to the actor, Rex Harrison. She died of leukaemia. She was of an acting family.

Landseer, Sir Edwin Henry (1802–1873)
St Paul's Cathedral, London.

Animal painter. Principally known for his 'Monarch of the Glen' and 'Stag at Bay' paintings, though his paintings of dogs, especially 'Suspense', which shows a dog watching at the closed door of his wounded master, and 'The Old Shepherd's Chief Mourner', are thought to be his finest achievements. He became a member of the Royal Academy in 1831, was knighted in 1850 and in 1867 unveiled the four lions which he had modelled for the base of Nelson's Column in Trafalgar Square.

Lawrence, Sir Thomas (1769–1830)
St Paul's Cathedral, London.

Portrait painter. He was encouraged by Sir Joshua Reynolds whom he later succeeded as Painter in Ordinary to King George III. He was made a Royal Academician in 1794 and painted most of the crowned heads of Europe, in 1818 going to Aix-la-Chapelle to paint the sovereigns and diplomats gathered there. Among his best-known works are those of George IV, and of his wife Caroline of Brunswick. He was knighted in 1815 and became President of the Royal Academy in 1820, a post he held until his death ten years later. As a portrait painter he ranks highly, though not now so highly as he did in his lifetime; but his more ambitious works, in the classical style, such as his celebrated 'Satan', are practically forgotten.

Leighton, Frederick, 1st Baron Leighton of Stretton (1830–1896)
St Paul's Cathedral, London.

Painter and sculptor. Studied in Italy, Germany and Paris. His first painting to gain fame was his 'Cimabue's Madonna carried in Procession through the Streets of Florence', which appeared at the Royal Academy in 1855, in the same year as Holman Hunt's 'Light of the World' and at a time when the public's interest was absorbed by the Pre-Raphaelite school. It created a sensation and was purchased by Queen Victoria. Thereafter his works became famous: 'Dante in Exile', 1864, 'Venus Disrobing for the Bath', 1867, and 'Captive Andromache', 1888. He also painted a few portraits, including that of Sir Richard Burton, the explorer. Among his sculptures are the celebrated 'Athlete struggling with a Python', 1877, and 'The Sluggard', 1886. His drawings, sketches and landscapes were also much admired. He settled in London in 1860 and in 1886 moved to a house at 12 Holland Road, Kensington, which is now a museum to his memory and contains many of his finest works. He was knighted in 1878, on being elected President of the Royal Academy, made a baronet in 1886 and created a baron in 1896, just a few days before his death.

Lely, Sir Peter (1618–1680)
St Paul's Church, Covent Garden, London.

Painter. Born at Soest, Westphalia, the son of an army captain named van der Vaes; the son adopting his nickname of Le Lys or Lely as a surname later. After studying at Haarlem he moved to England in 1641 to avail himself of the advanatage of Charles I's patronage of the arts. He soon gained a reputation for his landscapes and historical subjects and, shortly after the death of Van Dyck, Charles I requested Lely to paint his portrait. Later, he painted Cromwell. At the Restoration he won the favour of Charles II, who made him his State painter and gave him a knighthood. His most famous work is a collection of portraits of the ladies of the court of Charles II, known as the 'Beauties'. Of his few historical paintings the best is 'Susannah and the Elders'.

Lind, Johanna Maria, 'Jenny' (1820–1887)
The Cemetery, Great Malvern, Worcestershire, where her grave is covered by a plain slab of Swedish granite.

Singer. She was born in Sweden and was later known as 'the Swedish Nightingale' because of the remarkable range of her voice. Her professionalism distinguished her from her contemporaries but her immense popularity was due to the conviction she brought to her rôles, particularly when identifying with the favourite characters of Amina, Alice or Agathe. She sang throughout Europe and, from 1850 to 1852, in the United States, which she toured under the management of P. T. Barnum. She married Otto Goldschmidt and later settled in London where her husband conducted the Bach Choir, in which she also took an interest, and where she held the post of Professor of Singing at the Royal College of Music for some years.

Linley, Thomas (1732–1795)
Wells Cathedral, Wells, Somerset.

Musician. Born at Wells, he studied at Bath where he settled, becoming a singing master and conductor of concerts. From 1774 he was involved in the management of the Drury Lane Theatre where he composed many of the pieces of music produced there. He also wrote songs and madrigals and his work ranks high among English compositions. His children were also notable musicians: Thomas (1756–1778), a friend of Mozart, was a remarkable violinist and also a composer of songs and madrigals, later published in two volumes; William (1771–1835) held a writership at Madras but composed glees and songs; Elizabeth Anne (1754–1792) married Richard Brinsley Sheridan, but before her marriage was famous for the beauty of her voice, as well as her face. Her two sisters were also noted for their singing and their beauty.

Macready, William Charles (1793–1873)
Kensal Green Cemetery, Kensal Green, London.

Actor. Born at London and educated at Rugby. Instead of going to Oxford he helped his father in the running of his theatres and on 7 June 1810 made his first appearance as Romeo in Birmingham. His first London appearance was as Orestes in *The Distressed Mother* at Covent Garden on 16 September 1816. Thereafter he played many rôles, the most notable being his Richard III and Henry V. He managed both Covent Garden Theatre, 1837 to 1839, and the Drury Lane Theatre, 1841 to 1843. He travelled extensively in the United States but one of his visits to New York was marred by a riot at the Astor Opera House in 1849, inspired by a jealous actor, Edwin Forrest. He retired from the stage in a farewell performance of Macbeth at Drury Lane on 26 February 1851.

Matthews, Jessie (1907–1981)
St Martin's Church, Ruislip, Greater London, ashes in the Garden of Rest.

Stage and film actress born in Soho, London, who was one of the most popular performers of the 1930s, singing and dancing her way into the heart of cinema-goers as she had so appealed to theatre-goers in the twenties. She was a 'trim, musical star with a delicate face and a quivering, almost non-existent chin', Anthony Slide wrote of her. She was a dancer who should have but never did, partnered Fred Astaire, he believed. At age 12 she made her stage debut in *Bluebell in Fairyland*, going on to play in such plays and films as *This England* (1924), *The Good Companions* (1934), *Evergreen* (1935), Tom's mother in *Tom Thumb* (1958) and *The Hound of the Baskervilles* (1978). Her theme song was *Over My Shoulder*, which she sang to great applause in her solo concert at Los Angeles two years before she died of cancer. In 1970 she was awarded the OBE.

Millais, Sir John Everett (1829–1896)
St Paul's Cathedral, London.

Pre-Raphaelite painter. At the age of eleven he entered the Royal Academy schools where, at fifteen, he met and formed his lifelong friendship with Holman Hunt. In 1848, he and Hunt, with Dante Gabriel Rossetti and others, formed the Pre-Raphaelite Brotherhood which, according to Millais, had as its aim 'to present on canvas what they saw in Nature'. Ruskin espoused the movement's cause, showing his enthusiasm in letters to *The Times* and in a pamphlet entitled 'Pre-Raphaelism'. His most famous Pre-Raphaelite paintings are possibly 'Orphelia', 1852 and 'The Huguenot', also 1852. Of his later paintings the most popular include 'The Boyhood of Raleigh' and 'Bubbles'. After the annulment of her marriage, Millais married Effie Ruskin. He was knighted in 1885 at Gladstone's suggestion and died of cancer of the throat in 1896, a few months after he had been made President of the Royal Academy on the death of Lord Leighton.

Neagle, (Dame) Anna (1904–1986)
Central London Cemetery, 'Manor Park' (nearest station), London.

Actress who is perhaps best known for her rôle as Queen Victoria in the films *Victoria the Great* (1937) and *Sixty Glorious Years* (1938). She was also a great success in *Spring in Park Lane* (1948), for which she won the Picturegoer Medal. Born Majorie Robertson, she came to the stage via the chorus line and, married to the producer Herbert Wilcox, appeared in numerous films during the thirties, playing various heroines of history as in *Nell Gwyn* (1934), *Nurse Edith Cavell* (1939) and Amy Johnson in *They Flew Alone* (1942), plus many other highly acclaimed roles in *Goodnight Vienna* (1932), *Bitter Sweet* (1933), *Holiday Inn* (1936), *London Melody* (1937) and others. She cherished her rôle as the French resistance leader in *Odette* (1950) (Mrs Odette Hallowes, G.C.) whom she knew as a friend. It was considered one of her greatest portrayals. Another strong rôle a year later was her Florence Nightingale in *The Lady with the Lamp*. She was made a Dame of the British Empire in 1969 after her greatest stage success in *Charlie Girl* at the Adelphi. She was 'as much a part of Britain as Dover's white cliffs', Anthony Slide cited one critic as saying.

Novello, Ivor (Ivor Novello Davies) (1893–1951)
Golders Green Crematorium, Golders Green, London; ashes under the lilac tree in the Gardens, bust in the Cloisters.

Composer, actor and playwright, his mother being Clara Novello Davies who was a well-known singer. After being educated at the Magdalen College School at Oxford, at which he won a singing scholarship in its famous choir, he became a prodigy, composing and performing his own songs. Prior to obtaining a wartime commission in the Royal Naval Air Service he composed the patriotic song *Keep the Home Fires Burning* (or officially *Till the Boys Come Home*), which became an overnight success and was widely popular in both Britain and the USA, giving him financial independence. He acted on stage and in films but eventually made his major contributions to the theatre as a composer and actor in his own musical plays. His romantic Ruritanian plays were generally tuneful and romantically escapist; not so sophisticated as many of those of Noel Coward, his friend, to whom he could be theatrically compared. *Glamorous Night* (1935), *Crest of the Wave* (1937), *The Dancing Years* (1939), *Perchance to Dream* (1945) and *King's Rhapsody* (1949) were among his well-known musical plays. His song *We'll Gather Lilacs*, the hit of the year, which he wrote for *Perchance to Dream*, is sadly reprised by the commemorative tree under which his ashes were placed.

Olivier. Laurence Kerr Olivier, 1st Baron (1907–1989)
Westminster Abbey, London, ashes placed beneath plaque in 'Poets' Corner'.

An actor who was revered throughout the English-speaking world, he was also a director and producer. Born in Dorking, at 17 he studied on a scholarship at the London School of Dramatic Art, played his first professional rôle in *Byron* (1924) and took part in a sketch that toured England the same year; his last performance was in Benjamin Britten's *War Requiem* in 1989. His Shakespearian debut was as Macbeth, as a member of the Birmingham Repertory Company (1926–28), and his first film part was in *Too Many Crooks* (1930). Since then his stage, film and television appearances varied widely from a role with Marilyn Monroe (*The Prince and the Showgirl*) to his towering portraits in Shakespeare.

He served for four years in the Fleet Air Arm, being released in 1944 to codirect the Old Vic Theatre Company with Sir Ralph Richardson (whom see). Knighted in 1947, in recognition of his performances in the films *Henry V* and *Hamlet*, Olivier was either nominated for or received fifteen Best Actor awards. Married three times, his first marriage was to actress Jill Esmond, who bore him a son Tarquin. This marriage ended in divorce in 1940 when he married Vivien Leigh, from whom he was divorced in 1960. His third wife, actress Joan Plowright, bore him three children, Richard, Tamsin and Julie; he had married her in 1961 and his death widowed her.

Olivier's peerage came in 1981; he was the first actor ever to be so recognized. As Director of Chichester Festival, from 1962 he worked hard to raise money for a permanent home for the National Theatre, now on the South Bank of the Thames. Perhaps the only reservation made about his acting was that his remarkable virility and on-stage gusto were more physical than poetic; as John Gielgud said, 'I had the voice, but Larry had the legs'. Nevertheless theatre critic Eric Shorter wrote that as an actor Olivier 'conquered the world'.

Opie, John (1761–1807)
St Paul's Cathedral, London.

Historical and portrait painter. Born near Truro in Cornwall, by the age of twelve he had mastered Euclid and opened an evening school for arithmetic and writing. He showed an early talent for drawing and by 1780 he had gained a local reputation for painting portraits. He then went to London where he was introduced as 'the Cornish Wonder' and for a time enjoyed much fashionable patronage. When his popularity waned he once again began to study to correct the defects in his work, earning himself the praise of his rival, Northcote, who said of Opie, 'Other artists paint to live; Opie lives to paint'. In 1786 he exhibited his first important historical painting, the 'Assassination of James I', and in the following year the 'Murder of Rizzio', the merit of which earned him immediate election as an associate of the Royal Academy, of which he became a full member in 1788.

Orpen, Sir William (1878–1931)
Putney Cemetery, Putney, London. Grave is upright stone with flat top; easy to find.

Portrait painter whose work has been called the finest of the century for its accuracy, rendering of character and feeling. Born in Ireland, he studied art there and at the Slade School in London. An official peace-conference painter after the first world war, his sketches and paintings he did at the front during the war are displayed in the

Imperial War Museum, London. In 1918 he was knighted, and he was elected an RA the following year.

Pavlova, Anna (1881–1931)
Golders Green Crematorium, Golders Green, London; urn in Ernest George Columbarium with a shrine there. Also in the Cloisters there is an Anna Pavlova standard rose and a rosebed in the Gardens.

Ballerina born in St Petersburg (Leningrad), Russia, who became world famous as a dancer, performing in her own company after being a prima ballerina in the Imperial Ballet Company of Moscow. She left Russia permanently in 1913 and toured the world both during and after the war. Her most famous performance was *The Dying Swan* which, with her small delicate figure and exquisitely graceful dancing, made her three-minute solo adored everywhere she performed.

Purcell, Henry (c.1658–1695)
Westminster Abbey, London, in the north choir aisle of the Nave, where the shield to his memory is inscribed with the following epitaph, which may have been written either by Dryden, his wife, Lady Elizabeth Dryden, or her sister-in-law, Dame Annabella Howard, who erected the monument:

Here Lyes
HENRY PVRCELL. Esqr.
Who left his life
And is gone to that Blessed Place
Where only his Harmony
can be exceeded.

Composer and organist. Born in Westminster where his father was a gentleman of the Chapel Royal. Henry Purcell was admitted to the Chapel Royal as a chorister and in 1676 was appointed copyist at Westminster Abbey. He composed the music for Dryden's *Aurenge-Zebe* that same year and in 1678 produced what was considered to be a masterpiece of musical composition in the overture and masque for Shadwell's new version of Shakespeare's *Timon of Athens*. In 1680, his master, Dr Blow, resigned as organist of Westminster Abbey in favour of his pupil, and at twenty-two Purcell gained one of the most important musical posts in the country. His opera *Dido and Aeneas* formed an important landmark in the history of English operatic music.

Gravestone of Henry Purcell, Westminster Abbey, London

His great anthems, 'I was glad' and 'My heart is inditing', were written for the coronation of James II. His greatest work is undoubtedly his *Te Deum and Jubilate* written for St Cecilia's Day 1694, the first English *Te Deum* ever composed with orchestral accompaniments.

Reynolds, Sir Joshua (1723–1792)
St Paul's Cathedral, London.

Portrait painter. Born at Plympton Earl in Devon, he was apprenticed at seventeen to the popular portrait painter, Thomas Hudson, in London. The first portrait to gain him any attention was that of Captain the Hon John Hamilton. He returned to Devon on the death of his father in 1746 and settled with his sisters at Plymouth Dock, where he came under the influence of the works of William Gandy of Exeter, who had died in 1730. Northcote said of Gandy that his painting came 'nearer to nature in the texture of flesh than that of any artist who ever lived'. The influence of Gandy's painting on Reynolds may be seen in the early self-portrait, being so rich in impasto and strong in light and shade, in which the artist is seen shading his eyes with his hand. Reynolds travelled abroad, visiting Spain, North Africa and Italy, which had been the object of his trip, during the 1750s, returning to London and settling in Leicester Square. His portraits became famous and when in December 1768 the Royal Academy was founded, Reynolds became its first president, receiving a knighthood from the King as well as a commission to paint his and the Queen's portraits. His most important portraits are 'Mrs Siddons as the Tragic Muse', 'Johnson', 'Sterne', 'Lord Heathfield', 'Gibbon', 'Burke', 'Fox', 'Garrick' and 'Goldsmith'. Mention must also be made of the 'Angels' Heads' and 'Nelly O'Brien'.

Richardson, Sir Ralph (1902–1983)
Highgate Cemetery (New), Swain's Lane, Highgate, London, near path.

An actor whose successful career lasted over fifty years from 1926 when he made his London debut at the Haymarket. He was an actor who could 'make an ordinary character seem extraordinary' and vice versa, it was said. His first stage appearance was at Brighton at the age of 20 in *The Emperor's Candlesticks* and he later played more important parts in various Shakespearean productions there. His versatility saw him play a gamut of roles in scores of plays and films from Bulldog Drummond to Macbeth and Cyrano de Bergerac. His lifelong association with Sir John Gielgud began in 1930, and with Sir Laurence Olivier in 1938 at the Old Vic. He served with the latter during World War II in the Fleet Air Arm. Sir Peter Hall said of him, 'He was one of the greatest actors who ever lived – I'm sure of that.' He worked right up to the end of his life, which ended with a brief illness. He had been knighted in 1947 while he was a co-director with Olivier at the 'New' Old Vic. 'The art of acting', he once said, 'lies in keeping people from coughing.'

Romney, George (1734–1802)
St Mary's Church, Dalton-in-Furness, Cumbria.
  Portrait painter. Born in Dalton-in-Furness, he was the son of a builder and cabinet-maker. Apprenticed at nineteen to an itinerant portrait painter named Steele, he made little progress because of his master's erratic habits. In 1756 he impulsively married a young woman who had nursed him through a serious illness and to earn enough money took to portrait painting on his own account. In 1761, having saved £100, part of which he gave to his wife and family, he left for London alone to seek his fortune. He soon became popular in London, his 'Death of General Wolfe' winning second prize at the Society of Arts in 1766. A period of study in their schools about 1769, brought him greater experience and he was soon prosperous. As a portrait painter he was soon seen as a rival to Reynolds, Lord Thurlow remarking that 'All the town is divided into two factions, the Reynolds and the Romneys, and I am of the Romney faction'. One of his most famous sitters was Emma Hart, the future Lady Hamilton and mistress of Nelson, whose bewitching face smiles from numerous canvases, Romney confessing that she was the inspiration for what was most beautiful in his art. Towards the end of his life he withdrew from portrait painting, turning to subjects such as Seven Ages and Visions of Adam with the Angel. In the summer of 1799 his health deteriorated and he returned to Kendal to his long-deserted wife, who nursed him through the last three years of his life.

Rossetti, Dante Gabriel (1828–1882)
All Saints' Churchyard, Birchington, Kent. By the south door there is a monument designed by Ford Madox Brown in the form of a Celtic Cross.
  Painter and poet. The son of the Italian poet and liberal, Gabriele Rossetti, who had settled in London and married Frances Polidori, the sister of Byron's physician, Dr John Polidori. Their first son was christened Gabriel Charles Dante and from early childhood showed a marked aptitude for drawing and painting. He was impressed by some of Ford Madox Brown's early paintings and he went to study under him. He came into contact with Millais and Holman Hunt and with

them and others formed the Pre-Raphaelite Brotherhood in the autumn of 1848. His first Pre-Raphaelite painting was 'The Girlhood of Mary, Virgin', which was exhibited in March 1849 at Hyde Park Corner, whilst his 'Ecce Ancilla Domini!' is regarded as the one perfect outcome of the motives of the Pre-Raphaelite Brotherhood. Rossetti married his model, Elizabeth Siddal, and when she died he was so grief-stricken that he buried his collected poems with her. Later, these were exhumed and published. His poetry is strongly influenced by the revival of the romantic spirit in English poetry. His 'Sister Helen', 'The Blessed Damozel', 'Eden Bower', and 'Troy Town' all reflect this trend.

Sargent, Sir Malcolm (1895–1967)
Stamford Cemetery, Stamford, Lincolnshire.
Conductor. He was born at Stamford and made his debut as a conductor at the old Queen's Hall. He succeeded Sir Adrian Boult in 1950 as conductor of the BBC Symphony Orchestra, a post he held until 1957. During his long career he conducted the American NBC Symphony Orchestra, the Royal Choral Society, and many others including the D'Oyly Carte Opera Company.

Sellers, Peter Richard Henry (1925–1980)
Golders Green Crematorium, Golders Green, London, his ashes being placed next to those of his parents beneath rose bushes.
Actor. He was born into a theatrical family: his mother was a pianist and actress, whilst his grandmother and eight of his uncles were on the stage. He made a name for himself in the radio series, *The Goon Show*, in the 1950s. Thereafter he appeared frequently in films, the most popular being his rôle of the German scientist in *Dr Strangelove*, Inspector Clouseau in the *Pink Panther* series, in *I'm All Right, Jack* and *The Mouse That Roared*.

Siddons, Sarah (1755–1831)
St Mary on Paddington Green Churchyard, Paddingon, London. There is a monument to her on the Green, which was unveiled by Sir Henry Irving in 1897.
Actress. Daughter of the manager Roger Kemble, she was accustomed to appearing on the stage from childhood. She fell in love with William Siddons, an actor in her father's company, but her parents opposed their marriage and he was dismissed. However, the couple

eventually married in November 1773 and subsequently appeared in Cheltenham where Sarah attracted public notice. David Garrick sent his deputy to see her and she was engaged to appear at Drury Lane at a salary of £5 a week. Initially, she was not a great success and lost her position at Drury Lane, but, after touring and receiving much acclaim in Bath, she was engaged to appear at Drury Lane again in 1778. Thereafter her career was established and she played all the leading rôles of her day. She was greatly respected by many of her contemporaries and Dr Johnson wrote his name on the hem of the garment which she wore for her Reynolds' painting saying, 'I would not lose the honour this opportunity afforded to me for my name going down to posterity on the hem of your garment'.

Stubbs, George (1724–1806)
St Marylebone 'Old' Parish Church, Marylebone High Street, London. The site of the old parish church and its graveyard is now marked by the Garden of Rest in Marylebone High Street and contains a tablet commemorating some of the notable people buried there.

Animal painter and anatomist. Most famous for his paintings of horses, one of his best being 'Phaeton and Pair', which hangs in the National Gallery, Trafalgar Square, London. He was largely self-taught and it was an interest in comparative anatomy which led him to study horses, and eventually to the publishing of the *Anatomy of the Horse*, 1766, which still commands great respect. He also painted landscapes and some portraits, chief of which were those of Lord Grosvenor and the Duke of Richmond.

Sullivan, Sir Arthur Seymour (1842–1900)
St Paul's Cathedral, London.

Composer. Born in London, he was the son of an Irish musician who was bandmaster at the Royal Military College, Sandhurst. He won the Mendelssohn Scholarship at the Royal Academy in 1856, and he did so well at the Academy that he was given a two-year extension of his scholarship. He is popularly remembered for the music he wrote for light operas, with W. S. Gilbert as the librettist, especially *The Pirates of Penzance*, *The Mikado*, *The Yeomen of the Guard* and *The Gondoliers*. He also wrote a great deal of religious music and, with a friend, discovered Schubert's lost *Rosamunde* music. He was knighted in 1883.

Tauber, Richard (1891–1948)
Brompton Cemetery, West Brompton, London.

Singer. He was born in Austria and became world famous for his singing rôles in operetta. His English success was made in Franz Lehar's *Land of Smiles.*

Terry, Dame Ellen Alice (1847–1928)
St Paul's Church, Covent Garden, London.

Actress. Born into a prominent theatrical family she made her first stage appearance at nine years old. Thereafter she played juvenile rôles until her marriage to G. F. Watts, the artist, when she was sixteen. The marriage was a disaster and later he divorced her. She returned to acting and became famous for the rôles she played opposite Sir Henry Irving at the Lyceum Theatre and during tours of the United States. She had two children, neither by her husband, Gordon Craig, the stage designer, and Edith Craig.

Tilley, Vesta (1864–1952)
Golders Green Crematorium, Golders Green, London; ashes under a lilac tree.

Male impersonator (born Matilda Alice Powles), she was a child prodigy who made her first stage appearance at the age of five in Nottingham. In London she became famous as 'principal boy' in pantomimes. Small of stature, she never approved of vulgarity, nor did she ever become touched with any scandalous rumours. She became as popular in the USA as she was in England; her perfectionism, her immaculate dress and petite figure combined with her unique voice and diction made her performances and her songs a memorable event for all who saw her. Her farewell performance on 5 June 1920 was a joyous and virtually hysterical landmark for the London stage. She was happily married to a member of parliament, becoming Lady de Frece.

Tree, Sir Herbert Beerbohm (1853–1917)
St John's Churchyard extension, Church Row, Hampstead, London.

Actor manager. He was the actor-manager of the Haymarket Theatre until 1897 when he built his own theatre, His Majesty's Theatre.

Turner, Joseph Mallord William (1775–1851)
St Paul's Cathedral, London, in the crypt.

Painter who after studying under Sir Joshua Reynolds (whom see) exhibited his first drawing, 'View of Lambeth Palace', in 1790 at the Royal Academy. In his lifetime he is estimated to have produced over 1000 works, for which he visited Devonshire, the north of England, Scotland, Italy, France, Venice and Switzerland. Some of his famous paintings are 'The Battle of the Nile' (1799), 'The Fighting Temeraire' (1839), Venetian scenes and such strangely mystical works as 'War – the Exile' (1845) when he attempted to communicate vague thoughts by colour language. The son of a barber, he was considered to have been England's greatest painter of his time and style, which began to develop after his early stage when the Old Masters had influenced his work. He became a recluse toward the end of his life. There is a room in St Mary's Church, Battersea, where he used to sit for hours gazing across the Thames.

Van Dyck, Sir Anthony (1599–1641)
'Old' St Paul's Cathedral, London.

Painter. Born at Antwerp in Flanders, he studied under Rubens. He travelled extensively in Italy before settling in England where Charles I settled an annuity on him. He is principally known for his portraits of Charles I, his Queen, Henrietta Maria, their children and the court. He was knighted by Charles I. He died of the plague at Blackfriars.

Vaughan Williams, Ralph (1872–1958)
Westminster Abbey, London, in the north choir aisle of the Nave.

Composer. Born in Gloucestershire, he was educated at Charterhouse and Cambridge. Thereafter he studied under Max Bruch in Berlin and later under Ravel, in Paris. He wrote nine symphonies, besides a large number of choral and orchestral works, operas – *Hugh the Drover, Riders to the Sea* – ballets, chamber music, and songs. He was awarded the Order of Merit.

Walbrook, Anton (1900–1967)
St John's Churchyard extension, Church Row, Hampstead, London.

Actor. Born in Vienna, he first appeared on the English stage in Noel Coward's *Design for Living* at the Haymarket Theatre in 1939.

Thereafter he starred in films and on the stage, becoming famous both in England and in the United States.

Wheatley, Francis (1747–1801)

St Marylebone 'Old' Parish Church, Marylebone High Street, London. The site of the old parish church and its graveyard is now marked by the Garden of Rest in Marylebone High Street, and contains a tablet commemorating some of the notable people buried there.

Portrait and landscape painter. Born in Covent Garden, London, he studied at Shipley's drawing school and at the Royal Academy. He eloped to Ireland with the wife of the painter Gresse, and whilst in Dublin painted portraits as well as executing an interior of the Irish House of Commons. His scene of the 'Gordon riots in 1780' was admirably engraved by Heath, and is regarded as his best painting. He is well-known today for 'The London Cries', a series of London street scenes which lent themselves to engravings and are much valued by collectors.

Whistler, James Abbot McNeill (1834–1903)

St Nicholas's Churchyard, by the north wall of the new section, Chiswick Mall, Chiswick, London.

Painter. Born at Lowell in the United States, he studied in Paris before settling in England in 1859. His series of Thames etchings in 1859 disclosed a new vision of the great river. Of his oil paintings, the principals are 'Sarasate', 'Lady Archibald Campbell' and 'The Little Rose of Lyme Regis'. He was also a noted lithographer, his most popular being the 'nocturne' at Limehouse, and of the old Faubourg St Germain. He was a controversial figure and in 1878 he brought a libel action against Ruskin for the latter's remark that one of Whistler's nocturnes in the Grosvenor Gallery was 'a pot of paint flung in the public face'. After a long trial Whistler was awarded a farthing's damages.

Wood, Sir Henry Joseph (1869–1944)

Church of the Holy Sepulchre without Newgate, Holborn, London, in the Musicians' Chapel where his ashes lie under the central window to St Cecilia, the patron saint of music.

Conductor. Largely self-taught, as a child he deputised for the local organist. He is principally remembered as the founder of the Promenade Concerts at the Queen's Hall in 1895, which he conducted until his death, nearly fifty years later. He also conducted numerous orchestras both in England and abroad.

Zoffany, Johann (1733–1810)
St Anne's Church, Kew Green, Kew, Surrey.

   Painter. Born in Frankfurt-on-Main, he studied in Italy before journeying to London in 1758 where he obtained, after some initial hardship, royal patronage. In 1769 he was a founder member of the Royal Academy. He was given an introduction to the Grand Duke of Tuscany by George III and whilst resident in Florence received a commission from the Empress Maria Theresa to paint the Tuscan royal family. She was so pleased with the result that she made Zoffany a baron of the empire. From 1783 to 1790 he lived in India, to which period belong some of his best-known paintings. For the last twenty years of his life he lived in England. His portrait groups of dramatic personalities are the most esteemed of his works.

[8] Explorers, Sportsmen, Reformers, Outlaws, Heroines, Criminals and Miscellaneous

Beaton, Sir Cecil (1904–1980)
All Saints' Church, Broad Chalke, Wiltshire, blue slate headstone in churchyard.

Best remembered as a photographer, his brilliant talents included painting and writing. Better known as a portrayer of royalty and society personalities, he also photographed many film 'greats', including Marlene Dietrich and Gloria Swanson. In the theatre his skill as a costume designer was first seen in C. B. Cochran's *Streamline* review of 1934. The film *Gigi* (1959) won him his first Oscar for design, which was capped by another Oscar for the set design of the film version of *My Fair Lady*. He once proposed to Greta Garbo but, rejected, he died a bachelor.

Blondin, Charles (1824–1897)
Kensal Green Cemetery, Kensal Green, London.

Acrobat and tight-rope walker. Born in France, his real name was Jean François Gravelet. When he was nearly six he made his first appearance as an acrobat, being termed 'The Little Wonder'. In 1859 he first crossed the Niagara Falls, a feat he did again a number of times, but with different theatrical variations: blindfold, in a sack, trundling a wheelbarrow, on stilts, carrying a man on his back, sitting down midway while he made and ate an omelette. He first appeared in London at the Crystal Palace in 1861.

Booth, William, 'General' (1829–1912)
Abney Park Cemetery, Church Street, Stoke Newington, London.

Founder of the Salvation Army. He was born in Nottingham. In 1865, with the help of his wife, Catherine, he began mission work in the East End of London, which led in 1878 to the formation of the Salvation Army on military lines. It became an international organization, with members of his family organizing branches throughout the world.

Sir Cecil Beaton, Broad Chalke, Wiltshire

Brandon, Richard (d.1649)
St Mary Matfelon Churchyard, Alder Street, Whitechapel, London.

Executioner of Charles I. He was the son of the common hangman Gregory Brandon, known as 'Old Gregory', whilst Richard was known as 'Young Gregory'. He was apparently reluctant to execute the King but was forced to do so, receiving 'thirty pounds for his pains, all paid in half-crowns, within an hour after the blow was given', as well as an orange 'stuck full of cloves' and a handkerchief out of the King's pocket. He sold the orange for ten shillings in Rosemary Lane, where he lived. He also executed many other prominent nobles, including the Earl of Strafford, Archbishop Laud, the Duke of Hamilton, the Earl of Holland and Lord Capel. Although he confessed to the execution of the King, William Hulet was condemned for having dispatched the monarch. Brandon is reputed to have died of remorse for killing Charles I.

Buckingham. Henry Stafford, 2nd Duke of (1st creation)
(1454?–1483)
St Peter's Church, Britford, Wiltshire; in the chancel.

Is believed to have been the person who suggested the murder of the two Princes in the Tower to Richard, Duke of Gloucester. Buckingham married Catherine Woodville, sister of Edward IV's queen, but after Edward IV's death in 1483 he supported the claims of Edward's brother Richard to the throne and opposed those of Edward's son, the 13-year old Edward VI. Edward and his brother were imprisoned in the Tower of London and put to death and Richard was crowned in Edward's place. Richard has been accused of the murder of the two Princes and Buckingham of putting the idea into Richard's mind. Buckingham very quickly turned against Richard. Soon after the new king's coronation he led a rising in the West Country in support of Henry, Earl of Richmond, later Henry VII. The rising failed abysmally and Buckingham, a hunted man, took refuge in a hut near Wem. What gave him away was the richness and unusual nature of the provisions that were seen being taken to the hut by Ralph Bannaster, his retainer who, when Buckingham was discovered, was quite ready to accept the reward. The Duke was tried at Salisbury on Saturday, 1 November 1483, and beheaded in the market place on the Sunday, his vast estates being confiscated. There is some doubt whether his head was buried with his remains or not.

Burgess, Guy Francis de Moncy (1910–1963)
St John the Evangelist Church, West Meon, Hampshire, ashes sprinkled on his mother's grave at night-time ceremony.

English traitor, a spy for Russia who was a member of the ring of four who met at Cambridge University (with Blunt, Philby and Maclean). He fled to Moscow with Maclean (whom see) in 1951 after Philby warned them of their impending arrest. Philby followed them twelve years later. They were all senior members of the British security service MI5, Burgess being also with the BBC during most of the war. The son of a naval officer, he had been educated at Eton.

Burton, Sir Richard Francis (1821–1890)
St Mary Magdalen's Churchyard, North Worple Way, Mortlake, London. His monument is a life-size tent with a crucifix above the place where the entrance seems to be.

Explorer, writer and linguist. He is famous for the pilgrimage he made to Mecca and Medina in 1853 disguised as a Moslem. He explored Central Africa and translated the *Arabian Nights*, which ran into sixteen volumes.

Cavell, Edith Louisa (1865–1915)
Norwich Cathedral, Norwich, Norfolk, outside the south-east transept wall.

Nurse. She was shot by the Germans for helping Allied fugitives to escape during the Great War. At her trial she admitted that she had received letters from the men she had aided, and this sealed her fate. Despite strenuous attempts from the American and Spanish ambassadors in Brussels, as well as worldwide condemnation, the Germans executed her by firing squad at 2 AM on 12 October 1915. After the war her body was brought to England and a memorial service held in Westminster Abbey.

Cornwell, John Travers, VC (1900–1916)
Manor Park Cemetery, City of London but memorial monument in Portland Naval Cemetery, Dorset.

Tomb of Sir Richard Burton, St Mary Magdalen's Churchyard, North Worple Way, Mortlake, London (p 323)

Inscription on the monument to Sir Richard Burton (overleaf p 324)

CAPTAIN ✝ ISABEL
SIR RICHARD FRANCIS HIS WIFE
BURTON NÉE ARUNDELL
K.C.M.G. F.R.G.S. (OF WARDOUR)
BORN 19 MARCH DIED 22ND DAY OF
1821 MARCH 1896
DIED AT TRIESTE
20 OCTOBER R · I · P
1890
JESUS MERCY MARY HELP
R · I · P PRAY FOR HER.

RICHARD BURTON

"FAREWELL, DEAR FRIEND, DEAD HERO! THE GREAT LIFE
IS ENDED, THE GREAT PERILS, THE GREAT JOYS;
AND HE TO WHOM ADVENTURES WERE AS TOYS,
WHO SEEMED TO BEAR A CHARM 'GAINST SPEAR OR KNIFE
OR BULLET, NOW LIES SILENT FROM ALL STRIFE
OUT YONDER WHERE THE AUSTRIAN EAGLES POISE
ON ISTRIAN HILLS. BUT ENGLAND, AT THE NOISE
OF THAT DREAD FALL, WEEPS WITH THE HERO'S WIFE.
OH, LAST AND NOBLEST OF THE ERRANT KNIGHTS,
THE ENGLISH SOLDIER AND THE ARAB SHEIK!
OH, SINGER OF THE EAST WHO LOVED SO WELL
THE DEATHLESS WONDER OF THE ARABIAN NIGHTS,
WHO TOUCHED CAMOEN'S LUTE AND STILL WOULD SEEK
EVER NEW DEEDS UNTIL THE END! FAREWELL!"

JUSTIN HUNTLY McCARTHY.

Grave of Nurse Edith Cavell, Norwich Cathedral, Norfolk

The boy (1st class) hero of the Battle of Jutland 31 May 1916, who 'stood on the burning deck' of H.M.S. *Chester* (reminding us of the poem by Mrs Felicia Hemans about an earlier boy hero, Giacomo Casabianca at the Battle of the Nile). Admiral Sir David Beatty said: '. . . Cornwell was mortally wounded early in the action. He nevertheless remained standing alone at a most exposed post till the end of the action, with the gun crew dead and wounded all around him . . . I recommend his case for special recognition in justice to his memory, and as an acknowledgment of the high example set by him.' Cornwell survived for 24 hours to die in Grimsby hospital just before his mother arrived from London. He knew she was coming, however; 'Give her my love,' were his last words.

Darling, Grace Horsely (1815–1842)
St Aidan's Churchyard, Bamburgh, Northumberland, where there is a Gothic shrine with metal colonettes and a recumbent effigy.

Heroine. Famous for the part she played in the rescue of passengers from the Forfarshire steamboat which was wrecked on the rocks off the Farne Islands on 7 September 1838. Her father was the lighthouse keeper on the Farne Islands and espied some of the survivors of the boat huddled on a rock. With his daughter's help he launched and rowed a coble and managed to rescue four men and a woman, whom they returned to the lighthouse. Her father then returned to the rock and with the help of two men brought off four more survivors. Grace Darling received much public acclaim for her rôle in the rescue and was awarded a gold medal from the Humane Society. Subscriptions brought in money but throughout Miss Darling remained unspoiled by the publicity. She died of consumption.

Duval, Claude (1643–1670)
St Paul's Church, Covent Garden, London, in the centre aisle under a stone with the epitaph:

> Here lies Du Vall: Reader if male thou art,
> Look to thy purse: if female to thy heart.

Highwayman. He came to England from Normandy after the Restoration of Charles II in 1660, in attendance on the Duke of Richmond. He soon joined the ranks of highwaymen and became notorious not only for his gallantry to ladies but for his daring exploits.

He was captured and tried at the Old Bailey and sentenced to be hanged at Tyburn. Many ladies apparently interceded for his life but the King, Charles II, refused. After his death his body lay in state at the Tangier Tavern in St Giles's and so many people visited it amid much disorder that the exhibition was stopped on a judge's order. It is also claimed that he was buried in St Giles-in-the-Fields, Holborn.

Epstein, Brian (1934–1967)
Kirkdale Jewish Cemetery, Long Lane, Liverpool, Merseyside.

As The Beatles' first manager he was responsible for launching them on their phenomenal success. He was in charge of one of his father's music stores (NEMS: North End Road Music Stores) in Liverpool when he first heard them playing in The Cavern Club. This was only a few minutes walk from his shop. He managed others including Cilla Black, but became sole manager for The Beatles. Their overwhelming success, however, became too much for him. Unable to control their individual activities, he found he could not fit in with them.

Fayed, ('Dodi') Emad (1956–1997)
Originally interred at the interfaith cemetery, Brookwood, Surrey but then moved to a new family burial spot on the country estate of his father Mohammed Al Fayed at Oxted, Surrey.

Born in Gamrok, Alexandria, Egypt. The wealth and influence his father achieved in adult life allowed Dodi to follow his early passion for the cinema. His uncle was Adnan Khashoggi, a Saudi financier who was said at the time to be the world's richest man. In England Dodi became 'adopted' by the Broccoli family after meeting Barbara, the youngest daughter of Albert 'Cubby' Broccoli, producer of James Bond movies. After taking a summer course in film making at Loyola University in New Orleans, Dodi displayed a remarkable talent for the art. His first major film was *Chariots of Fire*, for which he won a 1982 Academy Award for Best Motion Picture as executive producer. He became the epitome of a rich man-of-the-world with global residences, expensive cars and beautiful girls. In 1986 just after Christmas he married an international model Suzanne Gregard whom he had met in New York. The marriage lasted only ten months. On the day of a fatal car crash in Paris, in which he and Princess Diana were killed, he had bought an engagement ring, which he had presumably intended to offer Diana later that night.

Fenton, Lavinia (Polly Peachum), later Duchess of Bolton
(1708–1809)
St Alfege's Church, Greenwich, London.

Actress who took London by storm with the part of Polly Peachum in John Gay's (whom see) *The Beggar's Opera* (1728) and became the mistress of Charles Paulet, third Duke of Bolton (1685–1754) whom she married when his first wife died. Lady Mary Montagu pointed out that the Duchess of Bolton was 'crammed with virtue and good qualities . . . despised by her husband and laughed at by the public', while 'Lavinia, bred in an alehouse and produced on the stage, found the way to be esteemed.'

Frobisher, St Martin (c.1535–1594)
St Giles' without Cripplegate, London Wall, City of London.

Explorer and navigator. He was the first British navigator to seek the north-west passage from the Atlantic to the Pacific through the Arctic seas. He is commemorated in Frobisher Bay on Baffin Island. He commanded the *Triumph*, the largest ship in the English fleet, during the battle with the Spanish Armada in 1588. Admiral Lord Howard had divided the fleet into four parts under himself, Drake, Hawkins and Frobisher, who was knighted for valour during the battle.

Fry, Elizabeth (1780–1845)
Friends' Burial Ground, Barking, Greater London.

Prison reformer. She was the daughter of John Gurney of Earlham Hall, Norfolk, a Quaker and banker. In August 1800 she married a London merchant, Joseph Fry. It was not until 1817 that the great work of her life began with the founding of the association for the Improvement of the Female Prisoners in Newgate prison. She soon, mostly through her own exertions, managed to bring about an amelioration in the conditions of the prisoners and her work was then extended throughout Britain. She toured the Continent, and received official permission to visit all the prisons in France.

Grace, William Gilbert ('W.G.') (1848–1915)
Beckenham Cemetery, Elmers, End Road, Beckenham, Kent (a cemetery plan is near the main gate). A traffic by-pass is planned that might eventually necessitate destruction of the burial ground.

A cricketer whose name came to be hallowed on the cricket pitches of England and wherever else the game is played. His record of scoring 1000s in season most times still stands along with at least two others. Born at Downend near Bristol, he came from a family that was also accomplished at cricket. His career lasted for 43 years, during which time he scored 54,896 runs, made 126 centuries and took 2876 wickets, making him one of the top all-round players in first-class cricket to this day. He was a 6ft–6in. 'giant', black bearded and full of agility and stamina virtually to the end of his cricketing days. He practised as a surgeon in Bristol for 20 years, having been trained at St Bartholomew's and Westminster Hospitals. He twice played in Australia and also took a team of amateurs to the USA and Canada. Bowler J. C. Shaw of Nottinghamshire is cited as saying, 'I puts the ball where I likes, and Grace, he puts it where he likes'. A memorial gateway at Lords was erected to him in 1923 by the Marylebone Cricket Club, of which he became a member when he was 21 years old.

Hammett, James (1811–1891)
St John the Evangelist Church, Tolpuddle, Dorset.

He was the only one of the six Tolpuddle Martyrs to settle here when he returned from Australia after being transported to the penal settlement there. Six farm labourers had formed a local Friendly Society of Agricultural Labourers in an effort to get more pay, but were arrested and accused of administering unlawful oaths, contrary to an Act of 1797. Tried at Dorchester Assizes in 1834, they were all sentenced to penal transportation to Australia. Hammett's grave can represent the other five, who were all given seven-year sentences. They were George Loveless and his brother James, Thomas Standfield and his son John, and James Brine.

Herbert, George Edward Stanhope Molyneux, fifth Earl of
Carnarvon (1866–1923)
Beacon Hill, Hampshire. Two miles west of Old Burghclere, just off the A343, the grave is on the top of the 853-ft hill; a stiff climb!

Discoverer of Tutankhamen's tomb, he had been born at Highclere

Castle, the family seat of the Carnarvons. A serious automobile accident saw him recuperating in Egypt, where he became interested in archaeology. Excavating in Thebes with help from Howard Carter (1873–1939), antiquities chief at Luxor, they found some minor tombs after five years of digging. In 1922 when they were on the point of ending the search they discovered Tutankhamen's tomb in the Valley of Kings. In the antechamber they found a prodigious quantity of artifacts. The king had been a minor one of the 18th dynasty who died about 1352 BC. Later they found a huge gilded wooden shrine in which the king's mummy had been deposited. Carnarvon was bitten by a mosquito and within a month he had died from blood poisoning. At his wish he was buried on top of Beacon Hill.

Herbert, Mary, Countess of Pembroke (1561–1621)
Salisbury Cathedral, Salisbury, Wiltshire. All the Herberts, earls of Pembroke, were buried in the family vault in the front of the altar (except first- and second-creation first earls). Until the floor surface was renewed in recent years a slab marked the burial location. It was incised: 'Underneath this sable herse, Lies the subject of all verse, Sidney's sister, Pembroke's mother . . .', and it is now mounted on the south wall of the chancel.

Sister of Sir Philip Sidney, the poet and 'jewel in Elizabeth I's crown'. Mary and her brother were 'in perfect accord' and spent their time in literary studies, she being fluent in Latin, Greek and Hebrew. He wrote *The Arcadia* mostly in her presence, dedicating it to her: 'For you, only for you.' She was grief-stricken when he was killed in 1586; her father had also just died. She had married the second Earl of Pembroke in 1577 and, recovering from her grief, she became a generous patron of poets and men of letters, including Ben Jonson and Samuel Daniel, who tutored her son William at Wilton House. There was a theory, now thought unlikely, that Shakepeare addressed his sonnets to her eldest son William who became the third Earl. When her husband died, he left her 'as bare as he could'; there had been disagreement between them in their later married life, it was rumoured. James I, however, was generous to her and granted her Ampthill Park in Bedfordshire, where she built a magnificent mansion.

Hobbs, Sir John Berry, 'Jack' (1882–1963)
Hove Cemetery, Old Shoreham Road, Hove, Sussex.
  Cricketer. He is considered to have been the most perfect batsman
ever to take part in the English game. His career extended over thirty
years, during which he played for the Surrey Cricket Club, and for
his country. He was knighted for his services to the game.

Hood, Robin (c.12th and 13th centuries)
Kirklees Abbey, Mirfield, Yorkshire. The grave is available for viewing
only on Saturday afternoons, and even then it is uncertain. Permission
should be obtained from the Estate Office, Kirklees Estate, Mirfield,
Yorkshire. Proposed development might change this availability.
  Legendary outlaw. Various attempts have been made to authenticate
his life but none has been successful. He was mentioned in *Piers
Plowman*, which says that the 'Rymes of Robyn Hood and Randolph
erle of Chestre' were popular with the English peasantry about 1377.
He has had many guises, both in myth and in drama and fiction, but
one legend has it that when ill, he went to Kirklees Abbey to have his
blood let by the Prioress, where he was allowed to bleed to death at
the suggestion of Sir Roger of Doncaster. He is said to have called for
his bow as he lay dying, shot an arrow through the window, and asked
to be buried at the spot where it landed.

Howard, John (1726–1790)
St Paul's Cathedral, London, monument only as he is buried in
Russia.
  Prison reformer. Having been imprisoned in France during the
1750s he experienced his first taste of prison life. In 1773 he was
made Sheriff of Bedford and he began to enquire into the conditions
of the prisons within his jurisdiction. This led him to enquire further
afield and in 1774 he gave evidence before a House of Commons
committee about conditions in the prisons, for which he received the
committee's commendation and which led to an immediate act of
Parliament to relieve conditions. He then travelled extensively abroad,
particularly on the Continent, and died at Dophinovka, near Kherson,
in southern Russia and there was buried.

Hoyle, Edmund (1672–1769)
St Marylebone 'Old' Parish Church, Marylebone High Street, London. The site of the old parish church and its graveyard is now marked by the Garden of Rest in Marylebone High Street, which contains a tablet commemorating some of the notable people buried there.

Codifier of the rules of whist. Whilst living in London he supported himself by giving instruction in the game of whist and for the use of his pupils drew up a *Short Treatise* on it, which was printed in November 1742. His authority is established by the phrase 'according to Hoyle', meaning 'on the highest authority'.

Jackson, 'Gentleman' John (1769–1845)
Brompton Cemetery, West Brompton, London, where his monument is surmounted by a recumbent lion.

Boxer. He was the English boxing champion from 1795 to 1803 and he opened a boxing academy in Bond Street, London, and numbered Lord Byron among his pupils.

Jack the Ripper? Druitt, John Montague, Prime suspect (1857–1888).
Wimborne Cemetery, Wimborne Minster, Dorset.

According to Sir Melville Macnaghten, Chief Constable of Scotland Yard in 1889, Druitt was The Ripper. At least fourteen Scotland Yard officials were involved. In the final version of Macnaghten's report not released until 1966, he says: 'Personally and after much careful and deliberate consideration' he exonerated other suspects and '(F)rom private information I have little doubt that his own family suspected this man of being the Whitechapel murderer, it was alleged that he was sexually insane.' Druitt, the son of a prosperous Wimborne surgeon, was a barrister and had been quite a brilliant student at Winchester College and New College, Oxford University. He was also a good cricketer; Winchester first eleven and a member of the Dorset County Cricket Club. He was found drowned as an apparent act of suicide in the Thames on 31 December 1888 by a Thames waterman. In 1973 a carefully correlated list appeared in *The Cricketer* of his cricketing activities and the murders, and although hard evidence against Druitt is less than for other suspects, there is the strongest of recognition that Scotland Yard both at the time and now believe Druitt was Jack the Ripper.

Jack the Ripper Victims:

Nichols, (née Walker) Mary Ann (Polly), the Ripper's first victim murdered August 31, buried September 6, 1888. Age 42 years, flat bronze marker in ground. City of London Cemetery, Manor Park.*

Chapman, Annie, buried September 14, 1888, Manor Park cemetery 'in secret', grave number 78.

Stride, (née Gulafsdotter) Elizabeth, born Gothenburg, Sweden 1843, murdered September 30, 1888. East London Cemetery, West Ham, white marble 'frame grave', no headstone. Attendants can help locate if available.

Eddowes, Catherine, born Wolverhampton 1842, buried City of London Cemetery, Manor Park, October 8, 1888.*

Kelly, Mary Jane, born Limerick, Ireland, 25 years old, buried November 19, 1888, Leytonstone, St Patrick's Roman Catholic cemetery, row 67, grave 16 (marker stolen).

There were thirteen other alleged victims.

*Graves only a few yards apart.

Liddell, Alice (Mrs Reginald Hargreaves) (1852–1934)
St Michael's Church, Lyndhurst, Hampshire.

She was the original for Alice in Lewis Carroll's *Alice's Adventures in Wonderland*. Being the daughter of the Dean of Christchurch, Oxford, she met Charles Dodgson (Lewis Carroll) whilst he was lecturing in mathematics and he used to tell her the stories of Alice's Adventures when they walked together.

Little, John, 'Little John' (c.1230)
St Michael's Churchyard, Hathersage, Derbyshire.

One of Robin Hood's two lieutenants, the other being Will Scarlett. A grave of a John Little at Hathersage was opened in 1728 to reveal a 32-inch thighbone, indicating he must have been about seven feet tall. A longbow, reputed to be that of Little John, is on display at the Cannon Hall Museum, near Barnsley, Yorkshire.

Livingstone, Dr David (1813–1873)
Westminster Abbey, London, in the centre of the Nave.

Scottish explorer. He discovered the course of the Zambesi River, the Victoria Falls and Lake Nyasa, now Lake Malawi. He roused public opinion against the slave trade. Whilst exploring in Africa he

Grave of Alice Liddell, the 'Alice' of *Alice in Wonderland*, St Michael's Church, Lyndhurst, Hampshire

was believed lost but was discovered by Sir Henry Morton Stanley, then a journalist on the *New York Herald*, at Ujiji on 13 October 1871. Together they explored Lake Tanganyika. Livingstone died in Africa and his body was borne to the coast by bearers, shipped to London, and buried in the Abbey eleven months after his death.

Lord, Thomas (1757–1832)
St John the Evangelist Churchyard, West Meon, Hampshire.
Sportsman. He is remembered as the founder of Lord's Cricket Ground, which took his name. He had, as ground-keeper for a London club, started a cricket ground on the site of the present-day Dorset Square, but in 1814 he moved to the present site of Lord's.

Maclean, Donald Duart (1913–1983)
Church of the Holy Trinity, Penn, Buckinghamshire, in family plot, ashes in urn decorated with hammer and sickle.
English traitor, a spy for Russia, who was recruited by Burgess

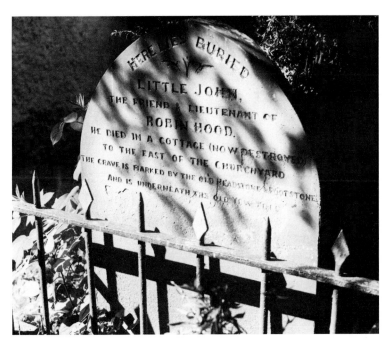

Grave of John Little, 'Little John', St Michael's Churchyard, Hathersage, Derbyshire

(whom see) and Anthony Blunt (1907–1982; cremated in London), of the quartet of spies (including Harold Adrian Russell and 'Kim' Philby (1911–1988), buried in Moscow who were all Cambridge University students in the thirties. They became senior officers in MI5, the British security service. Maclean and Burgess escaped to Russia in 1951 after being warned of their pending arrest by Philby. Maclean was the son of a Liberal cabinet minister.

Mills, Bertram Wagstaff (1873–1938)
St Giles's Church, Chalfont St Giles, Buckinghamshire.

Circus owner. He was the son of a Paddington coach builder and during the Great War of 1914–1918 he served in the Army Medical Corps. Bertram Mills' Circus became famous in Britain for its Christmas shows at Olympia in West London as well as for its provincial tours.

Grave of Thomas Lord, St John the Evangelist Churchyard, West Meon, Hampshire

Moody, Richard Clement (1813–1887)
St Peter's Churchyard, Bournemouth, Dorset; up the south-east steps and near to large white tomb of the Shelley-Godwins.

Founder of the town of New Westminster in British Columbia, Canada and first governor of the Falkland Islands. He was born at Barbados, became a colonel in the Royal Engineers and was sent to British Columbia in 1887 as Lieutenant Governor under Sir Edward Bulwer Lytton.

Nash, ('Beau') Richard (1674–1762)
Bath Abbey-church, Bath, Avon, under pew 33 in the nave; plaque on wall in aisle.

Man of fashion who became known as 'the King of Bath', where as Master of Ceremonies from 1704 he made the town a centre of attraction for the society of his day from royalty to gamblers. He himself had previously made a living by gambling. Born at Swansea, he was educated at Jesus College, Oxford, and in 1693 entered the Middle Temple.

Nightingale, Florence (1820–1910)
St Margaret's Churchyard, East Wellow, Hampshire; only her initials, 'FN', appear on her tombstone.

Nurse and pioneer of nursing reform. During the Crimean War of 1854–1855, she organized a nursing service to relieve the suffering of the war wounded. She earned herself the name of 'the lady with the lamp' from her grateful soldiers. Despite a great deal of initial Establishment opposition her nursing system was adopted and developed throughout the world. She was deemed to have 'raised the art of nursing from a menial employment to an honoured vocation'. In 1907 she received the Order of Merit, the first woman on whom it was bestowed. Her funeral service was held in St Paul's Cathedral.

Pankhurst, Emmeline (1858–1928)
Brompton Cemetery, West Brompton, London.

Suffragette. She was the leader of the militant movement for women's suffrage. With her daughters Christabel and Sylvia she organized the Women's Social and Political Union. She was constantly arrested for civil disobedience but resorted to hunger strikes during internment. At the outbreak of the Great War the campaign of civil disobedience ended and she worked tirelessly recruiting women for

Florence Nightingale, photograph by H. Heving

Grave of Florence Nightingale, St Margaret's Churchyard, East Wellow, Hampshire

THO: PARR OF Y COUNTY OF SALLOP BORNE IN AT 1483. HE LIVED IN Y REIGNES OF TEN PRINCES VIZ: K.EDW.4. K.ED.5.K.RICH.3. K.HEN.7.K.HEN.8.K.EDW.6.Q.MA.Q.ELIZ. K.IA.& K.CHARLES.ACED 152 YEARES. & WAS BURYED HERE NOVEMB.15.1635.

Gravestone of Thomas Parr, Westminster Abbey, London, in 'Poets' Corner'

munitions work. She travelled to the United States several times to gain support for her campaign. After the war she went to Canada but returned in 1926 and joined the Conservative Party. She died in London on 14 June 1928 shortly after the passing of the second Representation of the People Act which gave full and equal suffrage to men and women.

Parr, Thomas (c.1483–1635)
Westminster Abbey, London, in the South Transept now known as 'Poets' Corner'.

He was said to be 152 years old when he died and to have lived in the reigns of ten sovereigns, being reputedly born when Edward IV was still on the throne. His portrait was painted by Sir Anthony van Dyck. For most of his life he lived in Shropshire, where he was born, but in 1635 he was brought to London by the Earl of Arundel so that 'Old Parr', as he was known, could be presented to the King. The change of air affected him and he died shortly afterwards at Lord Arundel's house in London. The King ordered a post-mortem and Dr William Harvey found that his internal organs were in an unusually perfect state and his cartilages unossified.

Peel, John (1776–1854)
St Kentigern's Churchyard, Caldbeck, Cumbria.

Huntsman. His hunting prowess was enormous and his knowledge of the Cumbrian countryside faultless. As a young man he eloped with a Miss White and married her at Gretna Green. The marriage was extremely happy. The ballad, 'D'ye ken John Peel', was written by his friend, John Woodcock Graves, and happened by chance. One evening Graves and Peel were planning a hunting expedition when Graves's daughter asked whether they knew the words of an old Cumberland tune, 'Bonnie Annie'. Graves promptly wrote out the verses of 'D'ye ken John Peel', setting them to the tune of the traditional air.

Pembroke. William Herbert, 3rd Earl of (1580–1630)
Salisbury Cathedral, Salisbury, Wiltshire; family vault in front of altar.

Courtier and literary patron, he was born at Wilton House, Wilton, Wiltshire and shared the literary taste of his mother and his uncle, Sir Philip Sidney. Herbert was handsome and accomplished, matriculating from Oxford when he was only 13 years old. Often at Elizabeth I's court, he did not pander to her, displaying an independent spirit. Although he got along well with men, he was also said to be 'immoderately given up to women', and indulged himself in 'pleasures of all kinds, almost in excess'. At one time he had a secret romance with Mary Fitton, a great favourite of Elizabeth's, and after his own father's death, he became the father of an illegitimate child by her. The child died in infancy, and Pembroke was imprisoned briefly for his part in the scandal.

When Sir Walter Raleigh was imprisoned in the Tower, Herbert tried to secure his pardon; there is some evidence that he actually instigated the attack on the Mexican fleet for which Raleigh was executed. He continued his mother's patronage of poets and writers, being friendly with John Donne, the dramatist, Philip Massinger (his father's steward's son), and Ben Jonson. He knew Shakespeare but was not a personal patron of his. Herbert became very friendly with James I, entertaining him several times at Wilton House and showing him Stonehenge. He took part in Parliamentary debates, siding at times with the Duke of Buckingham, at other times disagreeing with him. Herbert was at James I's deathbed and carried the crown at Charles I's coronation. He had been deeply interested in New England explorations, becoming a member of the King's council for Virginia and sending immigrants and cattle there, and he had incorporated the North West Passage Company in 1612. He died suddenly of apoplexy in London after a 'full and cheerful' dinner the night before. He had been Chancellor of Oxford University since 1617.

Pocahontas, Mrs John Rolfe (c.1595–1617)
St George's Church, Gravesend, Kent.

Daughter of Powhattan, over-king of the Indian tribe in Virginia. In 1607 she was credited with having interceded with her father to save the life of Captain John Smith, who had been captured by the Indians. Her plea was granted. In his initial account, Captain Smith made no mention of Pocahontas's intercession, first mention being made when he re-wrote his account in 1622. What is certain, however, is that from 1608 onwards Pocahontas was a frequent visitor to Jamestown, was fond of the local children, and acted as a kind of go-between for her father and the settlers. In 1612 she was herself held hostage for the return of some prisoners her father had taken. Shortly afterwards she became a Christian, taking the name of Rebecca, and married John Rolfe, a settler. In 1616 she visited London and became a great favourite at court, especially with the Queen, Anne of Denmark. She died at Gravesend as she was about to embark to return to America.

Raleigh, Sir Walter (c.1552–1618)
St Margaret's Church, Westminster, London. His decapitated body lies buried before the altar, his head being interred at West Horsley in Surrey. The west window contains a full-length figure of Sir Walter Raleigh spreading his cloak.

Explorer and writer. He rose to prominence at the court of Queen Elizabeth I, legend having it that he came to the Queen's notice by spreading his cloak over a muddy patch for her to walk upon. In 1580 he helped to put down the Irish rebellion, and in 1584 began his colonization of Virginia. He was responsible for the introduction of tobacco and potatoes to England. He did not find favour with James I on his accession and was sent to the Tower, where he languished for many years. During that time he wrote his *History of the World*. He was released in 1615 to lead an expedition to the Orinoco, using the lure of treasure in his bargaining with the King. The expedition was a dismal failure and also brought the death of Raleigh's son. On his return he was executed. His wife is believed to have had his head embalmed and to have carried it with her until her own death.

Repton, Humphrey (1752–1818)
St Michael's Church, Aylsham, Norfolk.

Landscape gardener. After an unsuccessful attempt to be first a merchant, then involving himself in the postal service, as well as a brief spell as deputy-secretary to the Lord Lieutenant of Ireland, he decided to pursue landscape gardening to earn himself a living. He was guided by Lancelot Brown but gradually discarded Brown's formalism. His first major work was at Cobham in Kent in about 1790 and thereafter he laid out Russell Square and altered Kensington Gardens in London. He was the author of several works on gardening including *Sketches and Hints on Landscape Gardening*, 1794, as well as on local history and art.

Scathelock, William, 'Will Scarlett' (c.12th and 13th centuries)
St Mary's Churchyard, Blidworth, Nottinghamshire.
   One of Robin Hood's two lieutenants, the other being Little John. He was reputedly left behind, according to the manuscript of Bishop Percy, when Robin Hood and Little John went to Kirklees Abbey for Robin to be bled for 'the sickness that had come upon him'. In the village of Blidworth there is a house which is rumoured to have been where Maid Marion lived before her marriage to Robin Hood. Scarlett's gravestone marker is thought to be from the pinnacle of the church tower.

Sheppard, John, 'Jack' (1702–1724)
St Martin-in-the-Fields, St Martin's Place, London.
   Robber. Brought up in the Bishopsgate workhouse and later apprenticed as a carpenter. He fell in with Elizabeth Lyon, notorious as 'Edgeworth Bess' for her lack of morals. He lived with her and took to crime to gratify her tastes. He was arrested as a runaway apprentice and from then on he says 'I fell to robbing almost every one that stood in my way'. He twice escaped from jail and in mid-1724 was responsible for an almost daily robbery in or near London. He was captured and tried at the Old Bailey but with the help of Edgeworth Bess managed to escape the condemned cell. In September he was caught again and imprisoned in Newgate where he was chained to the floor. But he escaped up the chimney. Once more he was captured, hopelessly drunk, in the Clare Market tavern and was hanged at Tyburn on 16 November 1724. He was then not quite twenty-two. He was the hero of a novel by Harrison Ainsworth, entitled *Jack Sheppard*, 1839.

Southampton. Henry Wriothesley, 3rd Earl of (1573–1624)
St Peter's Church, Titchfield, Hampshire; in the crypt under the Southampton Monument. He is the kneeling figure on the west end of the monument, chancel side.

Famous as Shakespeare's only patron, he was a royal ward under Lord Burghley at five years of age, when he inherited his title. He was a brilliant student at St John's College, Cambridge and graduated at age 16. Southampton became a lover of literature and, it is said, of women. He was handsome, with blue eyes and dark auburn hair. He once hired Shakespeare's company to put on a performance of *Richard II* to incite the public to rise by presenting a royal abdication scene on stage. But the rising failed, and Southampton was imprisoned in the Tower of London for three years.

James I freed him as soon as he acceded, and under the new monarch he actively pioneered various colonies in America, including Virginia and those of New England, where he is commemorated in a town and river name; there was even an Indian tribe called 'Southampton' after him. He was a member of the East India Company, and in 1610 he helped to send Henry Hudson to seek the North-West Passage. In politics he strongly opposed George Villiers, Duke of Buckingham; once they nearly came to blows in the House of Lords. He had to devote much energy to championing the interests of the Virginia Company, in peril to hostile Spain. A treaty with the Netherlands against Spain allowed the Netherlands to raise 6,000 troops in England, and Southampton went with the English volunteers as their commander, taking his elder son James with him. They both caught a fever in the Low Countries and there died. Until the time of his death Southampton continued to be eulogized by poets and writers. He had been secretly married to his mistress Elizabeth Verdon, one of Elizabeth I's personal maids.

Stanley, Sir Henry Morton (1841–1904)
St Michael's Churchyard, Pirbright, Surrey, where a granite monolith above his grave bears the inscription, 'Henry Morton Stanley, 1841–1904,' with his African name 'Bula Matari' and, as an epitaph, one word, 'Africa'.

Born at Denbigh of English parents, he had a deprived childhood and went as a cabin boy to the United States where, in New Orleans, he took the name of the merchant for whom he worked, Henry Morton Stanley. He became a naturalized American citizen and fought in the Civil War on the Confederate side and was captured. He returned to England briefly, was rejected by his mother, and enlisted in the American navy in 1864. After that he became a journalist, eventually going to the *New York Herald* as a correspondent. He accompanied the British expedition to Abyssinia in 1867–1868 as a correspondent for the *Herald* and witnessed the fall of Magdala. He then received a roving commission from the newspaper and travelled extensively, until he was ordered to go and find Livingstone. They met at Ujiji on 10 November 1871, the young Stanley greeting the veteran Livingstone with the words, 'Dr Livingstone, I presume'. With Livingstone he navigated the shores of Lake Tanganyika and thereafter, having completed lecture and other tours, he returned to Africa from 1874 to 1877. This expedition led to the founding of the Congo Free State in 1879 and to the partition of hitherto unappropriated regions of Africa between the western states of Europe. He became a close friend and associate of King Leopold II of The Belgians, and, after once more becoming a British subject, was knighted in 1899 in recognition of his services to Africa. For five years he was Liberal Member of Parliament for Lambeth, from 1895 to 1900.

Turpin, Richard, 'Dick' (1706–1739)
St George's Churchyard, York, Yorkshire.

Highwayman. Born in Hempstead in Essex, he was apprenticed to a butcher in Whitechapel. He was caught stealing cattle and joined a gang of smugglers and deer-stealers who carried out some brutal robberies in Essex. He entered into partnership with the highwayman, Tom King, but inadvertently killed King when he tried to shoot the constable trying to arrest his friend. Before he died King must have given away some of Turpin's haunts, but he managed to evade arrest and got away to York, the journey presumably the basis for his 'famous ride to York' on his horse, Black Bess, of which much has been written. He was later apprehended in York and tried for horse-stealing, for which he was hanged at York on 7 April 1739, aged 33. His body was rescued from the clutches of the surgeon by the mob and buried in St George's Churchyard.

Tussaud, Madame Marie (1760–1850)
St Mary's Church, Cadogan Street, Chelsea, London. Her tomb is sealed in the vault and not visible, but there is a memorial tablet to her in the church.

Waxwork modeller. She learned her trade from her uncle in Paris and during the French Revolution she was forced to model many of the guillotined heads, and was, for a short time, herself imprisoned. She came to London in 1802 where, after touring for thirty-three years with her waxworks exhibition, she set up a permanent museum in Baker Street, where it still remains.

Wilson, Charles (1932–1990)
Streatham Cemetery, Garratt Lane, Tooting, south London.

Train robber, one of the five members of the gang who stole £5 million in the Great Train Robbery of 1963, a daring raid on the Glasgow to Euston train. Wilson was murdered in Spain because of suspected cheating in a drug-dealing activity. He had served about one-third of his prison sentence for his part in the robbery, being released in 1978, after which he lived in a luxury villa in Marbella where he was murdered.

Younghusband, Sir Francis Edward (1863–1942)
Parish Churchyard (previously St Peter ad Vincula before its destruction by fire), Lytchett Minster, Dorset. There is a bas-relief of Lhasa on his headstone.

Soldier, explorer, diplomat and mystic who was born at Murree, India. After receiving a commission in the 1st (King's) Dragoon Guards at the age of 19 – he had graduated from the Royal Military College at Sandhurst – he went on expeditions in the Himalayas, the Afghan border and Manchuria. From Peking he made an epic overland journey to India, becoming the first European to cross the Gobi desert. Appointed to the Indian foreign department in 1889, he was exploring in the northern part of India when he met a Russian patrol and was told to leave Russian territory. It was an area between that country, China and Afghanistan that had never been officially demarcated. Lord Salisbury, however, later received a Russian apology. As a man sensitive to the eastern religions he was able to penetrate into the then hostile territory of Tibet and sign a treaty in that country's mysterious capital of Lhasa. After retirement, Younghusband became the first chairman of the Mount Everest Committee and a founder of the Himalaya Club. He was awarded the Founder's Medal of the Royal Geographical Society and had been correspondent in Rhodesia and the Transvaal for *The Times*. He set down his religious philosophy in two books, *Life in the Stars* (1927) and *The Living Universe* (1933), and in 1936 he founded the World Congress of Faiths. Despite his beliefs in, and support of, mystic eastern religions, he chose to be buried in a Christian grave.

Geographical check-list by county

For speed of reference, this lists counties alphabetically rather than by geographical propinquity, as is sometimes done. But it is pointed out, especially for visitors from overseas, that three or four counties can often be visited within a relatively short distance, and convenient groupings can be made by using a map of England that clearly delineates county boundaries.

A few burial locations listed in the main entries are no longer physically marked. This applies mostly to London churches. St Martin-in-the-Fields, for example, was a burial place for thousands of people from all walks of life from the year 1222, burials being registered after 1525. When the old church was torn down in the sixteenth century, more than 3,000 coffins were cleared from the vaults. In 1853 the chuchyard, which used to extend across to where the National Gallery now stands, and in other directions too, was also cleared of graves by an Act of Parliament. Some of the coffins were claimed by relatives and reinterred in St Martin's Cemetery, Camden Town. One of the coffins thus discovered was that of Dr John Hunter; it was transferred to an honoured position next to Ben Jonson's mortal remains in Westminster Abbey.

St Paul's Cathedral is another place where some famous burial sites are no longer marked; and at Glastonbury Abbey ruins, where several kings other than Arthur were buried, exact grave locations are no longer known. Even so, the knowledge that an honoured and famous historical person was buried there (in the case of Queen Boadicea, for instance, under an otherwise prosaic railway platform) imbues a particular area with a powerful attraction.

This check-list will help you to plan your route to such places. You will find the relevant page numbers of each location in the general Index on page 359. A query in brackets indicates a claimed, but not authenticated, burial place.

AVON
Bath, Abbey Church: Thomas Robert Malthus; Richard ('Beau') Nash. *Walcot Cemetery*: William Beckford; Fanny Burney, Mme d'Arblay.

BERKSHIRE

Reading Abbey (ruins): Henry I. *Windsor Castle, St George's Chapel*: Charles I; Edward IV; Edward VII; George III; George IV; George V; George VI; Henry VI; Henry VIII; Queen Jane Seymour; William IV. *Windsor Home Park, Frogmore, Royal Cemetery*: Edward VIII; Duchess of Windsor. *Royal Mausoleum*: Prince Albert; Queen Victoria.

BUCKINGHAMSHIRE

Beaconsfield, Roman Catholic Cemetery: Gilbert Keith Chesterton. *St Mary and All Saints Church*: Edmund Burke; Edmund Waller. *Chalfont St Giles, St Giles' Church*: Bertram Mills. *Chalfont St Giles, Jordans, Quaker Meeting House*: William Penn. *Great Hampden, St Mary Magdalene's Church*: John Hampden. *Hughenden, St Michael's Churchyard*: Benjamin Disraeli, 1st Earl of Beaconsfield. *Little Marlow, Town Cemetery*: Edgar Wallace. *Olney, St Peter and St Paul's Church*: John Newton. *Penn, Church of the Holy Trinity Churchyard*: Donald Duart Maclean (*ashes in urn*). *Stoke Poges, St Giles' Churchyard*: Thomas Gray. *Upton, Slough, St Laurence's Church*: Sir William Herschel.

CAMBRIDGESHIRE

Cambridge, Sidney Sussex College: Oliver Cromwell (head only). *Ely Cathedral*: St Ethelreda. *Little Gidding, St John's Churchyard*: Nicholas Ferrar. *Peterborough Cathedral*: Catherine of Aragon. *Wicken Fen, St Laurence's Church*: Henry Cromwell.

CHESHIRE

Chester Cathedral: Ranulf Higden. *Chester, Holy Trinity Church*: Thomas Parnell. *Knutsford, Brook Street Chapel*: Elizabeth Gaskell. *Port Sunlight, Christ Church*: Lord Leverhulme, William Hesketh Lever.

CORNWALL

Fowey, St Nicholas's Church: Sir Arthur Quiller-Couch. *Trebetherick (north Cornwall), St Enodoc's Churchyard*: Sir John Betjeman.

CUMBRIA

Caldbeck, St Kentigern's Churchyard: John Peel. *Coniston, St Andrew's Churchyard*: John Ruskin. *Dalton-in-Furness, St Mary's Church*: George Romney. *Grasmere, St Oswald's Churchyard*: William Wordsworth. *Grasmere, Town Cemetery*: Dr William Archibald Spooner. *Keswick, Crosthwaite, St Kentigern's Churchyard*: Robert Southey. *Keswick, St John's Churchyard*: Hugh Walpole. *Lanercost Priory*: Thomas Addison.

DERBYSHIRE

Ault Hucknall, St John the Baptist Church: Thomas Hobbes. *Chesterfield, Trinity Church*: George Stephenson. *Cromford, St Mary's Church*: Sir Richard Arkwright. *Derby, Cathedral of All Saints*: Henry Cavendish. *Hathersage, St Michael's Churchyard*: John Little, ('Little John'). *Kedleston, All Saints' Church*: George Curzon, 1st Marquess of Kedleston. *Repton, St Wystan's Church*: Ethelbald I.

DEVONSHIRE
Exeter Cathedral: Bishop Leofric. *Hartland, St Nectan's Church*: John Lane.
Lew Trenchard, St Peter's Churchyard: Sabine Baring-Gould. *Paignton Cemetery*: Oliver Heaviside. *St Budeaux, Plymouth, St Budiana's Church*: Sir Ferdinando Gorges.

DORSET
Bournemouth, St Peter's Churchyard: William Godwin; Mary Wollstonecraft Shelley; Percy Bysshe Shelley (heart); Mary Wollstonecraft (Mrs Godwin); Richard Clement Moody. *Bournemouth, Wimborne Road Cemetery*: Evelyn Baring, 1st Earl of Cromer; John Nelson Darby. *Broadstone, Town Cemetery*: Alfred Russel Wallace. *Corscombe, in private field*: Thomas Hollis. *Dorchester, Holy Trinity Church*: John White. *Kingston, Old Church graveyard*: John Scott, 1st Earl of Eldon. *Lytchett Minster, Parish Churchyard*: Sir Francis Edward Younghusband. *Mappowder, St Peter and Paul Churchyard*: Theodore Francis Powys. *Morton St Nicholas's Church*: T. E. Lawrence. *Shaftesbury Abbey* (*ruins*): Edward the Martyr. *Sherborne, Abbey Church*: Ethelbald; Ethelbert; Sir Thomas Wyat. *Stinsford, St Michael's Churchyard*: Cecil Day-Lewis; Thomas Hardy (heart). *Swyre Head, near Chaldon Herring*: Llewelyn Powys (*ashes under monument*). *Tarrant Crawford, St Mary's Church*: Richard Poore, Bishop of Salisbury (body). *Tolpuddle, St John the Evangelist Churchyard*: James Hammett. *Wareham, Lady St Mary's Church*: Edward the Martyr(?). *Wimborne Minister, Minister Church*: John Beaufort, 1st Duke of Somerset; Ethelred I. *Wimborne St Giles, St Giles' Church*: Anthony Ashley Cooper, 7th Earl of Shaftesbury. *Winterborne Came, St Peter's Churchyard*: William Barnes. *Worth Matravers, St Nicholas Churchyard*: Leslie James Banks.

DURHAM, COUNTY
Durham Cathedral: The Venerable Bede; St Cuthbert; Ralph Neville, 1st Earl of Westmorland. *Houghton-le-Spring, St Michael and All Angels' Church*: Bernard Gilpin.

ESSEX
East Horndon, near Billericay, All Saints' Church: Anne Boleyn (heart?). *Hempstead, St Andrew's Church*: Sir Eliab Harvey; William Harvey. *Waltham Abbey*: Harold II.

GLOUCESTERSHIRE
Berkeley, St Mary's Church: Edward Jenner. *Daylesford, St Peter's Church*: Warren Hastings. *Gloucester Cathedral*: Edward II; Robert II, Duke of Normandy. *Sudeley Castle, Winchcombe*: Queen Catherine Parr.

HAMPSHIRE
Beacon Hill, near Old Burghclere: George Edward Stanhope Molyneaux Herbert, 5th Earl of Carnarvon. *Binsted, Holy Cross Churchyard*: Field-Marshal Viscount Montgomery of Alamein. *Catherington, All Saint's Church*: Charles John Kean; Sir Charles Napier. *East Wellow St Margaret's Churchyard*: Florence Nightingale. *Eversley, St Mary's Church*: Charles

Kingsley. *Exbury, St Catherine's Churchyard*: William Mitford. *Farnborough, Abbey Church of St Michael*: Napoleon III. *Fordingbridge, Town Cemetery*: Augustus Edwin John. *Hamble, St Andrew's Churchyard*: Sir Edwin Alliot Verdon-Roe. *Highcliffe, St Mark's Churchyard*: Harry Gordon Selfridge. *Hursley Church*: Richard Cromwell. *All Saint's Churchyard*: John Keble. *Little Somborne, Redundant Churchyard, near King's Somborne*: Sir Thomas Octave Murdoch Sopwith. *Lymington, Sir Thomas the Apostle Churchyard*: Caroline Ann Bowles (Mrs Robert Southey). *Lyndhurst, St Michael's Church*: Alice Liddell ('Alice in Wonderland'). *Micheldever, St Mary's Church*: Sir Francis Baring. *Minstead All Saint's Churchyard*: Sir Arthur Conan Doyle. *Old Alresford, St Mary's Church*: George Brydges Rodney, 1st Baron. *Otterbourne, St Matthew's Churchyard*: Charlotte Mary Yonge. *Portsmouth, Royal Garrison Church*: Sir Charles James Napier. *Portsmouth, St Thomas' Cathedral*: Sir John Kempthorne. *Romsey, Romsey Abbey Church*: Earl Mountbatten of Burma. *Selborne, St Mary's Churchyard*: Gilbert White. *Southampton, Old Cemetery*: George Saintsbury. *Titchfield, St Peter's Church*: Henry Wriothesley, 3rd Earl of Southampton. *West Meon, St John the Evangelist Churchyard*: Guy Francis de Moncy Burgess (ashes); Thomas Lord. *Winchester Cathedral*: Jane Austen; Henry Beaufort; Canute; Egbert; Ethelwulf; Earl Godwin; St Swithin; William of Wykeham. *Winchester College Chapel, in the Garth*: Archibald Wavell, 1st Earl Wavell. *Winchester, St Bartholomew's Church: Hyde Street and Hyde Abbey ruins?*: Alfred the Great. *Winchester, 'New Minister'*: Edward the Elder; Hardicanute. *'Old Minister'*: Edred; Edwy.

HEREFORD AND WORCESTER

Evesham, Abbey Ruins: Simon of Montfort, Earl of Leicester. *Great Malvern Cemetery*: Johanna Maria ('Jenny') Lind. *Hereford Cathedral*: St Thomas de Cantelupe. *Little Malvern, St Wulstan's Churchyard*: Sir Edward Elgar. *Ridge, St Margaret's Church*: Field Marshall Earl Alexander of Tunis. *Weobley, Church of St Peter and St Paul*: John Birch. *West Malvern, St James's Churchyard*: Peter Mark Roget. *Worcester Cathedral*: King John; Stanley Baldwin.

HERTFORDSHIRE

Ayot St Lawrence, Shaw's Corner: George Bernard Shaw. *Hertingfordbury Church*: William Cowper, 1st Earl. *King's Langley, St Mary's Dominican Friary (ruins)*: Piers Galveston, Earl of Cornwall. *St Albans Cathedral:* St Alban; Thomas De La Mare. *St Albans, St Michael's Church*: Francis Bacon.

HUMBERSIDE

Little Driffield Church: Alfred the Great. *Rudston, All Saints' Church*: Winifred Holtby.

ISLE OF WIGHT

Bonchurch, St Boniface's Church: Henry de Vere Stacpoole; Algernon Charles Swinburne. *Newport St Thomas' Church*: Princess Elizabeth.

KENT

Beckenham, Town Cemetery: William ('W. G.') Grace. *Birchington, All Saints' Churchyard*: Dante Gabriel Rossetti. *Boxley Abbey*: Sir Francis Wyatt.

Canterbury, Maugham Library, King's School: Somerset Maugham (ashes scattered near). *Canterbury, Roman Catholic Cemetery*: Joseph Conrad. *Canterbury, St Dunstan's Church*: Sir Thomas More (head only). *Canterbury Cathedral*: St Anselm; St Thomas à Becket; St Dunstan; Edward, Prince of Wales, 'The Black Prince'; Henry IV; Joan of Navarre; Lanfranc; Cosmo Gordon, Baron Lang of Lambeth; John Morton; Frederick Temple; William Temple; Hubert Walter. *Faversham Abbey*: King Stephen. *Gravesend, St George's Church*: Pocahontas (Mrs John Rolfe). *Keston Churchyard*: Dinah Maria Mulock, Mrs Craik. *Rochester Cathedral*: Walter de Merton. *Shipbourne, St Giles's Church*: Sir Henry Vane (the elder); Sir Henry Vane (the younger). *Shoreham, St Peter and St Paul's Churchyard*: Edward John Moreton Drax Plunkett Dunsany, 18th Baron.

LANCASHIRE
Old Jewish Cemetery, Manchester: Michael Marks.

LEICESTERSHIRE
Leicester Abbey: Richard III; Thomas Wolsey. *Lutterworth, St Mary's Church*: John Wycliffe.

LINCOLNSHIRE
Lincoln Cathedral: Robert Grosseteste; Hugh of Avalon. *Stamford Cemetery*: Sir Malcolm Sargent. *Stamford, St Martin's Church*: Lord Burghley, William Cecil.

LONDON AND GREATER LONDON
Aldgate, St Andrew Undershaft Church: John Stow. *Barking, Friends' Burial Ground*: Elizabeth Fry. *Barnes Cemetery*: Francis Turner Palgrave. *Battersea, St Mary's Church*: Benedict Arnold; St John Henry Bolingbroke, 1st Viscount. *Bishopsgate, St Helen's Church*: Sir Thomas Gresham; Robert Hooke. *Canon Street, St Michael's Paternoster*: Richard ('Dick') Whittington. *Chelsea, St Mary's Church, Cadogan Street*: Madame Marie Tussaud. *Chiswick Mall, St Nicholas's Church*: Barbara Villiers, Duchess of Cleveland; Oliver Cromwell; William Hogarth; James Abbott McNeill Whistler. *City Road, John Wesley Chapel*: John Wesley. *Covent Garden, St Paul's Church*: Thomas Arne; Samuel Butler; Claude Duval; Sir Peter Lely; Dame Ellen Alicia Terry. *Cripplegate, St Giles's Church*: Sir Martin Frobisher; John Milton. *Deptford, St Nicholas's Church*: Christopher Marlowe. *Edmonton, All Saints' Churchyard*: Charles Lamb. *Finchley Cemetery*: Thomas Henry Huxley; Alfred Charles William Harmsworth, Viscount Northcliffe. *Finsbury, Bunhill Fields Burial Ground*: William Blake; John Bunyan; Daniel Defoe; Isaac Watts. *Finsbury, John Wesley Chapel, City Road*: see *City Road*. *Fleet Street, St Dunstan's in the West*: George Calvert, 1st Baron Baltimore; Lord Northcliffe (bust). *Fleet Street, Temple Church*: Oliver Goldsmith; William Marshal, Earl of Pembroke; John Seldon. *Fortune Green Road*: see *Hampstead Cemetery*. *Golders Green Crematorium, East Columbarium*: Sigmund Freud. *Ernest George Columbarium*: Anna Pavlova (*with shrine and rosebed in Gardens*). *Gardens and Cloisters*: Ivor Novello (Davies). *Garden of Rest*: Eric Coates; Peter Sellers; Sir Bernard Spilsbury (*Book of Remembrance in Chapel of Memory*); Vesta Tilley (*ashes under lilac tree*). *Gower Street, University College, south cloister*: Jeremy Bentham.

Great Stanmore, St John the Evangelist Church: Sir William Gilbert. *Greenwich, Naval Hospital Mausoleum*: Sir Thomas Masterman Hardy; six other Admirals as listed under Hardy. *St Alfege's Church*: Lavinia Fenton (Polly Peachum); James Wolfe. *Hampstead, St John's Churchyard*: John Constable; George Palmella Burson Du Maurier; Sir Herbert Beerbohm Tree; Anton Walbrook. *Hampstead Cemetery, Fortune Green Road*: Gladys Cooper; Sebastian Ziani de Ferranti; Pamela Frankau; Kate Greenaway; Joseph Lister. *Hart Street, St Olave's Church*: Samuel Pepys. *Hendon, St Mary's Church*: Sir Thomas Stamford Raffles. *Highgate Cemetery 'new'*: George Eliot (Mary Ann Cross); William Friese-Green; John Galsworthy; Karl Marx; Sir Ralph Richardson. *Highgate Cemetery 'old'*: Michael Faraday; Radclyfe Hall (Mabel Veronica Batten). *Highgate, St Michael's Church (adjoining cemetery)*: Samuel Taylor Coleridge. *Holborn, Church of the Holy Sepulchre without Newgate*: Roger Ascham; Captain John Smith; Sir Henry Wood. *Holborn Circus, St Andrew's Church*: Henry Sacheverell. *Holborn, High Street, St Giles-in-the-fields*: Luke Hansard; Andrew Marvell. *Islington, St Luke's Church, Old Street*: William Caslon. *Ivydale Road, Nunhead Cemetery*: Sir Frederick Abel. *Kensal Green Cemetery*: Charles Babbage; Charles Blondin; Isambard Kingdom Brunel; Sir Mark Isambard Brunel; John Cassell; Wilkie Collins; William Charles Macready; John Murray; Sir William Siemens; William Makepeace Thackeray; Anthony Trollope. *Kensal Green, St Mary's Roman Catholic Cemetery*: Sir John Barbirolli. *Kensington, Church Street, St Mary Abbot's Church*: Robert Monckton. *King's Cross Railway Station, under platform 10*: Queen Boadicea. *Lambeth, Norwood Cemetery*: Mrs Beeton; Sir Henry Bessemer; Sir Hiram Stevens Maxim; Sir Henry Tate. *Lambeth, St Mary's Church*: Elias Ashmole; William Bligh; Thomas Tenison. *Leadenhall Street, St Andrew Undershaft*: John Stow. *Leadenhall Street, St Katherine Cree Church*: Hans Holbein (the younger); Sir Nicholas Throckmorton. *London Wall, St Giles's Church without Cripplegate*: See *Cripplegate*. *'Manor Park', (nearest station), Central London Cemetery*: Dame Anna Neagle. *Mortlake, St Mary Magdalen's Churchyard*: Sir Richard Francis Burton. *Mortlake, St Mary's Church*: John Dee. *Newgate Street, Christ Church*: Isabella of France; Sir Thomas Malory. *Paddington Green, St Mary's Churchyard*: Sarah Siddons. *Paul's Wharf, St Benet's Church*: Inigo Jones. *Pentoville, St James' Church (site of)*: Joseph Grimaldi. *Putney, Town Cemetery*: Sir William Orpen. *Piccadilly, St James's Church*: John Arbuthnot. *St Giles High Street*: see *Holborn*. *St John's Wood Chapel, Wellington Road*: John Sell Cotman. *St Marylebone 'Old' Parish Church*: Edmund Hoyle; George Stubbs; Francis Wheatley. *St Pancras Old Churchyard*: Johann Christian Bach. *St Paul's Cathedral*: Sir Max Beerbohm; John Donne; General Charles Gordon (effigy); John Howard; William Holman Hunt; Sir Edwin Landseer; Sir Thomas Lawrence; Frederick Leighton; Sir John Everett Millais; John Opie; Sir Joshua Reynolds; Sir Arthur Sullivan; Sir Christopher Wren. *St Paul's Cathedral Crypt*: David Beatty, 1st Earl; Cuthbert Collingwood, 1st Baron; Sir Alexander Fleming; Bernard Cyril Freyberg, 1st Baron; John Rushworth Jellicoe, Earl; Horatio Nelson; Frederick Roberts, 1st Earl of Kandahar; Joseph Mallord William Turner; Arthur Wellesley, 1st Duke of Wellington; Sir Henry Hughes Wilson. *St Paul's 'Old Cathedral'*: Sir Nicholas Bacon; Ethelred the Unready;

John of Gaunt; King Sebert; Sir Philip Sidney; Sir Francis Walsingham; Sir
Anthony van Dyck. *Ruislip, St Martin's Churchyard*: Jessie Matthews (*ashes in
Garden of Rest*). *Soho, St Anne's Churchyard, Dean Street*: William Hazlitt;
Dorothy Leigh Sayers. *Southwark Cathedral*: John Fletcher; John Gower.
Stoke Newington, Abney Park Cemetery: William Booth. *Strand, St Clement
Danes*: Harold Harefoot. *Teddington Cemetery*: Richard Doddridge
Blackmoore. *Tower of London, St Peter ad Vincula*: Anne Boleyn; St John
Fisher; Simon Fraser, Lord Lovat; Queen Catherine Howard; Lady Jane
Grey; Duke of Monmouth; Sir Thomas More; Edward Seymour, Duke of
Somerset; Thomas Seymour of Sudeley. *Trafalgar Square, St Martin-in-the-
Fields*: Robert Boyle; Thomas Chippendale; Sir Winston Churchill (ancester
of); Nell Gwyn; Jack Sheppard. *Twickenham, St Mary's Church*: Alexander
Pope. *Walbrook, St Stephen's Church*: Sir John Vanbrugh. *Waltham Abbey
(ruins)* see ESSEX. *West Brompton, Brompton Cemetery*: George Henty;
'Gentleman' John Jackson; Emmeline Pankhurst; John Snow; Richard
Tauber; Brandon Thomas. *West Hampstead*: see *Hampstead Cemetery*.
Westminster, St Margaret's Church: William Caxton; Sir Walter Raleigh;
Westminster Abbey, Edward the Confessor's Chapel: Edward the Confessor;
Edward I, Longshanks; Edward III; Eleanor of Castile; Henry III; Henry V;
Richard II. *Westminster Abbey, Henry VII's Chapel*: Queen Anne; Joseph
Addison; George Villiers, 2nd Duke of Buckingham; John Sheffield, 1st
Duke of Buckingham and Normandy; Caroline of Anspach; Charles II;
Edward VI; Elizabeth I; George II; Henry VII; James I; Mary I; Mary II:
Mary Queen of Scots; George Monck, 1st Duke of Albemarle; Prince
Rupert; William III (see also *RAF Chapel*). *Westminster Abbey, Innocents'
Corner*: Edward V; Richard, Duke of York. *Westminster Abbey, Nave, centre*:
William Thomson Kelvin, 1st Baron; Andrew Bonar Law; Dr David
Livingstone; Sir Isaac Newton; Ernest Rutherford. *Westminster Abbey, Nave,
west end*: William Pitt the Younger (monument); The Unknown Warrior.
Westminster Abbey, Nave, north aisle: Clement Attlee; Ernest Bevin; Sir John
Herschel; John Hunter; Ben Jonson. *Westminster Abbey, Nave, north choir
aisle*: Charles Darwin; Edward Elgar (memorial stone); Henry Purcell; Ralph
Vaughan Williams; William Wilberforce (monument). *Westminster Abbey,
Nave, south aisle*: John André; Neville Chamberlain; William Congreve.
Westminster Abbey, North Transept: Charles James Fox; W. E. Gladstone;
Henry John Temple Palmerston, Viscount; William Pitt the Elder; William
Pitt the Younger; William Wilberforce. *Westminster Abbey, Poets' Corner*:
Joseph Addison (monument); Francis Beaumont; Robert Browning; Geoffrey
Chaucer; Charles Dickens; John Dryden; T. S. Eliot (memorial stone);
David Garrick; George Frederick Handel; Thomas Hardy (ashes); Sir Henry
Irving; Dr Samuel Johnson; Ben Jonson; Rudyard Kipling; Thomas
Babington Macaulay; John Masefield; Laurence (Kerr) Olivier, 1st Baron
Olivier; Thomas Parr; Matthew Prior; Richard Brinsley Sheridan; Edmund
Spenser; Alfred, Lord Tennyson; William Makepeace Thackeray (bust);
William Wordsworth (monument); James Wyatt. *Westminster Abbey, Presbytery,
south side*: Anne of Cleves. *Westminster Abbey, RAF Chapel*: George Villiers,
1st Duke of Buckingham; Oliver Cromwell; Sir Hugh Caswell Dowding, 1st
Baron; Hugh Trenchard, 1st Viscount. *Westminster Abbey, St George's Chapel*:

Edmund Henry Hynman, Viscount Allenby. *Westminster Abbey, St Paul's Chapel*: Sir Rowland Hill. *Westminster Abbey, South Ambulatory*: King Sebert. *Westminster Abbey, Triforium*: John Gay. *Whitechapel, Jewish Burial Ground*: Nathan Mayer Rothschild. *Whitechapel, St Mary Matfelon Churchyard*: Richard Brandon. *Woolwich, St Mary's Churchyard*: Henry Maudslay.

NORFOLK
Aylsham, St Michael's Church: Humphrey Repton. *East Dereham, St Nicholas's Church*: William Cowper. *Elvedon Park Church*: Anne Boleyn (heart?). *Houghton Hall, St Martin's Church*: Robert Walpole, 1st Earl of Orford. *Lamas, Old Quaker Meeting House Garden*: Anna Sewell. *Langham, St Andrew and St Mary's Churchyard*: Captain Frederick Marryat. *Norwich Cathedral*: Nurse Edith Cavell; Henry Despenser. *Norwich, St George's Church, Colegate*: John Crome. *Salle, Boleyn Church*: Anne Boleyn (?). *Tittleshall, St Mary's Church*: Sir Edward Coke.

NORTHAMPTONSHIRE
Weedon Lois, St Mary's Churchyard extension: Dame Edith Sitwell.

NORTHUMBERLAND
Bamburgh, St Aidan's Churchyard: Grace Darling.

NOTTINGHAMSHIRE
Blidworth, St Mary's Churchyard: William Scathelock ('Will Scarlett'). *Hucknall Torkard, St Mary Magdalen Church*: George Gordon, Lord Byron. *Newark on Trent, Newark Cemetery*: Wladyslaw Sikorski.

OXFORDSHIRE
Bladon, St Martin's Churchyard: Lord Randolph Churchill; Sir Winston Churchill; Jenny Jerome (Lady Randolph Churchill). *Blenheim Palace Chapel*: John Churchill, 1st Duke of Marlborough. *Cholsey, St Mary's Churchyard*: Dame Agatha Christie. *Dorchester Abbey Church*: St Birinus. *Elsfield, St Thomas of Canterbury Churchyard*: John Buchan, 1st Baron Tweedsmuir. *Ewelme, St Mary's Churchyard*: Jerome K. Jerome. *Idbury, St Nicholas's Church*: Sir Benjamin Baker. *North Stroke, St Mary the Virgin Churchyard*: Dame Clara Butt. *Nuffield, Holy Trinity Church*: William Richard Morris, 1st Viscount Nuffield. *Oxford, Broad Street, opposite Balliol College*: The Three Martyrs. *Oxford, Merton College Chapel*: Sir Thomas Bodley. *Oxford, Oriel College Ante Chapel*: Sir Henry Tizard. *Oxford, St Cross's Churchyard*: Kenneth Grahame. *Oxford, St John's College Chapel*: William Laud. *Oriel College Anti-chapel*: Sir Henry Tizard. *Sutton Courtenay, All Saints' Churchyard*: Henry Asquith, 1st Earl of Oxford; George Orwell. *Swinbrook, St Mary's Churchyard*: Nancy Mitford. *Wroxton, All Saints' Church*: Frederick North, Earl of Guildford.

SHROPSHIRE (SALOP)
Brosley, All Saints' Church: Abraham Darby. *Ludlow, St Lawrence Church*: A. E. Housman. *Moreton Say, St Margaret's Church*: Robert Clive. *Tong, St Bartholomew's Church*: The Vernons of Pembruge.

SOMERSET
Combe Florey, St Peter and St Paul's Churchyard: Evelyn Waugh. *East Coker, St Michael's Church*: T. S. Eliot. *Glastonbury Abbey (ruins)*: King Arthur; Richard Bere; Edmund I, the Magnificent; Edmund II, Ironside; Queen Guinevere. *Mells, St Andrew's Parish Church*: Maurice Christopher Hollis; Ronald Arbuthnot Knox; Siegfried Sassoon. *Wells Cathedral*: Thomas Linley.

STAFFORDSHIRE
Burslem Cemetery, Stoke-on-Trent: Arnold Bennett. *Drayton Bassett, St Peter's Church*: Sir Robert Peel. *Whittingham, Litchfield, St Giles' Churchyard*: Thomas Spencer.

SUFFOLK
Aldeburgh, St Peter and St Paul's Churchyard: Benjamin Britten, 1st Lord Brittenof Aldeburgh. *Boulge, St Michael's Church*: Edward FitzGerald. *Bury St Edmund's Abbey (ruins)*: St Edmund. *Garboldisham, Soldier's Hill*: Queen Boadicea (?). *Playford, St Mary's Churchyard*: Sir George Airy. *Quidenham*: Queen Boadicea(?). *Sudbury, St Gregory's Church*: Simon of Sudbury. *Wingfield, St Andrew's Church*: William de la Pole, 1st Duke of Suffolk.

SURREY
Brookwood Cemetery: Sir Thomas Beecham; Dame Rebecca West; Dennis Yates Wheatley. *Burstow, St Bartholomew's Church*: John Flamsteed. *Compton Cemetery*: Aldous Huxley. *Dorking Cemetery*: George Meredith. *Farnham, St Andrew's Church*: William Cobbett. *Guildford Cemetery*: Lewis Carroll (Charles Dodgson). *Kew, St Anne's Church*: Thomas Gainsborough; Johann Zoffany. *Laleham, All Saints' Churchyard*: Matthew Arnold. *Leatherhead, St Mary and St Nicholas's Churchyard*: Anthony Hope. *Limpsfield, St Peter's Churchyard*: Frederick Delius. *Mickleham, St Michael's Churchyard*: Richard Bedford Bennett, 1st Viscount Bennett. *Pirbright, St Michael's Churchyard*: Sir Henry Stanley. *Richmond, St Matthias's Churchyard*: Edmund Kean. *West Horsley*: Sir Walter Raleigh (head). *Wotton, St John's Church*: John Evelyn.

SUSSEX EAST AND WEST
Fletching, St Mary and St Andrew's Church: Edward Gibbon. *Horstead Keynes, St Giles' Churchyard*: Harold Macmillan, 1st Earl of Stockton. *Hove Cemetery*: Jack Hobbs. *Ifield, St Margaret's Church*: Mark Lemon. *Lewis, St John's Church*: Gundrada de Warenne. *Rodmell, Monks House*: Virginia Woolf. *Salehurst, St Mary's Churchyard*: Lord Alfred Milner, K. G. *West Grinstead, Church of Our Lady and St Francis*: Hilaire Belloc. *West Lavington, St Mary Magdalene Churchyard*: Richard Cobden. *Worthing, Broadwater Cemetery*: John Richard Jefferies.

WEST MIDLANDS/WARWICKSHIRE
Birmingham, Church of England Cemetery chapel vaults: John Baskerville. *Bourneville, Friends Meeting House*: George Cadbury. *Birmingham General Cemetery*: Joseph Chamberlain. *Handsworth, St Mary's Church*: James Watt. *Stratford-on-Avon Cemetery*: Marie Corelli (Mary MacKay). *Stratford-on-Avon, Holy Trinity Church*: William Shakespeare.

WILTSHIRE
Alvediston, St Mary's Churchyard: Sir Anthony Eden, 1st Earl of Avon.
Bemerton, St Andrew's Church: George Herbert. *Britford, St Peter's Church*:
Henry Stafford, 2nd Duke of Buckingham (2nd creation). *Broad Chalke, All
Saints Church*: Sir Cecil Beaton; Maurice Henry Hewlett (*plaque, grave on
private site*). *Bromham, St Nicholas' Churchyard*: Thomas Moore. *Castle Combe,
St Andrew's Churchyard*: Sir John Eldon Gorst. *Corsham, St Bartholomew's
Churchyard*: Field Marshall Lord Methuen, Paul Sanford Methuen, 3rd
Baron. *Farley, All Saints Church*: Sir Stephen Fox. *Hardenhuish, St Nicholas'
Churchyard*: David Ricardo. *Lacock, Town Cemetery*: William Henry Fox
Talbot. *Malmesbury, Abbey Church*: King Athelstan. *Salisbury Cathedral*: Mary
Herbert, Countess of Pembroke; William Herbert, 3rd Earl of Pembroke; St
Osmund; Richard Poore (heart?). *Sevenhampton, St Andrew's Churchyard*: Ian
Fleming. *Stourton, St Peter's Churchyard*: Sir Richard Colt Hoare. *Trowbridge,
St James' Church*: George Crabbe. *Wilsford and Lake, St Michael's Churchyard*:
Sir Oliver Lodge.

WORCESTER see HEREFORD AND WORCESTER

YORKSHIRE (EAST)
All Saints' Church, Rudston: Winifred Holtby

YORKSHIRE (NORTH)
Coxwold, St Michael's Churchyard: Laurence Sterne. *Hubberholme, Upper
Wharfedale, St Michael and All Angels Church*: John Boynton Priestley.
Scarborough, St Mary's Churchyard: Anne Brontë. *Whitby Abbey (ruins)*: King
Oswy. *Whitby, St Mary's Churchyard*: Caedman. *York Minster*: Henry Bowett;
Thomas Rotherham; Richard le Scrope. *York, Society of Friends burial ground*:
Joseph Rowntree. *York, St George's Churchyard*: Richard ('Dick') Turpin.

YORKSHIRE (WEST)
Haworth Parish Church: Charlotte Bronte; Emily Bronte. *Heptanstall, Hebden
Bridge, St Thomas' Churchyard*: Sylvia Plath. *Kirklees Abbey, Mirfield*: Robin
Hood.

Index